RV TRAVELS
WITH MY GIRLS

SEEKING SOLACE IN THE GREAT OUTDOORS

STEVE GAZO

ISBN: 979-8-9928088-0-3 (Paperback)
ISBN: 979-8-9928088-1-0 (e-book)

Cover Art by: EBook Launch
Chapter illustration by: Rawpixel
Photography by: Steve Gazo\ Rhythms of Nature Photography

DEDICATION

This book is dedicated to my copilot and dear wife Jo, for your support, love, and inspiration. You've never steered me wrong.

TABLE OF CONTENTS

PREFACE

No, I am not some kind of sex maniac from Utah with multiple wives. I am a somewhat conservative fellow with fairly strong religious convictions. The most important of the girls in this book is my wonderful wife, Jo, who for whatever reason, decided to hook up with a fairly poor, average-looking Czechoslovakian with a nervous disorder and no great hope for achieving anything much as regarding success in the world. I've grown to have mediocre goals, mediocre finances, mediocre intelligence, and as we have lately discovered, mediocre health prospects. I used to think that all of these attributes were resting comfortably at a higher level, but after spending my life dealing with its harsh realities, I now realize that I will probably always be in the lower middle income bracket, have gotten used to the fact that my goals have now shrunk to just having some fun in life, and my intelligence, even while resting at a fairly high numerical number, is quite happy operating in the power-save mode. To put it more succinctly, my wife is happy to point out that "I have no common sense"

Jo is a beautiful woman, both inside and out. I was so enamored with her upon our first meeting that I told her we would be getting married in the near future. That sweet demeanor, the long golden tresses and those loving and compassionate blue eyes had pierced my heart like a hot knife through butter and I was overwhelmed – hook, line, and sinker. She probably didn't appreciate the "told her" part, but I like to think the she was impressed by my forceful directness. Eventually she came around and the wedding bells rang. She is stubborn, like eastern Europeans are apt to be, but is the most caring, sweet girl in the world. She will go out of her way to help anyone, at any time, much to my chafing, and is a fantastic cook, much to my glee. She loves nature and being in the outdoors. She is very grounded and practical and fills many of her hours crafting, gardening, painting or strumming her guitar. She loves to get out with me canoeing, sailing, or hiking the pines. As far as I am concerned – she is the perfect woman. She still does not quite appreciate my tendency to over-analyze everything, and doesn't

1

understand my propensity to plan and run my life using the "Helter-Skelter" method, but she is coming around. She has guided us through our marriage, through our health challenges, and I am sure will guide us safely through our travels and golden years. I love her deeply.

The second girl in the trio is my mom, Beatrice. She loved nature and the world around her, but spent most of her adult life, together with my dad, trying to raise five, somewhat unruly kids on a small farm in southern New Jersey, on a limited income. She probably wanted to travel and explore all her life, but putting family first, she spent her days trying to take care of us - dealing with the everyday struggles of making ends meet and seeing that we were raised in the proper manner. It was only in her later years that we discovered that she liked to travel when Jo and I finally convinced her to take a trip with us to a lakeside cabin in northern Vermont. She loved it. She loved walking through the woods identifying various trees and plant life. We took her for rowboat rides and she was as excited as a little kid. She reveled in the peace and quiet and we would sit on the deck in the evening just looking up at the stars and listening to the calls of the nighttime animals – the owls, the coyotes and the loons. She was born in the Tatra Mountains in Czechoslovakia and we didn't realize how much she missed the mountains. Armed with this new revelation, we tried to take her on all of our cabin trips and I think that we added a great deal of joy to what life she had left. It wasn't long after that, that she passed away. I like to think that we brought a little more happiness and some fond memories to her final years. We loved her dearly and miss her intensely. We named our motor home "Bea", hoping that she is still travelling with us and having fun, to make up for all those years of toil and sacrifice.

The third of my girls was named "Akasha". This had more to do with my wife insisting on a proper name rather than what we liked to call her. I think it means "great spirit in the sky" or something like that. Not keen on formality, I jokingly started calling her "Kasha" which I think means oatmeal in Czechoslovakian. Jo does not appreciate my dry sense of humor so after a bit of discussion, we eventually agreed to call her "Sparky". I don't know why, but anyone with dogs knows that sooner or later the right name just pops up. So we ended up with a nice, down home, American name that I knew how to spell and pronounce and didn't sound too pretentious. She possessed an unbounded supply of energy and sense of fun. She loved to go for runs and explore new areas. She didn't listen for a spit and was impossible to train. She seemed to be a mix of mainly wire-haired terrier and about one hundred other things. She was a medium-sized, black female with ears like a hound, tail like an Akita, webbed pads and two white circles around her eyes that gave her the comical look of being part raccoon. She did not have a sense of humor, and would give you a baleful, withering look when you referred to her as anything but the greatest dog in the world. Thankfully all those hundreds of genes mixed together allowed for a long and healthy life and she lived to be seventeen years old. I still can't believe all the years that we walked her, morning and night, through the rain, snow, cold, and heat. But we loved it, as we got to experience breathtaking sunrises and the ebbing breezes of the dusky summer nights. We spent most of our time with her and her passing broke our hearts.

These were my companions on my travels – spiritually and physically.

As for myself, I am a semi-retired CPA with a strong sense of tradition, a sarcastic sense of humor and I am generally a romantic at heart. If you looked up my birth sign – Leo – you would think I am a bold, fearless, leader who thrives on social interaction and has bus loads of friends. I must have been born prematurely or really late because I am the opposite of everything a Leo is supposed to be. I am an introvert and squirm at any hint of an upcoming social interaction. I am more than happy to labor in the shadows and let someone else take all the credit. I am not bold, am not fearless and instead of bus loads of friends, I probably have a maximum of about 2 – and that's on a good week. I revel in peace and quiet. I love fishing the small lakes and streams of Southern New Jersey in my kayak and love photography, sailing, mushroom picking and just being outdoors. I also love reading as Jo constantly attests to by yelling about our overflowing bookcases. I used to be an optimist and was generally happy with the way my life turned out even though it wasn't exactly as I had planned. Slowly, old age is creeping up and things are starting to crumble a bit.

Physical ailments seem to be popping up faster than the advertisements on my internet feed and my mental acumen and memory seem to be fading faster than invisible ink. My skin is beginning to take on the look of a wet plastic bag, my teeth are crumbling like our border wall and I have to struggle like a gymnast to cut my toenails. Sometimes I just look around and wonder what the hell is happening. Our parents lied to us – getting older sucks. Everything begins to hurt, you don't get any wiser, and in the distance you can see the light from that proverbial train that's coming to run you over. Now let me say, it's not all bad but you can get the sense that you are in a vise that is slowly tightening on you. You watch with a feeling of helplessness as your mental and physical abilities become compressed, your finances get squeezed and your hopes and dreams are squashed. What to do?

Jo and I decided to head out into the great outdoors. We are both amazed by nature and the overwhelming beauty of this country and decided that it would be the cure for our problems. Gobs of fresh air, peace and quiet, and getting away from life's entanglements would surely reinvigorate our bodies and calm our restless minds. Would it work?

We really hoped so.

CHAPTER 1

SWIMMING WITH THE LOONS

It looked to be a beautiful day. The sun was breaking out and a stiff, cool breeze was playing upon the surface of the lake. A chill was in the air. We rubbed our hands for warmth while our early morning exhalations, crystallized by the cold, rose as a foggy testament to autumn's chill in the northern forests. The grass near the landing was coated with frosty white decorations and a thin rime covered the fallen logs along the water's edge. The leaves were turning, splattered with red, orange and yellow daubs like an artist's renderings and a silent mist crept across the emerald waters. The promise of a beautiful fall day played in my mind as I sat at the picnic table drinking my coffee and pondering life.

Big Bear Lake is a beautiful lake in upper Minnesota, known to be the gateway for the Boundary Waters wilderness. After a two week journey, we were finally here. I looked forward to getting out on the lake, hoping to absorb some of that "wilderness aura" that surrounds the "Land of a Thousand Lakes" in the Minnesota north woods.

Hundreds of years ago the French-Canadian voyageurs plied their trade here: hunting and trapping for pelts to be sold at the scattered rendezvous posts. They travelled in sturdy birch-bark canoes which were large enough to carry the hundreds of pounds of furs and required supplies. They travelled for months at a time, from lake to lake, harvesting pelts of beaver, lynx, and mink from their traps. For sustenance, they relied mostly on pemmican (a mixture of dried meat and animal fat), foraging for plants and berries and hunting game. It was a tough, dangerous job. Being a dreamer, I pictured myself in those times

– wrestling bears, running rapids, and breaking new trails. I wanted to experience sitting at the campfire and listening to the howling of the wolves on a moonlit night and conversing with the crazy loons plying the lonely waters of the great north.

My early morning ponderings were over and I jumped into Bea (our RV) to wake Jo from her slumbers and to put the coffee on. She prepared a hardy meal of bacon and eggs while I dressed in warm layers and renewed our plans for the day. This was my big chance.

The previous day I had reserved 2 kayaks for our excursion. After breakfast we headed to the office to pick up our paddles and life jackets and proceeded to the landing area. The kayaks were very small and shaky. Cheap plastic, they were short and rode high in the water. Being a somewhat proficient kayaker myself, I soon convinced Jo that she would be ok and pushed her off into the lake. I have been a kayaker for many years and never had any problems, but these were very tipsy and made me pause for a moment. I shrugged it off and headed out onto the lake with my fishing gear and camera. Chuckling to myself, I told the Lord that if anyone flipped over today, let it be me, as I was older and not as good of a person as my wife. I hoped this small act of beneficence toward another would be rewarded with his grace. Little did I know: Be careful what you pray for!

It was a perfect setting for a paddle. A lone eagle soared above the pines and a quiet engulfed the waters. A hint of smoke from the early morning campfires drifted across the lake. The breeze was a little stiff, but not enough to mar the beautiful day. The sun was shining brightly and the reeds along the water's edge bowed and danced to the rhythm of the wind. I slowly drifted across the lake taking pictures and casting for what I hoped would be a nice pike or bass. The rocky, pine studded shores were unlike the sandy, flat beaches of South Jersey lakes and I snapped away with my new camera as the silence and fresh air engulfed my senses. Jo was slowly floating along the opposite shore searching for driftwood or anything else interesting that she could find. Not having much luck fishing, I decided to cross over to fish by my "sweetness". She saw me coming towards her and decided to paddle out to meet me in the middle of the lake as she wasn't having much luck either. As she approached in a perpendicular line, the breeze was at her back and pushing her quite swiftly while I bobbed along in between the wave crests trying to keep my boat somewhat stable. As she got closer, I warned her to slow down, but then realized I was too late and we were going to collide. As I leaned over to keep her kayak from crashing into me, the world turned upside down.

Moments later, shouting expletives (#!??!#!), I arose from the murky depths, realizing that my camera gear and fishing tackle were now sinking to the bottom of the lake. For the moment I was just pissed at the whole situation while I thrashed in the waters of Big Bear Lake. I wanted to experience the lake, but not this way!

After a few minutes of kicking and paddling my brains out, I began to realize that I had bigger problems. It was quite chilly out on this October day and I had dressed appropriately – layers and layers of clothing with thick socks and my hiking boots on. I was using my life jacket as a seat cushion – not a particularly intelligent move at the present moment! My wet clothes must have weighed 500 pounds and I was sinking like a rock. I kept trying to climb up on the nose of the kayak, which was floating mostly submerged because it had no inner flotation. It wouldn't hold my weight and every time I climbed up, it would sink back beneath the waves. This happened repeatedly and after a short while I was quickly running out of energy. My legs were turning into frozen sausages from the frigid autumn waters as I struggled to stay afloat. This 65 year old smoker with COPD was gasping and wheezing like an old accordion and my legs were numb and cramping. This was getting serious. I told Jo to stay away as I did not want to overturn her as well, for then we would both be goners. I was getting scared.

I could hear the children laughing and playing in the campground, the dogs barking, and somewhere far off – music playing. I was pondering once again, only this time the thin juxtaposition between life and death, as opposed to the beautiful day.

It slowly dawned on me that I WAS GOING TO DROWN! I could still see the eagle circling in the air currents above as I was swallowing little bits of Big Bear Lake and trying to keep my head above the waves. I told Jo I didn't think I was going to make it. I was starting to feel a warm and a serene calm permeate my body. Fond memories flashed through my mind. I said to Jo: "I love you honey", as I continued to struggle, exhausted and beaten.

WHAT THE HELL HAD HAPPENED????

HOW THE HELL HAD I GOTTEN HERE????

CHAPTER 2

INTRODUCTION

I grew up in a relatively poor household. It was a struggle just to make ends meet and extravagances, like travel, were definitely out of the budget. The most we could manage were irregular visits to my relative's homes in the Catskill Mountains of New York or the infrequent wedding or funeral out of town. We mostly had to entertain ourselves when it came to free time, of which we had little. Hunting and traipsing through the woods, swimming at the local lake and fishing the small ponds and streams were about the extent of my travels. I still have scars from being shot in the head with a BB-gun and being hit in the butt from a spear my brother threw at me. But, hey, we had to get our fun where we could find it. As I reached my teens, I joined the local scout troop with my two best friends who lived in my neighborhood. It was great learning all about woodsman lore and camping out in the great outdoors. It also let me see a bit of the outside world. We travelled to nearby states and it opened up brand new possibilities for fun and excitement outside of my normal realm. I really enjoyed seeing and experiencing new places and new activities. All too quickly, I transitioned into my mid teens and had to begin working during my free time to try and save up for college. I worked at night during my college semesters and summer days, to put money aside for my continuing education expenses. I more or less forgot about the excitement of travel and concentrated on my education and career. The memories of those brief travels did not desert me, but merely burrowed down in my mind to be resurrected at some future date.

Graduating college, finding my first "professional" job and getting married consumed the next decade of my life, but around this time my almost forgotten fond memories of travel started to grow like small seeds in my mind. During our first few years of marriage, Jo and I managed to get out occasionally to go camping and we really enjoyed it. As our finances improved, we graduated to renting cabins for a week here or there throughout the northeast. We made week-long trips once or twice a year to the New York Catskills and Adirondacks, the Green Mountains of Vermont and the coast of Maine. We even made a trip to Florida and the southern states. We enjoyed travelling but were somewhat limited in our expenditures, as we concentrated on paying off our mortgage and saving for retirement.

Eventually, after 15 years of work, we both decided we needed a bigger break from our structured lives and planned a 6 week trip out west. We couldn't wait to begin our trip after researching some of our nation's beautiful national parks like Zion, Bryce, the Grand Canyon and the Tetons. It took quite a bit of planning as we only had a pick-up truck to travel in and limited resources. This was in the days before the internet and I spent months writing away for travel and lodging brochures. My boss's deadpan reply to my request for a six week vacation was: "I guess its ok, nobody has ever asked for that long of a vacation before".

So, off we went on our cross country jaunt with our golden retriever, Sporty. We had a fantastic time. We spent a few days camping on the north rim of the Grand Canyon and the breathtaking vistas were awe-inspiring. Hiking down and through the hoodoos in Bryce canyon was unbelievably beautiful and listening to the elk bugle at Oxbow Bend in the Tetons as the sun was rising was an incredible experience. The beautiful animals were scattered across the frosted meadow, their foggy exhalations rising with the early morning mists. I will never forget those moments. What most people don't talk about on a trip like that is the sense of calm and peacefulness that pervades your body. More than the incredible sights, what my wife and I talked about the most was the incredible feeling of relaxation that we experienced long after we returned home. No TV, no newspapers, and little interaction with day-to-day tribulations for an extended period of time resulted in a wonderful de-stressing of the body and mind. We became totally relaxed and our minds calmed to an almost imperceptible level. We forgot about work, our bills, our home projects and our everyday problems. Our trip was the best thing we ever did and we vowed to do it again.

Of course, once you get home and return back to work, the serenity and memories begin to fade. We were back in the grind, but this time we held onto those memories tightly and refused to let them go. We planned to resume our travels in retirement, once our goals were achieved and everything was ready to go. All we had to do was keep up with our current health and financial plans for 10 years and then everything would be wonderful. Well, you know what happens with the "best laid plans". Tragedy was heading our way like an ominous storm cloud and our lives would soon be upended.

CHAPTER 3

PLANS GO AWRY

It was pleasant day in December 2009. A chill engulfed our house, but it was nice and warm inside. The fireplace was going and we were having a good time putting up the Christmas ornaments and preparing for the holidays. Towards evening the phone rang and just like that our lives were upended. It was a call from the imaging company to inform my wife that her breast scan had come back positive for a nodule. She was instructed to get it checked out as soon as possible. Like the air going out of a tire, our festive mood evaporated and an impending feeling of doom descended on our home. The following week we visited the doctors and they took a biopsy of the nodule. Already being in panic mode, I tried to shield Jo from seeing the biopsy needle perched on the exam room table. It looked to be the length of my forearm and the needle the size of a straw. Jo, being as brave as ever, calmly laid on the examination table. While the doctor proceeded to implant the needle into the nodule, we watched on the room monitor as he removed a small piece for the biopsy. As Christmas approached, we spent another tense week awaiting the results of the test.

The bad news arrived a few days before Christmas Eve. Yes, the biopsy revealed my wife did in fact have breast cancer and plans had to be made to move forward. As you can imagine, our Christmas holidays were now totally destroyed. We held each other and cried, trying to imagine the path forward. We never finished the holiday decorations. Our tree was only half adorned with lights and bulbs and our packages lay unopened as the holiday passed by. We were scared and our dreams began to crumble.

The weeks turned into a blur as the wheels of big medicine kicked into gear. Appointments with surgeons, radiologists, cancer specialists, and dieticians filled our days. After various tests and exams, surgery was scheduled for February of 2010. As the day approached, our anxiety increased. The ride to the hospital in the dark pre-dawn hours was silent as we both thought about this new path we were heading down. We held each others hands. There wasn't much to say. I think we were both in shock. I remember my wife yelling in pain as they inserted 4 needles into her chest, during pre-op. The surgery was pretty straightforward – cut out a flap of the breast and remove the tumor as well as the surrounding nodes. Then they made us wait until they tested the remaining nodes to see if any were positive for cancer. After a couple more tests, a few more nodes were removed from under my wife's arm and the surgery was completed. The recovery was fairly straightforward as to rest and recuperation and she was feeling pretty good after a few weeks. She did have some pain and weakness in her arm as a result of the surgery but other than that, it seemed the surgery was a success. We were both feeling good about the results. Part of the journey was completed but we still had a long way to go.

Little did we know that the surgery was the easy part of the process. After rehabilitating for a month to get back into shape, the radiation regimen was started. As treatments progressed, my stoic wife refused to knuckle under and continued to work while dealing with the nightmare. Rising early for her radiation treatments, she would dress and make herself a lunch, then go get the treatments before going to work. It was exhausting and painful and began to take a toll on her. The treatments literally burned the skin of her breast.

After the radiation, the chemo treatments started. What did we think about the radiation treatments then? They were a walk in the park. The chemo literally kills the cells in your body. The theory being, as your good cells are killed, the cancer cells will also die and hopefully you have enough good cells to survive and come back. It is like a war being fought between your body and the chemotherapy. Your bodily systems go berserk. Red cells, white cells, liver function, platelets, immune cells and nerve cells go haywire. They run amok trying to repel the invading army of chemotherapy. Your bodily systems begin to break down. As a result of the treatments, her veins had shrunk, her bones were more fragile and her immune system was destroyed. She fought daily nausea, her nerves were screaming, she felt constant aches and pains and was so tired she felt like collapsing. My wife lost her hair – she had beautiful long blond hair down to her waist and I used to kid her that that is why I married her. There was nothing left to kid about. She was going bald. She came down the steps in our home holding big piles of her hair in her hand that began coming out in clumps as she was showering. Tears streamed down both of our eyes. My heart cried out.

My beautiful, effervescent girl was now a bald, ghostly shadow of her former self. Dark circles under her eyes, walking hunched over in pain, she looked like a refugee from a concentration camp. Her skin turned a grayish pallor and she lost a lot of weight. She was wasting away before my eyes and there was not much I could do about it. I tried to help her outside so that she could sit in the sun under a blanket and get some fresh air. She was sick to her stomach, exhausted and shaking. Watching her suffer was heartbreaking. The mental anguish of watching your loved one go through something like that is excruciating.

After a couple of months, the treatments finally stopped and a return to some sense of normality ensued while we waited through the healing process. We prayed that she would regain her strength and that the cancer was gone.

Finally, after a year of worry, stress, and complete disarray in our lives, my wife's situation began to improve. The cancer had not yet reappeared and she was beginning to get back into shape. She finally felt well enough to eat good, healthy meals and was beginning to walk and practice her yoga. Things were looking up. Our minds and finances began to heal. Had we won the cancer war?

CHAPTER 4

MR. GLASS HALF-EMPTY

Now people always ask me why I have a glass half-empty attitude about life. I will tell you why. Jo's situation was improving and we spent time trying to get our lives back on track. Another year passed and I began having pains in my stomach and constant constipation and diarrhea. Shrugging off the symptoms as due to IBS or stress, I continued my life as before: trying to save up some money for retirement and trying to get our lives back to normal. As a celebration of my wife's recuperation, I went out and bought an older sailboat, because I knew she loved sailing from the few trips we had gone on in the past. Never having operated a sail boat before, I put all my efforts into learning how to sail so that we could enjoy some recuperative, calm moments sailing in the bays in South Jersey. As the year progressed, my sailing got a bit better. I continued to hone my seamanship skills, all the while being nagged by stomach problems which did not seem to be improving.

By the fall of that year, my stomach cramping had become severe and something had to be done. I scheduled a colonoscopy and began to worry a bit. Well, Mr. Glass half-empty's instincts proved right again. I had a tumor in my rectum and once again the wheels of big medicine started to spin. Could this possibly be happening again? I was diagnosed with stage 3 rectal cancer. To begin with I would have to undergo 33 rounds of radiation to try and shrink the tumor. So for a few months I received radiation in the mornings. It did not hurt, but the embarrassment of dropping your drawers everyday and lying on a table, while what looked like 18 year old girls operated the equipment, was

17

overwhelming. I kidded with them about taking videos and showing them to their classmates in school. Towards the end of the treatments, the diarrhea became severe and to avoid total embarrassment I skipped the last 2 sessions. A person's pride can only take so much. My last treatment, I drew a smiley face on my butt so that the aides would have something to remember me by.

After the radiation, dozens of meetings ensued with a colorectal surgeon for examinations, consultations and CT Scans. The 100 mile trips just aggravated an already horrendous nightmare. It was to be quite an operation, so of course many tests were scheduled and my life became a week-by-week gauntlet of specialist visits and tests. Lung tests, heart tests, blood tests, vascular tests, and stress tests ensued. Running on a treadmill until I just about fell over from fatigue, blowing into the little tube until I thought my lungs would explode, having instruments jammed up my butt hole and having every orifice in my body probed and palpitated was humiliating and very stressful. When you are very sick, you are no longer a person – you are an object.

Finally the day came and I reported for surgery. Unbelievably for me, I only had to take one "Xanax" and I made it to the hospital without collapsing from stress. Did I tell you that I suffer from anxiety? You can imagine what the years of stress were doing to my mind and body. Well, I made it thru the 6 hour operation - barely. My wife told me that as I was being wheeled out of the operating room, I was cursing everyone and everybody in the hospital. She had to turn her head in embarrassment. They must have been a little chintzy with the gas.

I was awakened the next day by a pretty, 18 year old nurse. I shrunk under the covers in embarrassment as she tried to get the catheter in place. The shave that followed did not help. After a stay in a hospital you have no dignity left. By the end of the week I was strolling thru the hallways for exercise, flashing my supposed cute butt (according to my wife), for all to see. Thankfully, I didn't have the giant scar down my chest because they had performed robotic surgery.

Did I tell you that up to this point I had never been in a hospital before? I don't know if I will ever go willingly again. I was always in perfect shape. The first time I get sick, they radiate my body for a month, cut out half my intestines and I end up with a hernia and a body that felt like I had been in a war. I was hurting, was weak, and stressed out of my mind. Just like with Jo, the war was only half over and the surgery was the easy part.

I now had to get back into "good shape" so that I could survive the months of chemotherapy. Not to belabor the point, let me just tell you it was bad. I felt sick every day, was very weak, was always nauseous, and lost a lot of weight. When you do chemo you get sores in your mouth and on your lips. You are constantly cold. When I went outside to try and get some fresh air, I had to bundle up like I was trekking across Antarctica. If your hands are in the refrigerator for even a moment, they become painfully cold. You can not eat with normal utensils as the metal taste makes you want to vomit. I lost about 35 pounds during treatment. I always felt sick to my stomach and never wanted to eat. I end up subsisting on protein milkshakes and soup.

After a horrendous spring and summer, I slowly began to try and return to normal. I exercised and started practicing yoga, not only for the physical benefits, but also to try and heal my mind which at this point was a total cluster-fxxx! I was confused, stressed, depressed, and probably a tad suicidal. My wife had just endured her cancer ordeal and now I was going through it also. I remember sitting in the chemo room bundled up under blankets because I was freezing. I watched the drips of chemo entering the tube and wondered if each drip was bringing me closer to death or healing. It was like sitting on death row and pondering your certain death while waiting for a last minute reprieve.

I lost my job and of course at this point the bills were once again pouring in. Just trying to keep track of the old bills, new bills, paid bills, deductibles, co-pays and bills from wherever was a full time job. We both had giant folders full of paperwork. We received a bill from the anesthesiologist for $14,000. It seems that he did not accept my insurance. Billing $14,000 for a six hour job where you don't even do anything except monitor a machine. Is the whole world going crazy?

My chemo was approximately $3,000 a week for a bag of solution to be dripped into my arm. Why don't our useless politicians do something about this medical extortion? Even if insurance pays for most of it, we are all paying for it in one way or the other.

Well, to get back on track, it was not a good year. Once again my retirement account was streaming out the door, being used for other than retirement. I eventually was feeling better and learned how to live with the idea that both my wife and I had now had cancer and an uncertain future hovered over our heads. A third of our retirement savings had been spent on medical and living expenses and we were now in our mid-fifties. Being a CPA and numbers man, all our finances had been well planned out and structured for that retirement payday. Everything was now in disarray. As we tried to get along with our lives, our financial plan was out the window, our healthy retirement plan was out the window, and our work plans were out the window. I felt like I had post-traumatic stress syndrome. I could not plan anymore. You learn to live day by day, not knowing if your cancer or other ailments associated with the treatments would strike. I felt like my safe little nest had just been run over with a lawnmower. Joy had left our lives.

I began to doubt my religion. I consider ourselves to be a decent, faithful couple. What kind of God would bring this catastrophe down on us? Why was I praying? What was I praying for? Could it get any worse? You begin to realize that you are on your own in life. You will never feel as lonely as when you are suffering from cancer. People begin to avoid you. You sit at home, for the most part, all alone – for months. People have nothing to talk to you about. You never go out. They know you feel terrible. Your future goals and plans are wrecked. You are depressing to be around. You are not happy, you have all types of aches and pains that they don't understand and your life is a general shit hole. Of course some of the dedicated friends and family do try but it is an insurmountable wall to overcome. The world goes on and other people are happy, having parties, going to weddings, and accomplishing their goals. Your life is crumbling around you as you try to stay alive. More than just the physical pain, the mental anguish is almost unbearable. You are on your own, and must deal with it alone.

Had god abandoned us also? It felt like it.

CHAPTER 5

A REORDERING OF PRIORITIES

Eventually you start all over again. In order to survive, both mentally and physically we took Stephen King's advice and "got busy living". We slowly worked to get our mind and bodies back to where they should be. We began to set goals again, albeit much smaller. As we broached our 60's, we realized that our finances would never be in good shape again, so we tried to save for small things. For me that meant a camera, some fishing gear, and maybe a week up in the Vermont woods. I started taking small walks and set up a light exercise regimen so that my body would heal. I started meditating to try and heal my mind which felt like a scrambled egg. Our "new normal" was depression and despair. It was hard to overcome.

After living like this for awhile, I began to realize that there were some good things that happened as a result of the cancer. I began to see life in a new light – as a temporary gift which might be taken away at any moment. I began to appreciate the smaller things in life, which I now realized meant more to me than my savings and plans. Watching the birds in the yard, taking a quiet walk in the woods, or enjoying a good meal was now more important and more delightful. I appreciated the closeness and love of family and friends. I don't think I would have survived without my wife. Our marriage grew stronger.

I started a small tax practice at home to try and make a few bucks. I could no longer face the stress of 60 hour tax weeks in the spring or client meetings with lawyers and IRS agents. It is amazing what you can live on when you have to. We realized we could get by on very little and be happy! We never go out to dinner any more. In my downtime I learned how to cook. So between my wife (who is a great cook) and me, it feels like a waste of money going out to eat. We eat great meals at home and are more comfortable.

We discovered that you don't need "new" things to feel better about life. Now we appreciate the older things. I love kayaking and fishing the small ponds around our house. I love picking mushrooms and even raking the leaves on a fall day. The costs are minimal and the joy is greater.

I never buy new clothes. I love putting on an old shirt that brings back cherished memories of walking with my dog or feeling the pull of a 5 lb. largemouth on the end of my fishing pole. My wife cans and sews to save a bit of money. We now have time to enjoy life. Some people will argue that you need a lot of money to enjoy life. They are wrong. As long as you can pay for the daily necessities, that is all you need. There is nothing better than enjoying a hot cup of coffee and cream on a cold winter day, as you read a good book.

We now had the luxury of actually sitting down and talking together – not about the unimportant crap, but our feelings and thoughts and dreams.

Things come and go. Memories stay with you forever. I drive a pick-up truck that is 21 years old. It's still in good shape. It also brings back many memories of bygone trips and explorations: sinking in a puddle one winter day and having giant ice bergs scraping its hood, sleeping in the back and roaming the desert southwest, or driving up in the N.J. Pine Barrens and finding a quiet little oasis along a stream to spend an afternoon. I love my truck. It has been a loyal servant and friend for many years. Why should I get a new one?

I am a romantic at heart. I had tears in my eyes when I recently had to junk my RCA color console TV and I get a bit sentimental when my wife throws out my old ripped, favorite pants or a shirt. Sometimes I hide stuff for sentimental reasons, but Jo eventually finds and tosses them. I have 3 cast iron sinks lying in the garage and around the house. I'll use them some day, won't I? The older I get, the worse I get. I guess that is how we try to hold onto the past.

The new thing is to "de-clutter". That's a great idea but you also de-clutter your mind of all your great, old, cherished memories. Not this guy. When we pass it on, it's going to take them a year to get rid of all our old "stuff". They might think of it as junk, but I like to think of it as treasure to be carefully picked through, caressed and salted away for future memories. I would not deny my heirs the joyous hours they will spend picking through my clutter. I am sure they will thank me some day. They will have to work for that inheritance.

We had finally reached the golden years and looked forward to collecting our Social Security payments. Now everyone complains about how little it is and I would agree. However for those who are making minimal income and have a large old farmhouse to support, it is a godsend. We had to sign up early, due to our health problems and lack of income. It is not much, but that, along with a small IRA distribution is enough for us to survive and actually do some of the things we like. Our priorities quickly changed.

We have always wanted to travel and see this wonderful country. In the past, work and life's priorities always seemed to get in the way and we never had the time. Now was our chance – the only problem being that we finally had the time but not so much the money.

CHAPTER 6

FRUGAL – NOT CHEAP!

After the ravages of cancer on our lives, our attitudes about the future began to change. We had spent our entire lives purchasing very carefully, trying to save for retirement and we passed up buying all those things one feels entitled to as they work hard and get older. We started with nothing. We even had to use our wedding gifts to pay for our wedding reception. We worked hard for 30 plus years to gain some kind of sense of financial stability. We scrimped and saved our entire marriage. Some people snidely refer to us as being "cheap", but I like to think that we are just being "frugal".

The house we bought was a "fixer upper" to put it mildly. The outside window frames were unpainted and rotting away. The vegetation surrounding the house was overgrown and the grass was knee-high. Upon entering the house we were greeted with a single cabinet sink in the kitchen that was sinking into the floor from water damage. The upstairs toilet was clogged and unusable. The walls were covered in ten layers of wallpaper, the molding in ten layers of paint and the wooden floors covered with ten layers of linoleum. Some deranged person had run about the house firing staples into all the woodwork. Working our way up into the attic, we found a couple of dead blackbirds lying between the rafters which contained no insulation. They must have gotten in through the broken windows. Glancing up we could see bits of sunlight filtering through the holes in the roof. The rooms were very dark and thick window coverings blocked out the light. We felt as though we had entered some medieval horror show. Jo just looked at me like I was crazy for even considering living there. But my theory was that we were poor, full of energy, and needed a house in the country to raise our planned-for five children. It was on a nice piece of land in the neighborhood I grew up in and I eventually convinced her that with a "little" elbow grease, a small amount of money and a bit of help we would eventually have a castle in the woods.

Well after 40 years, no children and countless hours spent fixing the homestead we do indeed have our "castle". Beauty is in the eye of the beholder. Some might consider it a bit scary looking but I consider it comfortable. It has treated us well through the years. Even the resident ghost that lives in the attic likes the job we did on his habitat and occasionally he raps his pleasure on the attic walls. We still have quite a bit to do after all this time but have decided we will leave some of the fixing up to future owners as we are now out of money and elbow grease. I can tell because usually my wallet is empty and my joints make some kind of strange creaking sound when I move about.

The plan mostly worked out as projected. I thought that purchasing the house would be a good deal, as we could put less down and have smaller monthly mortgage payments. We could use the savings from the smaller payments to pay for some of the capital improvements we expected to make. Every night and on weekends we worked on the house, budgeting about $500 a month for improvements. Being a CPA, home reconstruction is not my strong point. However, with the help of friends and family, I learned quickly. We put on a new roof, ripped out all the interior walls and insulated them. Then we added new plumbing and wiring – most of it done with the help of others. A wood stove was installed to save on the heating bills.

It is a big old farm house, so furnishing it was a challenge. We went to estate sales and yard sales, and gladly accepted any contributions of used items if they could be put to use. The result was that we furnished the entire house for less than $10,000. That included a beautiful, hand made bedroom suite crafted by the Amish that we got for the same price as your normal store bought junk. It was expensive, but we knew it would last forever. We also bought a new living room set, mattress, stove, refrigerator, sink, bathroom tub and shower. Donations included a dish washer, oil tank and a recliner. For $500 we bought a beautiful dining room table, chairs, china cabinet, hutch, 3 bedroom dressers and a vanity at an estate sale. We had to replace all the kitchen cabinets (The old houses only had 1 or 2 cabinets). After a bit of effort, we discovered an out of work, alcoholic cabinetmaker that agreed to custom build two walls of full kitchen cabinets for the price of $2000, which was less than store bought manufactured cabinets. Knowing his past history, we paid as things were completed and budgeted 3 months for the job. That was a good move on our part as it took him all summer to complete the work. Occasionally he would arrive, completely disheveled and hung-over, but eventually he would get some work done. He was quite a craftsman when he was sober. He would show up for two or three days and then we would not see him for a week. But as long as you keep your expectations low and have some patience, you will not be disappointed. Eventually we had beautiful custom cabinets installed at a very reasonable price.

The house is very old and has hardwood floors throughout. The estimate to refurbish them was very expensive, so I decided to tackle the job myself. What a job – dust everywhere and I think I lost some of my hearing in the process of running the sander 8 hours a day for a month. But the result was very pleasing. Are there imperfections? Sure, but these only add to the charm of the old house. When I was staining the floor I was also painting the staircase banisters and steps a beautiful forest green color. Without our knowledge, our cat (Slick Nick) decided to exit her temporary imprisonment in an upstairs bedroom while we were sleeping. The result was a couple of beautiful green cat prints permanently imposed on my shiny foyer floor. Did I get mad? Of course I did. But time heals all wounds and now I think they are beautiful. Slick Nick is no longer with us, but we have fond memories whenever we see those green paw prints on the floor.

Since it was an old house, it had beautiful old wooden molding around the rooms and tin ceilings. We scraped and repainted the old ceilings and sanded the old molding through many layers of paint. The result was beautiful and could not be replaced these days. Of course my brain has been addled ever since, sanding that old lead-based paint.

We took out most of the old windows and replaced them with inserts as our budget allowed, and added a nice large bow window to our dining room. Eventually a new heater was added and completed our major purchases. Was it all worth it? We spent thousands of hours rehabbing our house, skipped vacations for 5 years, endured endless minor bruises, washed our plates and silverware in the downstairs tub for months, spent endless hours reading electrical and plumbing books, and missed many a gathering and parties. My wife honed her sewing abilities and made all the window treatments in the house. The result was we got a house finished to our liking, paid off our mortgage in 7 years and were debt free most of our lives. Sure, the old homestead still has its quirks – as most old homes do, but that just makes it more special in our eyes. It probably made our marriage stronger and it united us in a monumental job for years that surely gave us plenty of exercise and experience that we would not have gotten otherwise. My friends are just now paying off the mortgages on the new houses they bought back then.

We have always been frugal. After you operate that way for a while, it becomes ingrained like muscle memory. We rarely go out to eat, cook all our meals at home, have a garden for vegetables and rarely go shopping. We try to pay for our vehicles mostly in cash, and avoid credit cards as much as possible. When I see the current crop of entitled children (and grown-ups) I just shake my head in bewilderment. Most families in America today have no savings and are in debt up to their eyeballs. They spend everything they make and are partying like it's the 1920's. I was taught to work hard and save hard. We are not entitled to anything except life and liberty. When the "Great Reset" comes, the entitled will be crying all the way to the soup lines as governmental resources run dry and the economy collapses from debt and runaway spending. We looked forward to a decent, leisurely retirement.

What happens when health issues derail your plans? It is not pretty. You feel as though you have been sucker-punched in the gut. After both of us having back-to-back cancers, our plans were in total disarray. We spent tens of thousands of dollars on operations and doctors. I lost my job. Try to get medical insurance when you both have had cancer. Our first year premium for a cheap medical plan was $28,000 with a $15,000 deductible. We withdrew approximately $200,000 from our IRA's for living expenses. The life plan we had was a good one and works most of the time. However, in cases like ours, it makes you wonder. Thankfully we had the financial resources to pay our bills. We had both worked and saved since our early teens. Now it felt like it was all for nothing. Our dream of a long, leisurely retirement was destroyed and our finances were draining away at a rapid pace. Our health had taken a serious hit, and the future was getting somewhat cloudy. The clock was ticking.

CHAPTER 7

"ROUGHING" OUT THE PLAN

We had always dreamed of traveling the country but never felt that we had the time or the savings to afford it. We compensated by spending many hours roaming through our native Pine Barrens and occasionally taking short trips to the northeast to visit relatives or to relax fishing and unwinding. Now with the clock ticking, it was time to accelerate our plans for travel and adventure. Our illnesses were a glaring warning signal that sometimes things don't go as planned and banking on a life of longevity was not always in the cards. I started planning some trips, but soon realized how expensive major get-a-ways in luxury cabins or resorts could be. Still determined to push on, I started to consider camping as an alternative option to achieve our dreams. Jo was not quite on board, but I kept reading and researching how we could travel without spending a million dollars to do it.

When we first got married, we had occasionally gone tent camping with minimal supplies. It was fun to be in the great outdoors, but it definitely had its trials and tribulations. It was almost impossible to cook on the little gas stove and the menus were pretty limited. Having only a few small coolers, the gastronomic selections were minimal. Hot dogs and hamburgers, eggs, cereal, milk and lunchmeat were about the most we could handle along with the 10 pounds of required ice.

Trying to get a restful sleep on a cold, damp night was impossible. We had a lumpy mattress and our old tent leaked. Many a night was spent huddled with our retrievers in our quest for warmth.

We did not want to spend our retirement years starving on meager rations, getting eaten by bugs or freezing to death in the remote wilds of America. Was it possible to comfortably travel this great country of ours while camping and not break the budget? After attending various camping equipment expos and talking with fellow campers, we decided that yes, it was possible. We discovered that modern camping trailers and motor homes were not astronomically expensive and are loaded with comfortable amenities: bathrooms, showers, TVs, stoves, refrigerators, heaters and air conditioners. We marveled at the equipment now available to those who wanted to "rough it". Jo was impressed, so our search began in earnest.

First, I considered camping trailers. They were beautiful and loaded with everything we needed. They were relatively inexpensive as compared to motor homes. They would definitely fit our budget except for one small problem - my twenty year old pick-up truck. I love my truck, it has treated me well and I have endearing faith in its ability to keep on chugging forever. However, hitching a couple tons to the back of it and driving around the country on its rusty frame did not seem like a good idea. It was wheezing worse than me and after a quick discussion with my long time, green, metallic friend, I decided it was not capable of handling the job required.

Have you seen the cost of a new pick-up truck today? I was soon experiencing convulsions, both physically and mentally, after visiting a few of the local dealerships. Had the world suddenly gone crazy? The asking prices were more than the cost of my house. The payments on a new truck and camper would last into my afterlife. Maybe that is the definition of hell. Oh well, Plan "A" was not going to work, so I switched to plan "B".

Plan "B" was to consider buying a small motor home. Though considerably more expensive than a trailer, they contained everything we needed, were self-contained and I would not have to purchase a new truck.

So we spent many weeks at various dealerships, touring the units while trying to decide what amenities we required and which were too outlandish and a waste of money. We took some for rides to see if we could handle a large vehicle on the road. We compared how the various systems worked and the comfort of the rides.

We had detailed discussions with the salesmen regarding the different units' reliability and options. Now listening to them, owning a new motor home was equivalent to attaining the gates of heaven during your lifetime - and only for a small amount down and low payments forever. They didn't realize they were talking with Mr. and Mrs. "Frugal".

While doing all this, I also began researching motor home reliability and discovered one big problem – their tendency to arrive from the manufacturers and promptly fall apart. Leaky water systems, cabinets falling off walls, things hooked up backwards and shoddy workmanship seemed to afflict all the newer units. The lack of pride in workmanship today is unbelievable. After purchasing one, a buyer could expect to spend many months at the dealership getting things fixed, hoping to someday travel.

I am a CPA, not a rocket scientist. I did not relish the idea of buying a prohibitively expensive vehicle, loaded with a myriad of complex mechanical systems that needed constant repair and maintenance and of which I knew nothing. I was feeling a bit bewildered.

The motor home option was not looking too attractive. After many days of pondering, a great idea exploded in my mind – buy a used one! The owners would have already addressed any manufacturing defects. Since they are relatively expensive, owners tend to baby their unit with annual tune-ups, oil changes, waxing and servicing. Most campers only put 5,000 or 10,000 miles a year on their rigs, as they are too busy working and making those eternal payments to actually take the time to enjoy them. My frugal mind also smiled, knowing that I would save a ton of money. So began our search for a used motor home.

It was a bit scary. Would we be able to ascertain a great unit from a piece of junk? I spent hours researching how to inspect a used unit for major deficiencies. How much did it cost? I spent more hours comparing the prices of used units and what the various equipment options were worth.

I drew up a list of what size unit we were looking for and the options we wanted, all the while knowing that finding the perfect fit would be difficult in the used market.

We decided on a smaller, gasoline-powered unit in the 20 to 25 foot range. We were comfortable driving that size motor home and since we only expected to be travelling for 4 or 5 years, did not want the expense or require the durability of a diesel engine. The unit had to have air conditioning and heat, a rooftop ladder, oven, full bathroom, heated tanks, generator, outside shower and a porcelain toilet.

Obviously we needed heat and air conditioning to comfortably travel the highways at different times of the year. Some motor homes don't have rooftop ladders and I didn't relish the idea of taking up valuable storage space toting around a ladder on our journeys. We needed the oven – we both love cooking and it would save us a ton of money if we didn't have to eat out. As regarding the full bathroom, we're both in our sixties. Neither of us relished the idea of trekking to the bathhouse at 3:00 in the morning, if you know what I mean. Now I wouldn't mind just taking a pee out the door in the middle of the night, but Jo doesn't quite get my attraction to nature and nixed that idea. I thought the heated tanks would come in handy for any early spring and late fall trips.

Now Jo and I like camping in the great outdoors with some peace and quiet and room to get around. We had planned on mostly camping in state and federal parks. They are usually roomier, quieter, cheaper and more spacious than commercial campgrounds. We didn't care about the amenities – we don't need a playground, swimming pool, or organized activities. Some commercial campgrounds allow people to stay for months and they eventually begin to resemble small cities with the attendant trash and noise. They are always cramped and usually filled with partying drunks screaming and blasting music all night. That might be fine for some people but we were searching for something different. We were searching for solace. I'm sure there are exceptions but we haven't come across any as of yet. All we really wanted was some quiet time in the woods. The problem with a lot of state and federal parks is that they do not have hook-ups. Therefore, a generator would definitely be required.

We didn't really need an outside shower, but a single, beautiful vision kept flittering about my mind: a baking hot day in the barren desert, my sweetie and I cavorting about, beneath our outside shower, the cool sprinkles caressing our wrinkly skin - just two old hippies having some fun. Can't you see it? That picture alone was worth the extra cost and yes, I am still waiting as I write this, but waiting expectantly. Jo doesn't seem to share my artistic vision, but I'm working on it and it gives me another reason to keep on traveling.

As for the porcelain toilet, I don't think that it requires much explanation. Suffice it to say I don't feel like risking my life while uncomfortably perching my derriere on a flimsy piece of plastic. I have nightmares......

So for 2 years we looked and looked, always being too scared and frugal to pull the trigger. We fell back on the "it's in Gods hands theory" and continued our search with no results and time passing by. The urge to travel was becoming more urgent but we weren't getting anywhere.

We spent the time dreaming of our up-and-coming travels. The national parks and monuments, great landscapes, lonely scenic roads and windswept coasts pervaded our thoughts. Imagining quiet nights around the campfire, listening to the loons and the wolves, or watching the meteors streak by on a starry night bought peace to our minds. We were ready, but reality, not quite yet.

CHAPTER 8

SUCCESS!

Finally, in the fall of the third year of searching, I got a call from my sister, who lives in North Jersey. It is an interesting story, so I will fill you in on the details. God does indeed seem to work in mysterious ways.

It seems that my sister had left my mother's memorial card in a book she was reading when she returned it to the local library. Lo, and behold, an old friend who she hadn't talked to in quite a few years, took the same book out of the library and found the card. Recognizing the last name, she called my sister to inquire about the card. Yes, it was hers, and a long conversation ensued about catching up on old times. In the matter of chatting and what they were doing, the friend mentioned they spent quite a few weeks camping and were just now selling their motor home and up-sizing to something bigger, because of children and grandchildren. My sister inquired about a few details, knowing that we had been looking for a couple years and indicated we might be interested and would give us a call. Upon receiving the call, we were excited, but remembering past searches to no avail, were hesitant to drive the two hours to look at the motor home, expecting to be disappointed once again. After talking to the owner, we learned he would be camping down by us in the Cape May area and would be passing near our home on his travels. I made a deal to meet him at the nearest rest stop on the local highway, just for a quick look.

The day came and I arrived at the rest stop not really expecting much, but hoping none the less. After three years of looking, I was just about ready to give up.

I THOUGHT IT WAS BEAUTIFUL - the right size and all the required must-haves. I told him I was very interested and now I was nervous because he had the big "for sale" sign in the window. After almost three years of looking, could we finally have found it? I rushed home and told my wife all about it and told her we had to go see it as soon as possible. So the next day, we were on our way to North Jersey in the pouring rain.

Actually the rain was good because we could easily check for any leaks, which is one of the most serious problems encountered when purchasing a used recreational vehicle. Nothing leaked and the cabinets and woodwork were still in beautiful condition.

It had a full shower, oven, microwave, gas engine, outside shower, large refrigerator, heated tanks, generator, and a porcelain toilet! I saluted the gentleman's taste in motor homes. Of course there was a ladder on the back and I went up on top to give a cursory inspection in the pouring rain. It also had a ton of extras I did not expect to be able to afford. That is another reason to buy used if you can. You get all the extras for just about nothing. It had tinted windows, a hard fiberglass roof, heated side view mirrors, back up camera, in-dash GPS and CD player, a revolving passenger seat, Sealy Posturpedic mattress, ducted a/c vents, LED lighting, a curved dining table (which probably works as good as the normal rectangular one, but is much "cooler"), fold-away Roku TV, tire valve extensions, surround sound stereo, pleated shades, screen door, a deadbolt lock on the side door, extra chassis battery, overhead vented fans and an inverter for running the refrigerator off the engine instead of using up your propane. It also had a full size generator and an emergency switch for the house batteries to start the engine if, god forbid, your unit would not start. In addition the gentleman had added a bike rack, had installed 6 new tires and had the brakes relined. He also had an appointment for getting the generator serviced and checked. WOW. I was somewhat overcome with all the extras and we were quite impressed with the unit and its owners. Being late in the year, the owner was also in the process of winterizing the unit and showed me how it was done. The unit was 4 years old - a bit older than I wanted and had a bit more mileage, at 30,000 miles, but I figured this would get us a reduced price and on the road. The outside was beautiful and in almost mint condition except for a little dimple where they had bumped into a tree. Being a bit older, the seating was a bit worn and there were a few nicks on the woodwork, but all-in-all it was a beautifully kept unit. The owner brought out a folder which held a record of all of the annual checkups, oil changes and grease jobs, any minor repairs and receipts for anything he had purchased for the unit and its price. The man was impressive.

So, the wife and I had a quick out-of-the way discussion and decided to make an offer, knowing that this unit would not last long on the market. After haggling for a few moments about the price, we agreed to what I thought was a very reasonable approximate figure and we left the owners with a deposit and an agreement to return the following week to pick up the unit after he had the generator serviced and we could take some time to go over the unit in more detail. The price could be adjusted for any minor problems or deficiencies that we came across in our final review.

The following weekend we returned for a thorough inspection of the camper, along with a check for the purchase. The owner simultaneously was using our check as a down payment on his camper and needed to sell quickly. I am not an expert negotiator, but I do know that if someone is in a hurry to sell and you have the cash, then you are in a good negotiating position. Another one of my financial suggestions to individuals is to always try to have an open line of credit. This way you can write a check immediately if it helps in your negotiations. The sellers were very helpful and showed us how all the systems worked on the unit. My wife also videotaped the process for future review. After a bit more negotiating we agreed on a final price and the transaction proceeded.

The purchase was a fairly large transaction for us financially. Now due to my lack of mechanical skills, and the fact that I am from the sticks in South Jersey, I think somewhere along the line I might have threatened the poor man's life (in a nice way) if the unit had any major problems that he was hiding from us. In hindsight, it was an awful thing to do as the owners went out of their way to explain things to us and were very nice people. I guess I am just becoming one of those paranoid old geezers that are always scared of people ripping them off. I am sure he thought I was a nut. I was just a bit scared about spending a large part of our savings on something I did not have the ability to properly inspect or appreciate. At this point, after using and driving the motor home, I realize that they took excellent care of it and I owe them a great big thank you, for bringing a lot of joy to our lives and saving us lots of headaches.

Anyway, we concluded the transaction, ran over to the local motor vehicle station, transferred the title, and were the proud new owners of a motor home. Now I had to drive it home and of course I was a nervous wreck. As we zigzagged our way through the city and traffic, I was shaking like a leaf. Because of the weather, the wind was howling over North Jersey's Raritan Bridge that we had to cross to get home. I stayed in the right lane at 40 mph as the unit swayed its way over the bridge and I peered down at the churning water far below. We crossed over, crept through the skinny toll booth and then relaxed a bit for the long drive home. We eventually made it home, let out a collective sigh of relief, and excitedly discussed our future travel plans.

CHAPTER 9

GETTING PREPPED

Christmas was now rolling around and what better way to spend our Xmas allowance than on buying items for the camper. Instead of the usual boring clothes and knick-knacks that most people spend their hard earned money on, I now had a list of things we needed for the camper that were required necessities as opposed to the useless garbage of most years. Since the prior owners of the motor home were buying a new unit, one thing it did not come with was the usual supplies that are sold with a used unit. After spending my time on the RV blogs, I had put together what I thought was a pretty comprehensive list of required RV supplies. It was exciting to actually be buying things that would add to our joy throughout the year and made it feel like we were not just throwing our money out the window. I was like a kid in a candy shop and actually felt good about our list of Christmas expenditures, as our gifts to each other consisted of camping supplies and gear.

The list included a water filter, water pressure regulator, electrical surge protector, water hose, split water spigot adapter, waste hose and support, heavy duty electrical cords, a 30 amp to 50 amp adapter, tarps, non-spigot hose adapter, caulking for sealing the camper, fiberglass cleaner and wax, rugs for the interior, flashlights and lanterns, emergency gear, medical emergency kit, fuses, plastic scrapers and funnels, various cleaners, extra wiper blades, electric air pump, and most importantly the plastic wine glasses. The whole list totaled about $700 and I felt that it was money well spent. In addition, since we had lived in our house for over 30 years and had spent some time in the past camping, we had saved some equipment for that "we can use it some time in the future" theory that never quite pans out, but in this case did. Thank God that we didn't de-clutter. We had extra bedding and pillows, pots and pans and old camping gear such as a gas stove, fireplace grill, emergency road cones, glassware and dishes, old sleeping bags, backpacks and canteens, binoculars, caulking guns, axe and saw, and some small tools. Of course these lists are not all inclusive as I am writing from memory only, and ever since I turned 65 it seems like my memory is not quite what it used to be. I rarely know what day it is and occasionally wander into an adjoining room in our house and forget what I was looking for. But that is a matter for future discussions. Getting back to the supplies, I think that about $1500 would be a good estimate for outfitting your rig with the small necessities.

One purchase I forgot to mention for those cooks out there is a pizza stone. RV stoves are notorious for uneven and inefficient heating. If you decide you will be preparing meals mostly in the RV, it is a good investment. It evens out the heat distribution and allows you to cook almost anything you want without burning your meals. Jo even bakes cakes in ours.

Now some people out there might think that food preparation is not that important to your plans. But for those of you trying to live on a social security income, I figured our greatest savings would be in the food department. Eating out a couple times a week could surely run into the thousands of dollars if camping for extended periods. Now some would say "who wants to eat in when travelling?" We do. I think our meals are better than most restaurants and we are much more comfortable when dining. When we travel, we do not want to be running around looking for restaurants, standing in lines, and overpaying for those surprisingly blah meals. It is much more pleasurable for us to be sitting by the side of a lake, eating a wonderful meal and drinking wine while watching the sun set.

Does this plan limit you to just basic meals? Not in the least. When we go camping we have enough food and beverages to outlast Armageddon. RV refrigerators are surprisingly large. Before we go on an extended trip, we spend the prior week cooking up all our favorites, and for the most part stacking our freezer with enough frozen entrees to last quite some time. On our last trip we prepared and stored the following meals and accoutrements: containers of homemade spaghetti sauce, meatballs, homemade pizza dough, beef stew, chicken and dumplings, pepper steak, crab cakes, shrimp and scallops, chicken soup, fish and the usual hot dogs and hamburgers, steaks, pork chops, kielbasa and poultry. My wife makes multiple tins of cookies, dozens of blueberry, apple, and corn muffins, apple pies, and zucchini and banana breads. Occasionally I'll throw in a couple loves of artisan bread if I am feeling ambitious. I recently read in another book a foreigners amazement regarding American bread – "it lasts for months and never goes bad"! Food for thought? We try to stick with the home made stuff as much as possible. So, as one can see, it is possible to eat healthy and quite well without busting the budget. Our normal meals for a week might consist of homemade pizza one night, crab cakes with shrimp bombs, steak, baked rosemary chicken with vegetables and potatoes, breaded seafood combo, shrimp or chicken fried rice, lasagna, and beef stew. Not a bad selection and hundreds of dollars less than eating out. So you may still decide to call us cheap, but I still prefer frugal and husbanding of the worlds resources. We never throw out any excess food as we always cook our own portions and we try to buy organic fruits and vegetables while on the road. We don't only eat meat as the inside of our RV can attest to. My wife is never one to pass up any reasonable amount of fresh vegetables or fruits. Every nook and cranny of our dining area or seating area is filled with cabbages, lettuce, carrots, spinach, and broccoli. Little zucchinis can be seen peeking out amidst the pillows and the sweet potatoes and baking potatoes keep engaged in an entertaining dialogue as we roll down the highways and they surf the dishware in the cabinets. Oranges, apples, and bananas dance to our Sinatra CD's and occasionally one will escape and roll up between our seats to let us know it is time to stop and take a break. So our plan allows us to partake in some fantastic meals at a frugal price while actually making us healthier. What a deal. Why would one want to eat out?

There is a few more things I would like to have that are important for travel and camping: a good pair of hiking and walking boots, a weather alert radio, a pair of new off road bicycles and a tire monitor system. Alas, my frugality forces me to bide my time and stay within my budget. Since our early attempts at getting into shape by walking and riding are still in the infant stage, I am fairly sure that we can get by with sneakers and beat up bikes, but for us to progress to the "professional camper" stage, the right equipment is important. At my age and with my physical prowess being what it is, it might behoove me to hold off a bit on those expensive purchases as I might not make it to get into any kind of shape before I keel over from walking or riding too much. I will let you know how that is going in further chapters. However, if my wife takes over writing this book, you know what happened.

Of course, part of the prepping stage is vehicle maintenance. I try to do as much as I can, but not being a mechanic is a hindrance. So if you are like me, your salvation is to find a reasonable, able, prompt, and expert mechanic. I searched around awhile and was able to do just that. This all came about when I called the nearest RV dealership trying to get an oil change and check up. Due to the recent boom in camping, I was told I could get an appointment – in three months! Holy Mackerel! How can you plan camping trips when you are not sure if your unit can be serviced for months at a time. Most car dealerships or mechanics will not work on a motor home as their bays cannot fit one and their equipment cannot lift one. After searching and searching I came up with a great mechanic. He is reasonable and able and has the tools and equipment to work on our RV. I would tell you his name, but I do not want him to get swamped with work. I hope he forgives me, but I prefer to think of him as a passionate artist: one who pours his heart and soul into my camper's repairs, while singularly achieving that high level of self-actualization that results from the masterful care and maintenance he administers to my RV, Bea. He performs like a virtuoso, not for mere money, but for the love of the game itself. Of course I say this somewhat jokingly as the poor fellow has lately become a member of our extended family. Maybe that is why he helps me out. Whatever the reason is not important, but he is a great guy and I look forward to having a new "best friend".

Now that we have covered some of the prepping for travel, I will be moving on to the reason for this book – traveling tales.

CHAPTER 10

A RULE TO LIVE BY

Well, to pick up where I left off on page one, the valiant wife came through! She must have realized that she was close to losing her faithful man – the one who drives Bea across the country, keeps her feet warm on those cold nights and occasionally whips up a dinner feast for her to eat.

She paddled around my kayak, grabbed the life vest that was floating away and slowly worked the useless "seat cushion" strap down around my shoulder. Then she paddled around the other side and hooked the other loop around my other shoulder. Finally, I couldn't pull it down and hook it, but it provided enough buoyancy that I could somewhat float, as long as I kept kicking my legs. She then turned and headed for shore as I held onto the back of her kayak loop with my frozen fingers. After what seemed like an eternity, we made it to shore, where I unceremoniously collapsed in the sand; frozen, totally expended, and still cursing the loss of $2,000 worth of gear.

What happened? How could this beautiful day have been destroyed? We were having such a great trip. Moral of the story:

NEVER BRING YOUR WIFE ON A FISHING TRIP!

The next time my doctor advises a stress test I am going to tell him to forget it – I passed the natural one with flying colors.

CHAPTER 11

WHAT'S OUT THERE?

We had always planned on traveling in retirement and now the time had arrived. Obviously the time arrived quite a bit sooner than we planned and in quite different circumstances, but we needed to get going. Our finances were stressed, our health was stressed and of course our minds were beyond stressed. We needed a break. We were searching for solace but it was not to be found at home. It was out there somewhere and we had to find it. We needed a breath of fresh air and we had to get back into the rhythm of life that we had lost. The good thing was that our marriage had gotten stronger. We had a base to build on and armed with our new theories of less is more, enjoy life while you can and the clock is constantly ticking, we were ready.

We spent weeks discussing where we wanted to travel. There are so many beautiful areas in this country that it is actually hard to decide where to begin. The national park system consists of 63 national parks, 84 national monuments, 11 national battlefields, 4 national battlefield parks, 1 national battlefield site, 9 national military parks, 62 national historic parks, 73 national historic sites, 3 national lake shores, 31 national memorials, 4 national parkways, 19 national preserves, 2 national reserves, 18 national recreation areas, 4 national rivers, 10 national wild and scenic rivers, 3 national scenic trails, 10 national seashores, and 11 miscellaneous designations. In addition, there are 2,475 state parks not including state forests, historic sites, wildlife refuges and recreation areas in this great land.

It is amazing that there is any land left for us to live on. Most of the parks are amazingly beautiful and the diversity of landscapes is amazing. Our priorities were to get out in nature, visit small rural and rustic towns, get back in shape a bit, and also really relax for extended periods. We did not plan on visiting any large cities and extreme sports are not what are on your typical retiree's bucket list.

I am one of those people who can't understand some people's desire for foreign travel. Our country is so vast and beautiful it would take a lifetime to really explore. Travel to Paris, London, or Venice? No way. Maybe in my next lifetime, but in this lifetime I am spending my travel time exploring the good old USA. It is cheaper, at least as beautiful, and everyone speaks the language. It may be cool to say you spent your vacation in Los Cabos, Mexico, but I think it is even "cooler" to say I spent my vacation in Glacier National Park or camped in the Redwood forests. I don't have to worry about being inadvertently thrown into a Mexican prison or being shot by a cocaine cartel member. Of course there might be a few crazies out there, but in most instances they won't shoot you and they spend most of their time in our big cities.

I started to lay out a plan to cover this great country of ours in an efficient and practical manner. Since we are starting our travels at a somewhat later stage in life and since we have both battled cancer, I wanted to see the whole country, but we were somewhat limited as to time and health. I figured 5 years would be enough time and hopefully our health would at least last that long. This meant that we could not spend weeks and months just meandering about the old USA, but had to have a plan of visiting all the places we wanted to go to in a somewhat shorter time span. At our age and with our finances, full timing traveling was not something we are interested in. Not having travelled together extensively in a 24 foot box, we also worried about potentially killing each other as we joyously made our way around the country. As people reach their later years, they tend to get a bit crankier. Remember, we live in an old 2800 sq. ft. farm house with 11 rooms, a full attic and basement, two porches, and five acres. We were used to having freedom of motion and a place to escape to, should the need arise. It definitely helped in our attempts at marital bliss and is probably one big reason we are still happily married after 39 years. Inhabiting a small box on wheels in all types of weather and unknown challenges could present a problem, but we were willing to face up to the challenge.

Another aspect of the golden years is that your hearing tends to go and you begin to sleep more. Therefore, we hoped that these newfound traits would help offset some of the tension of being crowded into a small space like 2 rats.

I drew 3 boxes across the United States: the southern, middle and northern areas and begin laying out points of interest and sites we wanted to visit. We planned on making 1 long trip per year of approximately 2 months and 1 shorter trip per year of approximately 1 month. We felt that two months might be the maximum length of time we would feel comfortable being away from home. Who knows, if all our plans work out well and we really enjoy our time being cooped up together, the travel times could be extended. We will see how it progresses.

Our short trips would consist of a southern loop, a Florida trip, and a trip to Nova Scotia. On our long trips, we would crisscross the country. That more or less covered it all. Of course in the back of our minds the "big Alaska trip" awaits in the shadows of our neurons, but that will only be tackled if we are still alive in 5 years, the motor home has not blown up, we have successfully conquered our fears of close-quarter living for an extended period and we still have any money left.

CHAPTER 12

PLOTTING OUR JOURNEYS

I gleefully spent weeks and months plotting out our travels: what they would cost, what we would eat, and the sights and sounds we could hope to explore. I didn't use one of those new-fangled, modern, mapping apps. I love messing around with paper maps. Maps are amazing. I have gigantic maps, medium maps and tiny maps. There are dozens of little colored numbers, notations, and routes to explore.

To start, first you need a gigantic map of the whole country to forge an overall travel plan. Then you break it down by geographic area and devise your routes and site goals using the medium maps. Finally you delve into the smaller maps to pick interesting side trips, campgrounds, and exploration areas. It is a ball of fun. It is also a monumental task if you are anal retentive like myself. I did not want to miss any great spots, whizz by any small rustic towns, or god forbid, not have some of those "small gems known only to the locals" on my list. When you feel like you only have one shot to see all the best places on this continent, the pressure is immense. We will probably only make 1 trip to California or Oregon. What are all the "can't miss" places that we will only get to see once in our remaining lifetimes? I am constantly adding or subtracting potential stops to our journeys. The amount of information to be consumed is mind-boggling. Now I know why only retired people do this – it is like a full time job.

Now that the campgrounds are also overrun, due to Covid and government handouts, the times of pulling into various campgrounds at your leisure are gone. Reservations must be made months and months in advance, seconds after the sites are available for booking, especially in the state and national park campgrounds. On a typical longer trip like our expected trip to California and up the Oregon coast, I am planning on staying at approximately 25 campgrounds in 10 different states. To get a decent site and not have to worry about where we are staying meant that I had to reserve at least 25 sites in 10 different states, all opening up their reservation windows at different times. I have a detailed calendar with check-in and check-out dates, what months and what hour they open up for booking and what hook-ups are available.

My living room coffee table resembles the archives of a great educational institution. At any given moment it is covered with 3 USA atlases, one gigantic wall map, mileage and time charts and various books related to our planned trips: the "Alaskan Milepost", "USA's Best Trips", the "Pacific Northwest's Best Trips", the "American Southwest", "Michigan's Upper Peninsula", a "Guide to the National Parks", "British Columbia and the Canadian Rockies", "Scenic Highways and Byways", the "National Park Guide", the "Corp of Engineer Parks", and campground guides for Michigan, Wisconsin, Wyoming, Maine, and the north central USA, all of which ooze out from underneath the table and pile like mountains on its top. Of course this is only a part of the country. I still have quite a ways to go. I also have boxes of travel guides from all of the 50 states including my home state of New Jersey.

I never realized there were so many things to see just in my home state. Did I say this was a monumental job? Some people wonder what they will do in their retirement. Just take up travelling and you will have more than enough to fill your spare moments.

Of course, when I was growing up I also read and treasured a few well known travel novels. Reading "A Life on the Road", "the Longest Road", "On the Road", and my favorite, "Travels with Charley" filled many a quiet moment with the desire to see and experience this great country. Unlike Kuralt, Kerouac, Caputo or Steinbeck, my desire was not to find out what the people feel or think at moments in our history, but to just see what was out there. My mind functions at a lower level. Liking peace and quiet and being somewhat socially inhibited, I just want to see nature's grandeur and experience the various topographies and local customs. I really don't give a fig about what contemporary people think as I truly believe at any given time most people have their heads up their asses. Of course that includes me, but since you can't trust the media, the government or the internet, we all wander around in a fog with no idea of what the hell is going on. The only way to break this fog is to head out into the woods and the experience life for oneself.

CHAPTER 13

BABY STEPS

Finally, after a long winter of plotting and dreaming of our travels to come, we were ready to get going. We had spent a couple evenings camped out in our front yard just for practice. We tried to figure out what additional supplies we would need and where everything would go. It is amazing that when you look at an empty 24 foot motor home, you feel as though you could fit tons of supplies and food and clothes into all the cabinets and nooks and crannies. The reality is that you can fit a minimal supply of stuff. After loading the pots and pans, utensils, dishes and glassware, the kitchen cabinets were stuffed. Add food supplies, water, trash can, garbage bags, food wrapping supplies, coffee pot, spices and herbs, condiments and kitchen gadgets and you are maxed out. I don't see how a family of four could travel comfortably in one of these units. Just the two of us and the unit was filled.

What was interesting was when I started a campfire on my front lawn. Eventually, over the next couple of nights, all the neighbors stopped by to have a drink and chit-chat. People just can't resist a nice campfire. In addition, maybe because of our pioneering heritage, most people long to travel and explore, even if precluded from doing so because of their jobs or financial situations. I could see the far-off longing in their eyes as we discussed our planned upcoming journeys. We sat beneath the stars while listening to the crackle of the flames. I also burned a big hole in my front lawn, but since I'm not some sort of "neighborhood elitist", I didn't care.

In those few days we basically learned how to use the air conditioner and heater, how quickly the water gets used, when to put on the dc power and how to use the generator and stove. It took us a while to figure out the TV and CD system and how to raise the antenna. When it was over we had a basic understanding of the unit and how most things worked. We also got a sense of how fast the propane was used up and how comfortable it was sleeping in the bed. I had read horror stories about backing into trees, gigantic poop geysers, supply shortages and dead batteries. Of course you don't want to look like an idiot the first time you are out camping, so all the practice made us feel a little bit more comfortable that we were not going to be the laughing stock of the campground. It was a fun learning experience and we now wanted to take Bea out and try some actual camping.

We decided on a campground around an hour away and fairly close to where we still have our old sailboat docked. The thought was that we could accomplish our early spring jobs on the boat without having to drive so far every day, as the campground was only about ten minutes from the marina. It was a good idea and we got quite a bit done on the boat in a fairly short amount of time. We had been planning to sand and varnish all the woodwork and having to put on a new coat of varnish everyday was made much easier by the proximity of the campground.

The campground itself was somewhat disappointing. All the units were packed in with barely 10ft. between campers. It was noisy, offered no privacy and was very expensive. After that trip we vowed to stay in state or national campgrounds as much as possible in our future travels. It was fun staying in our new camper. We cooked up some great meals, relaxed by the fire and went for walks in the Pine Barrens.

They say campers are very friendly and it is true. Within minutes of our arrival, my wife, Jo, was talking with the neighbors and making plans for dinner. They lived locally and decided to bring back a big pile of clams for a clambake. Not having any seafood at the moment to offer up, I volunteered to make a couple of pizzas and we all had a good time at the makeshift camping feast. We had talked a bit about our health problems as it seems all retirees do. My neighbor went on for an extended period about his problems with cancer, operations and back problems. The poor fellow had scars on his back, some type of implant, and could barely bend over or sit up straight. It is amazing what some people have to persevere with. It also amazes me how just being out in nature can help one overcome the various mental and physical maladies that we are afflicted with.

We finally got to bed and enjoyed a peaceful, comfortable snooze out in the pines. The next morning the neighbors were over again inviting us to a barbecue at their house. We are generally friendly and sociable people, but now we were feeling a bit uncomfortable. They were inviting us to their home for a barbecue and to meet the family. We had just met them and were feeling a bit uneasy. Thoughts of redneck killings in the pines or robbery were starting to flit through our minds and we eventually begged off visiting them. The old survival mode was kicking in and I didn't want to be the main course at some ritualistic "Piney" barbecue. We felt bad, but decided self preservation was the safer route for the time being. They were really nice people, and we hope that we didn't insult them by refusing their invitation. We ended up having a very nice time on our first trip and managed to get some of our boat chores out of the way also. Bea's systems performed perfectly.

If you are ever in the Pine Barrens, check them out. Find a nice, secluded campground in the pines somewhere. There are many trails and small streams to hike and wade in. Canoeing is very popular and a better day can't be found then floating down a Pine Barrens stream, beneath the overgrown limbs, listening to the chuckling of the stream and watching the sun gleam off the tannin-filled waters. The quiet is profound and you will think you are hundreds of miles out in the wilderness, when in fact in most cases you are less than a mile from the nearest road. The wind offers up a definite sigh as it courses through the pine trees. Multi-color dragonflies sit perched on your canoe and supplies and turtles plop into the water intermittently as you float around the deadfalls. Watch out for the Jersey Devil though. He does like to occasionally pick off and eat some unsuspecting canoeing tourist, back in the dark, foreboding swamps.

We decided to try a long weekend trip to hone our skills so we planned on visiting my father-in-law where he parked his camper for the summer, in the Pocono Mountains of Pennsylvania. Well if anyone knows South Jersey, taking route 206 into Pennsylvania is always a test of situational awareness. The highway sort of peters out in downtown Trenton and disappears as you drive through the "hood". I may be biased or an old fogey, but I don't know what else to call an area that has weekly shootings and looks like bombed-out Iraq. Burned out buildings, broken windows, graffiti and collapsing structures greeted us as we made a wrong turn somewhere along the route. I guess it is too expensive for the city to put up a sign or two as they are probably spending all their money trying to fix up the city itself. Now mind you, I had never previously driven the motor home on other than a highway or back country road. I was petrified. Besides worrying about crashing my motor home, I was pondering the thought of never leaving Trenton alive. Of course I gunned it down the streets and around the corners as our phone GPS was telling us to go all over the place and I was scared someone would jump on the side of our rig and shoot us full of bullet holes. As we careened around the corners I hit a pothole the size of the Grand Canyon and the pie Jo had baked for her father-in-law flew out of its holding place in the microwave and landed upside down on the floor. Splattering across the rug, at least we now had the sweet aroma of apples and cinnamon wafting over us as we fled for our lives while being chased by the neighborhood dogs. Eventually we ended up on some cobblestone street beneath overhanging trees, which I believe might have been some kind of park. Requiring immediate assistance, I decided to swerve into a barricaded lot with an I.D. pass requirement. Within a minute, we were surrounded by cop cars and security guards who probably thought we were 60 year old terrorists in a motor home in down-town Trenton. After a quick discussion, they were happy to give us directions back to the highway, so presumably they could go back to their naps. Thanking the Lord, we then drove the rest of the way to Pennsylvania and our objective campground. It was a tough lesson, but as Jo commented: "you can now drive anywhere honey". So I smiled justifiably as I knew driving through downtown Trenton, N.J. in a motor home, while under extreme duress, could not be accomplished by just anyone. Major test number one was successfully completed.

We arrived at the campground late in the afternoon and were squeezed in amongst 3 campers on all sides. We had to share a water spigot and electric post and had to be careful putting out our awning so that we did not hit the camper next to us. Of course his sewer pipe was positioned 10 feet from our picnic table so we could inhale the fine aroma of sewerage as we lounged outside and prepared our dinner. What a delight. I still fail to see why some campers choose private campgrounds for their vacations.

Maybe it's just me, but I prefer the scent of pines and peace and quiet as opposed to sewer hoses and our neighbor's conversations. Nothing exciting happened over the weekend as we practiced our camping and picked up a few tidbits of knowledge from my father-in-law. Wanting to spend a few idle hours fishing, I was astounded to find out that you had to pay for every fish caught in their pond. These private parks will stoop to any depth to try and part their customers with every dollar they have. If it wasn't for my visiting my father-in-law, I would not even have paid them for the site, let alone for each fish I caught.

So that was more or less our first bigger camping expedition and we headed home after a few days. We were somewhat wiser, but between the getting lost and the tight quarters in the campground, somewhat less relaxed.

CHAPTER 14

WATKINS GLEN
& THE FINGER LAKES

The summer was soon over and we now planned our first "real trip" in the camper. We did not want to go too far, but wanted to get out in the woods and get in some serious relaxation and fishing. We decided on a trip to the Finger Lakes Region of New York. Building upon our recent camping experiences, we had decided that state parks were the only way to go. State parks are cheaper, give you more room and are generally populated by families and nature lovers as opposed to weekend partiers and drunks. Of course this now entailed the arduous process of making reservations well in advance for any trips. It took months, but I finally prevailed in figuring out how to carry out the process in a somewhat efficient manner. Everything was finally set, we packed up and were ready to go, full of expectations of a fun-filled adventure.

It actually turned out that way. Our first night we spent camped out on a nice peninsula in Promised Land State Park in Pennsylvania, our half way point. It had a beautiful lake and it was beautiful, sunny weather. We had a nice night and the next morning took a walk around the lake with our dog Sparky. She loved new places and happily romped around on the beach and the paths.

I also managed to get a few casts in, as the lake seemed to be a well-known bass haven. Alas, I caught no bass and seriously rued not bringing my kayak along. But it was nice and I did not have to buy a fishing license as I only buy one after I know there are fish in the lake, and I didn't see a one. All the crazy states think it is no problem to charge you exorbitant amounts of money to be able to throw a lure into their lakes whether there are fish or not. Not this cheapskate (frugal individual). I'm not paying anybody ten or twenty dollars for the privilege of casting a few lines for a few minutes of fun. By my quick CPA calculations, the government is paying me approximately .05 cents a minute based on the size of my social security check. Why should I pay them $1.00 a minute for a few practice casts on land that we, as taxpayers, own? If I am staying for a few days or can see the fish actually jumping out of the water, I am happy to pay. Besides, I think paying seven to ten dollars for 50 cents worth of wood should cover the price of the fishing also. What about the wood? Remember I live in the sticks and know you can get a cord of split hardwood for $150 to $200. A cord of wood is a rectangle 4 feet high, 4 feet wide and 8 feet long. My guesstimate is that a cord is made up of many hundreds of pieces of split wood. They sell you about seven pieces of crappy pine for ten bucks that burns up in about an hour or two. On top of that, they probably get it for nothing from cleaning the campgrounds. Of course you can't bring your own from the cords of wood stacked in your yard. They say it is to stop the spread of invasive species from spreading to different areas. After having a long chat with the local population of bugs, it was generally agreed that they could not read a map or knew where the state boundaries were. In addition, if they were not already in the area, the local weather was probably not conducive to their survival. They are not in any rush to relocate from where they were comfortable. But hey, maybe that is just my convoluted way of thinking and I don't necessarily recommend it to any of my readers. All I know is that trying to stop the spread of an invasive species as it moves its way across the country is like trying to stick your finger in a hole of the proverbial dam that's leaking all about you.

Anyway, the day passed quickly and we proceeded to head up to the Thousand Island area. I know it's not the Finger Lakes, but we had never been up there either and it was not too far of an extra drive. We had a reservation at Wellesley Island State Park and after a four or five hour drive we arrived at the bridge to our final destination. The park sits on an island between Canada and the U. S. on the St. Lawrence River. Well

I discovered another major stress point as regarding driving an RV across the U.S. - bridges. As I paid my toll at the booth, I looked ahead and could not even see the top of the bridge as it seemed to rise into the clouds. If I could have turned around right there, I would have except Jo reminded me we had fully paid for 4 nights at the park. To ease my anxiety, the booth attendant then proceeded to inform me that it might be to our benefit to pull in our side mirrors as we might lose them to the oncoming tractor trailers coming down the bridge. The road looked like a skinny ribbon running to the sky with very little in the way of guards along the shoulder-less edges. It didn't even look like two trucks or campers could safely pass by on the bridge without the shrieking of metal and flying of sparks. Did I also tell you that a have a small anxiety problem? As I proceeded to go, I was shaking like a leaf and had a death grip on the steering wheel. I visualized a tractor trailer driven by some young trucking student pushing us over the railing of the Thousand Island Bridge and us soaring on the crosswinds to crash a couple hundred feet below. I scrunched up in my seat and leaned forward. A prayer ushered from my clenched teeth. Of course my dog Sparky had a big smile on her face as she looked out over the river and my wife was commenting on the wonderful view as we drove high above the tiny islands below. I saw nothing except straight ahead and was sweating like a condemned prisoner. Up in the clouds I felt like I was soaring towards the pearly gates as the islands below got smaller and smaller and I watched the resident hawks spiral below us. I think that at one point I even closed my eyes when I saw the Space Shuttle drift by. Okay, so maybe I am exaggerating a bit, but you get the idea. Eventually we made it over and after a small distance proceeded to our site in the park.

The park was huge, having over 400 sites, but it was quite nice. I would have been happier with a little more vegetation between sites, but they were quite large and we had a pretty view of the river. After a couple drinks and a seat by the campfire, I finally started to relax. We did not go anywhere for a few days just so we could relax and enjoy some quiet time (I couldn't get up enough courage to go back over the bridge). Finally after Jo convinced me that we could not stay in the campground forever, and to go home we had to go over the bridge, I mustered the courage to sally forth for a scenic drive.

So, after downing a few Xanax, we spent a day taking a nice scenic jaunt. We stopped in some of the older, quaint towns like Alexandria Bay and Cape Vincent. We strolled along the walkways and visited a few stores. We also visited the Tibbett's Point Lighthouse which was built in 1827 and has beautiful views of the St. Lawrence Seaway and Lake Ontario with the waves crashing along the banks. The area also boasts two scenic, old castles: Boldt Castle and Singer Castle.

According to the Boldt Castle website, the structure was built at the turn of the century by George Boldt, who along with other things owned the Waldorf-Astoria hotel. Built in the classical style, it looks like a castle complete with block towers, massive granite walls and a terra cotta roof. It consists of 120 rooms with 365 windows and is 6 stories high. A beautiful arched stone walkway connects the Power house to the island. Alster tower was meant to be the Boldt's playroom. It was designed to include a dance room, billiard area, bowling alley, café and bedrooms. An underground tunnel leads out to the boat docking area and the grounds are surrounded by Italian gardens and extensive verandas. Poor George was building the castle as a Valentine's day gift for his wife, Louise, who passed away during the construction of the castle. With a broken heart, George stopped construction on the castle never to return. Eventually the Thousand Island Bridge Authority acquired the property and continues to maintain it as a tourist attraction. It is now fully handicapped-accessible with complete restroom facilities, picnic spots, and a food and beverage area. You can tour the spacious grounds as well as the castle rooms and a museum which has been added.

The Singer castle on nearby Dark Island is another beautiful castle which looms over the island like a medieval fortress. Showcasing huge granite blocks topped with red Italian tiles, it was built in 1905 by the owner of the Singer sewing machine company. The multitude of rooms includes a great hall decorated with armor and antiques, a library, wine cellar, dining room, breakfast room, wicker room and even a dungeon. Why a dungeon? Nobody knows. It also has a multitude of secret passageways. Outside are a rose garden, fountain, squash court and boat and boathouses. The grounds are beautiful and rooms can actually be rented in the castle if you decide on an extended visit.

Those are our highlights of the area. We did not see any gobsmacking, holy cow sites in the Thousand Islands, but the beauty of the area combined with many interesting attractions made it a worthwhile visit and well worth the trip. We only visited three of the 1,864 islands but had a very enjoyable and scenic rest and we planned to revisit the area in the future.

For our next leg of the journey we headed south towards Watkins Glen in the Finger Lakes Region of New York. It was a beautiful drive mostly along the shores of Lake Ontario. We stopped for a couple of rests and one of the areas was the town of Pulaski. We happened to be there in the fall and therefore the great salmon run was on. I don't know if anyone has been there at that time, but the town is filled with thousands of crazed salmon "fishermen". Now this is not my kind of fishing where you challenge your quarry one-on-one with your fishing acumen and ability while drinking in the beauty of nature. Yes, in the fall this area of the country is beautiful but it is ruined by the lunatics standing elbow to elbow along miles of waterway hurling giant snag hooks across the river hoping to snag into any of the thousands of salmon streaming by. Screaming, yelling, littering the banks with garbage and beer cans, they fill their coolers with salmon in an annual lust for the "kill". As far as I am concerned, it was quite disgusting and a horrible depiction of man's cruel destruction of nature. It made me ashamed to be a fisherman. It is an annual slaughter. It is not sport. Why do they do it? Who knows? Maybe a couple of individuals are actually poor and can use the salmon to offset a meager diet, but the majority, with their $50,000 SUV's and hundreds of dollars of equipment can only be lusting for the kill. What motivates these people? A beautiful day spent on the river? Hardly. They must have their reasons, but I for one could not figure it out and we promptly left in disgust after a short visit.

Eventually we reached Watkins Glen and the Finger Lakes. Now I don't know why these cities promote these beautiful areas all around the country with millions of dollars of ads, yet can't seem to spend a few bucks on signs. Of course we promptly got lost and spent a couple hours driving around the city trying to find the entrance to the campground. We spent an hour or so at the top of the gorge in a nice picnic area but could not find our way down to the bottom of the gorge where the campground is. Asking a few of our fellow picnickers for directions produced no results and we tried various routes to find the entrance. Pulling out on one small road we were faced with a low bridge with a sign reading 11 ft. high. Now the height of our motor home is 11' 3" and therefore I was a bit worried. I stopped in front of the bridge and it looked like we could make it, but not wanting to take any chances I ordered (requested) my assistant navigator, Jo, to get out and check the height. After struggling up the side of the bridge in flip-flops and shorts and nearly filleting herself on the concrete and stones, she lovingly declared that it looked like we could make it. So I rolled under the bridge and tooted the horn for her to hurry up so we could get going. After a rough slide back down the stones and concrete, I won't repeat her response to my "hurry up", but suffice it to say the bonds of our marriage were not strengthened at that moment.

As we cruised down around the mountainside, I decided one road looked like it could be an entryway to the park. Not so. It turned into a small residential side street barely hanging on to the side of the steep mountain and barely wide enough for our camper. I quickly decided to turn right at the next roadway and then we were in real trouble. The road rose up, at what looked to me like a 45 degree angle. After nearly rolling over on the turn, we were stuck. I could not back up or turn around. So with the engine straining and my foot to the metal, we slowly crept up the mountainside as Bea huffed and puffed. Eventually all of our luggage and clothes fell off the overhead sleeping area and went bouncing down towards the back of our rig. Throwing caution to the wind, I was too scared to stop at the stop sign at the top and proceeded to keep going onto the intersecting road. We almost turned over again after another 90 degree turn. Well, luckily nothing was coming and I am still here to write about our travels. Eventually we started over, went all the way back around the bottom of the mountain and finally stumbled upon the entrance. After once again straining up a long descent, we made it to what was quite a nice campground.

Watkins Glen State Park has been nominated as one of the best state parks in the United States. Large treed sights are arranged along the mountain rim near a gorge. The Park offers tent and trailer sites as well as an Olympic pool, picnic facilities and a playground. Trails run throughout the park and along the gorge.

The gorge is absolutely beautiful. A stream descends 400 feet down into the gorge, past cliffs and eroded rock as it winds its way to the bottom, encompassing over 19 waterfalls and many small pools. You can follow a beautiful stone walkway up and through the gorge for a total length of about 2 miles. The amazing stone trails were constructed by the Civilian Conservation Corps in the 1930's and wind their way up and along the gorge walls with intermittent stone bridges spanning the gorge and chiseled walkways cut in behind some of the waterfalls. Deep in the gorge all you hear is the running water traversing the moss-laden, shale cliffs. Small waterfalls leap from the rocks and the moss covered stones glisten green in the bright sunshine. Did I tell you how many stairs on this beautiful walk? There are approximately 900 as you huff and puff your way to the top. I wasn't sure I would make it, but the beauty was worth the effort. I eventually met up with Jo and our dog Sparky at the top of the gorge and we sat down for a while to catch our breaths. After a bit, we meandered our way back to the bottom, still somewhat gasping for air but at least heading in the right direction – down. We had a picnic lunch near the visitor entrance and relaxed in the late afternoon, fall sunshine. Both Sparky and I had a wry smile on our faces, happy with our accomplishments, but at what cost? At this point Sparky was 16 years old and her handler was a 65 year old smoker with COPD and herniated discs, but we made it. We both loved a challenge and being in the outdoors, we felt good. Of course it didn't faze Jo too much as she is one of those never get old women who eats right, dances, does yoga and generally tries to take care of herself. Then again she didn't get that same feeling of satisfaction that one gets when risking death as Sparky and I had. We drove back to the campsite as the sun was setting and I dished up a feast of crab cakes, homemade French fries and spinach accompanied with a nice bottle of Bully Hill Goat white wine.

I only bring up the wine because it is one of our favorites and a little hard to come by in the sticks of South Jersey. But guess what? After perusing the local tourist stops and wineries we discovered that the Bully Hill winery was actually located in the Finger Lakes region. So the next day we took a nice scenic drive around a few of the lakes and stopped in to get some wine. Now I am not a big spender, but being retired and on vacation I splurged for a whole case and we loaded up the camper for the rest of the trip.

Reading a travelogue on the region I was impressed to find that the area contains over 1,000 waterfalls and gorges, 400 registered historic sites and landmarks, 135 museums, 80 art galleries, 650 miles of shoreline, 50 farmers markets, over 100 restaurants, over 100 wineries and many craft beer facilities, 40 nature centers, 95 campgrounds, over 2,000 miles of hiking and biking trails and even 100 miles of the Erie canal. Now if you can't find something to do in this area you have a problem. The fall days were gorgeous and the trees wore a riotous explosion of colored hues.

We planned to visit the Corning glass museum the next day. The Corning Museum of Glass was established in 1951 as a gift to the nation from the Corning Glass works, a non-profit organization dedicated to exploring the history and use of glass. According to their internet site, the Museum consists of over 50,000 glass objects representing over 3,500 years of glass history ranging from ancient Egyptian glass to modern contemporary creations. It stages daily glass-working demonstrations and visitors can learn about the optics, technology, and methods used to create beautiful glass shapes and figurines. It is situated on a 10 acre campus in the town of Corning just south of Keuka Lake. We were ready to go but alas, the dreaded Covid virus had closed it down. What a bummer.

The lousy virus was not good for retired travelers. Besides making everyone sick, it flooded the campgrounds with millions of out-of-work employees now free to roam about with their stimulus checks. Some campgrounds and scenic areas were shut down. The ones that were open were crammed with people out to enjoy nature. In addition, a lot of the areas were open but the visitor and bathroom facilities were closed. The restaurants, bars and entertainment areas were also closed. Now being in our 60's, the need to use the restroom seems to be cropping up a little more frequently. Growing up in the sticks I am not averse to taking a quick pee behind a tree, but Jo, being somewhat more prudent, does not relish the idea of dropping her drawers in places teeming with thousands of tourists, even if there are quite a few trees. So our choice of destinations became somewhat limited.

In addition, camping is exploding in popularity. I've recently read that there are over 80 million camping households in the United States. I also seem to remember reading that there are about 16,000 public and private campgrounds in the country. Now if you take the 80 million households and add to that all the foreign tourists from Canada, Europe, South America and the Far East to that number and divide by 16,000 you seem to have a problem. These numbers were from before the pandemic. Add another couple million campers to the rolls and you can see why it is becoming increasingly difficult to find a nice camp site. The RV industry estimates it will sell over 600,000 units this year alone. It sucks to be at the end of the baby boom.

Not too long ago you could just drive around anywhere and find a nice site for the evening. Not anymore. Now you are competing with at least 80 million people who are also looking for a nice site. Being at the end of the baby boom means everything related to retirement spending is catastrophically high due to the numbers of retirees. Of course most of these retirees have their nice pensions and annuities to spend at will. When you are trying to compete with just your social security check, you are at a severe financial disadvantage. You can't afford the camper or the equipment, can't afford to eat out, and you can't afford the site rentals or the various entrance fees and sightseeing tours. The entrance fees for some sights are in the hundreds of dollars. The site fees in some of the private campgrounds are also reaching the hundreds and a nice meal out for two is in the hundred dollar range. What the hell. Campers can cost hundreds of thousands and to get one fixed will cost you $100/ hour at your favorite repairman. I really screwed up somewhere along the line with my job selection. I think we need a good old depression to bring everything back into perspective. Just remember, as the tail end of these boomers start retiring and spending all their money on travel and supporting their kids, imagine what the stock market is going to look like in a couple years. Just one of my many financial tips I like to throw in here and there. Anyway, where were we?

We couldn't make it to the museum of glass, so we spent the next couple of days touring the nearby sites and relaxing by the camper. Eventually the time came to pack it up and head home. We had a great time on our first big trip and were real happy with our camping experience and the equipment. We thoroughly enjoyed ourselves, learned a little and totally relaxed. Maybe there was something to this "retirement" other than sitting home watching TV and getting bored out of our minds. We headed back to sunny South Jersey with a smile on our faces, a skip in our hearts, and a few thousand dollars in the hole. What the hell. This is what you save for, right?

As for the trip home, what usually happens is that your relaxation and the good mood you feel vanishes as you get closer to home. Going down the N.Y. Thruway towards N.Y. City, the traffic slowly builds into a crescendo until you're in three lanes of bumper-to-bumper traffic packed with crazy N.Y. state drivers all racing back to the city. After about a half-hour of this you exit and are disgorged onto the N.J. Parkway. The traffic once again builds until 3 lanes of lunatics are funneled through the "Oranges". Here there is the inevitable traffic jam and you slowly crawl your way through this section until you are vomited out onto six lanes of crazy New Jersey state drivers. They are just like their New York counterparts only I don't think many of them have ever passed a driving test. Doing 60 miles an hour you might be pulled over for driving too slow. The average speed is probably 75 to 85 miles per hour. It is like being in some kind of road race game where your only objective is to survive. Slow pokes in the left lane too petrified to get back to the right, crazies doing 90 mph while passing on your right, all kinds of wannabe Dale Earnhardt's swerving in an out of all six lanes and the more than occasional rust bucket wobbling down the highway at top speed, spewing out smoke and noise. Wrecks and broken down vehicles alongside the highway give you something to peer at and remind you to say a few prayers. Merging traffic every mile or two means if you want to stay to the right you will be slowing down every exit or entrance or risk getting the front of your vehicle ripped off. If you pull into the middle lanes, the crazies will ride your bumper for the next two hours, six inches behind you while they flash their high beams on and off. Of course by now, the nuts that have merged onto the Parkway are doing 90 mph also, so you are sort of stuck in the middle. Eventually you pass over the Raritan River hoping no one pushes you over the meager 3 foot guardrail into the river below while they are swerving and changing lanes, and all of this spews out into what must be twenty lanes of toll booths. It then all gets crammed back into about 6 lanes consisting of an "express" lane and "local" lane. The express lanes immediately get clogged up and you spend the next part of the day alternately going at least 70 mph or jamming on the brakes for the inevitable, every twenty minute traffic jam. It is approximately a 100 mile drive from northern New Jersey to sunny, bucolic South Jersey. You will notice I capitalized "South" because I believe it is actually quite different than north Jersey and we should have seceded years ago. Anyway, it once took us 6.5 hours to travel that distance. That works out to about an average speed of 15 mph. Yeah, it's great living in New Jersey.

Hoping to avoid the above, on this trip we decided to take route 287 which parallels the Parkway and eventually curves around and joins the Parkway at the Raritan river bridge. Was there any difference? No. A steady stream of traffic merges onto 287 which is even more packed than the Parkway. Trucks are also allowed on this road meaning your likelihood of dying is increased. Now you have tractor trailers riding your bumper and swerving in and out of lanes. The shoulders are littered with blown tractor trailer tires. You begin to wonder if maybe the road is paved in recycled roofing shingles filled with nails, or the truck drivers are too cheap to replace their obviously bald tires. You can envision either blowing a couple of your tires on the nail laden road or a crazy truck driver blowing his tires and crushing you flat with 40 tons of gardening supplies or steel beams. What a way to go.

On this particular trip, dark clouds were heading our way and the wind was picking up. It didn't look good. Lightening flashed in the distance and it started to sprinkle. Being the ever cautious one, I pulled into the right lane and slowed down (after being stuck in the middle between 2 behemoths). Within a few minutes it started - an unbelievable downpour with 60 mph winds. It became pitch dark and the wipers were totally useless. We could not see where we were going and crawled along at 10 mph. All you could see were smeary lights all over the place with the tractor trailers still doing 60 mph, while covering your windshield with a constant fire hose stream of water. I pulled over onto the shoulder which was about nine foot in width and up against a 20 foot high retaining wall, and we prayed for our lives. The branches of the trees overhead were whipping about in a frenzy and threatened to fall and crush our camper at any minute. Did I mention our motor home is 8.5 feet wide? In the blackened maelstrom of horrendous fury, this left about 6 inches of clearance between the side of my camper and the highway where the rest of the lunatics were still going 50 mph and could see nothing. I prayed some more while a thought about the left side of my camper being ripped off played through my mind. I popped a couple Xanax and tried to calm the adrenalin surging through my veins. Well, God must have been listening, because after about an hour the clouds started to break up, the rain slowed to a drizzle and we were still alive. We continued on our route and yes, were eventually spewed out onto the six lane Raritan Bridge and spent the next 5 hours trying to get home safely. We eventually arrived at home passed dinnertime and unpacked a few vital essentials and collapsed in the relative safety of our little nest. I swear, after that drive I was tighter than a guitar string. I was exhausted, shaky, my back hurt, my head hurt, my eyes hurt and I swore-off ever going through north Jersey on vacation again. Were we even on a vacation? I couldn't remember. All the peace and serenity were long gone and our visions of sugar plums were crushed beneath the reality of everyday New Jersey living.

CHAPTER 15

WINTER MUSINGS

Winter came and went in sunny South Jersey. Like everyone else, we spent the late fall cleaning up around the house, making our minor repairs, cutting and splitting wood and taking care of the yard. Now in our yard we have trees – many massive trees. When the leaves fall in autumn the leaves can reach up to your knees. Without burning your yard up there is no way to easily get rid of the leaves. There are different methods of leaf collection and removal. The first, which my neighbor uses, is to use the power blower to blow all the leaves out onto the street and hope the township picks them up before they all blow back again. It works if you timing is right, but the noise is horrendous. Sitting in my yard and listening to that horrible whining for hours on end is enough to make you want to rip your eyeballs out or commit suicide. Sometimes I just bang my head against the wall until I am unconscious and cannot hear the horrible drone of the blower.

Another method my other neighbor uses is the drop cloth method. In this method you spread out a 10 square foot tarp and rake huge piles of leaves onto it. Then you drag it out to the road where you hope the township eventually picks it up before it blows back again. Depending on the timing, that method works quite well and is thankfully quiet. My preferred method, though, is the "grind-them-up method". After the leaves get about 4 inches high, I take my lawn tractor and cut up all the leaves and grass going round and round until I've covered the lawn about 4 times. I then let the dust settle until the leaves get another 4 inches high. Then I repeat the process. After a month or so all the leaves have fallen and my lawn is covered in about 2 inches of mulch. I then rake most of the leaves and mulch out to the street, once again waiting for the township to come around before they all blow away again. The difference is that my mulched leaves barely blow around unless there is a very heavy wind. In addition, I try to do my raking on a damp or drizzly day so that the sodden mountain of mulch out front usually stays put for quite a while. Raking the mulch is difficult as a lot remains due to falling between the rake tines. Some we save for throwing out back in the woods so that our friends the woodchucks and rabbits have enough to winter over in. However, I believe some mulch on the lawn is good over the winter and helps protect and enrich the grass. Jo thinks I am just too lazy to rake it properly. However I disagree and believe my method is best. The lawn is properly mulched, my mound of shredded leaves out front is fairly stable and I've gotten quite a bit of exercise raking for a week – all of this in comparable silence.

Now, I mention the leaves blowing away because we live in what is usually considered the back-water area of the township. We are not hip and trendy and growing rapidly like the other end of the township. We are the local backwoods hicks. Most of the area is zoned industrial in the hopes some business would ever like to relocate here. We like peace and quiet and like to be left alone. We don't attend township meetings and don't spend our lives sucking up to the local politicians. As a result, we are on the bottom of the leaf pick-up process. We have a very large township and it takes them forever to pick up leaves. Those who live in the eastern part of the township have their leaves picked up expeditiously as soon as the last leaf falls out of the tree. Out by us they schedule two pick-ups. One, very early in the season, which means they come and pick up the first five leaves that fall off your trees and the other 3 feet of leaves that eventually fall don't get picked up until just before or after Christmas. That means if you try to rake all your leaves in October or November, they inevitably blow back all over the place by the time pick-up takes place the second time. Your second option is to rake them very late in the season after they have lain on the ground for two months and totally killed your lawn. That is why I think my method works the best.

In addition to raking, a lot of my neighbors and we have wood stoves or fireplaces. I spend a lot of time every year cutting and splitting wood.

We have a small woodstove and it doesn't really heat our whole house but it provides nice, extra warmth on those cold days and provides the perfect ambiance for having that hot coffee with a splash of Irish Crème while doing a puzzle or reading a book. Some neighbors just order piles of split wood that they leave dumped in their yard for the winter. That is a perfectly good method however when you are trying to eke out a living on social security, not a very good plan as it can get a bit expensive. I prefer to use the "gather-whatever-falls-down-in-your-yard" method. We have a decent five acre lot that is packed with trees of every kind. Usually, every winter a few cherries or maples or apple trees will tumble to their deaths. I cut them up and leave a pile of wood to be split the following fall after letting them dry for a year or so. Once again, this is not the most efficient method of heating your home and we really could get by without it and just use our heater. However the burning of the cherry or apple wood does leave a nice aroma in the house during the winter. In addition I also get quite a bit of exercise out of the woodcutting and stacking. If there ever is an electrical black out, we still have our old wood stove to heat the house and I slowly get to clear some of the dead trees out of our woods.

Some people just cut down all their trees and burn them. To me that is sacrilegious. Why some individuals move out to "the country" only to cut down all their trees and cover their yards in tar, to me, is inexplicable. I just don't get it. I love all my trees. What's better than walking barefoot in the summer on cool, green grass? I don't want to be burning my feet on tar. Trees provide important shade in the summer months which enables us to get by with very little air conditioning our contribution in fighting global warming. They provide a playground for the vast number of birds in our yard that we love to feed and watch every day. Since moving here, I have recorded over 35 different species of birds in our yard and the surrounding woodlands. I love looking out over a large grove of trees. Who doesn't? Would you rather look out over an empty lot? I have huge trees surrounding my house and I feel as though they are hugging and protecting us. Yes, one eventually falls and bounces off our roof causing damage. But to me that is worth putting up with. Most of these behemoths have been here long before me and I don't feel it is in my right to determine their deaths. They provide for the air we breathe, actually hold the earth's soil in place and provide a playground for our animals. I've seen deer, foxes, raccoons, skunks, turkeys, snakes, birds, coyotes, rabbits, woodchucks and opossums in my woods and invite all of them to stay. What would we see with an empty lot? The most important thing about trees is their connection to the ultimate energy of the earth. Sometimes, when things are very still, sit and listen to the trees. You will hear a subtle sigh as the wind frolics in their branches and if you listen close you may soon hear the "holes" in the silence. This is not a topic I will dwell on, but for those who have heard it, you know what I mean. From the trees and their occupants is why some of us love to travel and be out in nature and I feel we owe them a lot. Trees support and nourish us and the earth. Take care of and love them and they will take care of you.

Fall is soon over and the cold and ice and snow begin. Sometimes on these cold mornings I hike up the small hill by our house that sits near a small pond. I reminisce of cold, frosty days spent on our Flexible Flyers racing down that hill, all bundled up and warm, our faces tingling red from the chill winds and snow. Many evenings were spent skating on the pond with a fire blazing and laughter echoing in the dark. One night we were running low on nearby wood and decided to use all the dried vines lying amongst the old rotted limbs. We laughed and chatted, enveloped by huge black clouds and smoke. Little did we know we were burning poison ivy vines – that was a big mistake. The next day we suffered with red welts and scratching and a couple of my friends actually had to go to the hospital. Their faces were swollen like basketballs and their eyes were swelled shut.

In those days is was the norm for country folks to have firearms and it is hard to understand the limits placed on those freedoms today. We were twelve and thirteen and would sometimes walk down to the pond with our 22 caliber rifles. All the boys had them. We would shoot at small varmints, pine cones, signs and just at the ice for the hell of it. It was great fun. It also made us feel safe and secure. Any potential deviant would have thought twice about grabbing any of the children skating at the pond because it would have looked like the shootout at the OK Corral if he did. Playing crack the whip, racing, and jumping holes in the ice was a great way to spend a cold snowy evening. Gliding down the ice on an inky black night with your arms out under a star studded sky is a memory not to be forgotten.

I met my first girlfriend skating at the pond on a cold, snowy night. I jumped a few large holes in the ice, and performed a couple of backward figure eights to catch her eye. I am sure she was impressed with my fire building ability and prowess on the ice skates. A few tepid smooches near the dark side of the pond sealed the deal and made for a very happy few years to follow as I advanced through my early teens.

Of course the cold and snow were not all fun. We had a long driveway that ran passed our house that was approximately 300 hundred yards in length. It seemed to snow more back in those days, or maybe we were just shorter. Right after an early breakfast of cream of wheat or oatmeal, my brothers and I would be directed to clear the driveway. We could not just clear a small area out the shortest end of the driveway to the road. My dad liked to keep his boys active and in shape. So with dread we would file out with our shovels to begin clearing what looked like a mile long avalanche with snow up to our waists, and howling winds swirling the snow crystals around us. We did not even have "snow" shovels. We had the old iron coal shovels that picked up about six inches of snow at a time and weighed about twenty-five pounds apiece. The snow would stick to the metal and every other time you heaved a big shovel full, the shovel would go with it. After an all day onslaught and myriad snow ball fights the driveway would finally be cleared and we would traipse back into the kitchen; frozen, soaking wet and exhausted. Our clothing was frozen hard like armor, snot would be frozen to our upper lips and red welts on our faces were worn like badges from the myriad snowballs that had hit their mark. We would pile on top of the coal stove to try and get warm while mom cooked up some chicken dumplings to "stick to our ribs" and warm us up. Would we rather have been sitting in our centrally heated homes streaming videos or chatting to our friends online? Not for a million dollars. Great memories of cold and ice and snow that warm our hearts and minds and bring us solace in our golden years. A joyful, simple life, a relic of the past, but a treasure trove of hard work, love, fun and happiness, never to be regained, but to always be remembered.

CHAPTER 16

SAYING GOODBYE
TO AN OLD FRIEND

During the winter, our dear Sparky left us. After our last trip it seemed like she was slowing down considerably. Her legs started dragging and the spark left her eyes. We brought her to the Vet but she could find nothing wrong. She actually stated that she had never seen such great blood test results from a dog so old. She was just getting old and running out of gas. The vet offered to "put her down" if we liked, but we recoiled in horror. That's not exactly how I pictured taking care of my best friend. There was no way we were going to end her life until she was ready to go. We took her home and tried to make her as comfortable as possible. She had valiantly made it through our first big camping trip with us, as though she wanted to share in our joy. Diet and health were now out the window and we made her feasts to eat and revel in. She smiled and licked her lips in a thank you, even as we had to hold her up to eat. She slowly got worse and worse until we had to carry her out every day so that she could relieve herself. We covered our futon with old towels so that she could enjoy her favorite spot while watching television with us. We took turns sitting with her, brushing her and hugging her. I tearfully tried to explain life and death to her and why I could not help her this time around. She stared at me with those beautiful, soulful eyes and I like to think that she understood. Days came and went. Thankfully I was retired and had the time to spend with her in those waning hours. Jo and I both cried constantly. She was sleeping more and more and got progressively weaker and weaker. We could tell nothing was hurting her – she was just too old. She had lived her life to the fullest and the longest age possible. On the last morning, I came down from upstairs and she could barely raise her head to say good morning. She struggled to do so and it was her last good-bye. After Jo and I had breakfast, we returned to the living room and she was at ease. I gave her a big hug and we cried for an hour. Our valiant friend had spent 17 years with us, enriching our lives and filling us with joy.

I remembered running through the pine forests with her, canoeing the streams with her and sitting beneath the beautiful Linden tree on our front lawn while pondering life. Many a deep conversation we had together. We were soul mates. I knew she would give her life to protect me and that I would do the same. A warm feeling settled in my heart as I remembered drifting in a row boat on a certain, cold Vermont evening, gazing up at the stars as we sat side-by-side listening to the silence. We floated across the stilled waters which reflected the glistening starlight as if in another world.

Our conversations were often one-sided but I knew she was listening and understood what I was saying. She would snuggle down in the warm grasses and occasionally glance up with one eye as if to reassure me in my musings. She suffered through my illnesses with me and would lay by my side for days when I was sick. She taught me what was important in life – which was not me. She tried to teach me to live for the moment, to enjoy life and not stress over what I couldn't control. Did I listen? No, but that just shows you that she was also smarter than me. She was my best friend, my protector, my psychiatrist and an immense source of joy in my life. She did not judge me and accepted and loved me with all my faults.

My dear old friend was gone….. A piece of my heart was torn away and gone also. Even as I type this, tears spill down my cheeks.

I have to stop now.

We buried her out in the back yard, under the creeping Vinca vines and beneath the wild Dogwood tree. She is with her brother and sisters – Cleopatra, Rusty, Sporty, Max, Nicky, Pookey, Squeaky and Spooky. Yes, I have a veritable pet cemetery in my yard, but unlike a Stephen King novel, ours is filled with love and serenity. We had loved all of them over the years, but they had all given us a greater love in return. Sometimes I sit out in the woods, amidst the tall cedars and pines and converse with my dear old friends. I am afraid that they might be the last, as my heart cannot withstand the pain anymore. I think we all get a bit more sentimental in our old age and a dear pet's death eventually becomes too much to bear. That is why I could never sell my house – I could never leave my old friends. I take comfort in them being near and I will never abandon them.

It is somewhat against Catholic religious doctrine to believe that animals go to heaven. That is a belief that I can't accept. I pray that they were all granted a happy and loving eternity and fervently believe that some day we will be together again. What could make for a greater happiness in heaven? We miss all our boys and girls and the yearning will never cease. I hope that they are all riding along with us on our journeys.

Sparky – My Best Buddy

CHAPTER 17

SPRING'S ARRIVAL

Spring was arriving. The fragrant lilacs in the yard were blooming, the birds were busy gathering down and sticks for their nests and the puddles were sinking in the now thawing ground. For the camper and traveler, like all other outdoorsman, farmers, and nature lovers, this means that the juices begin to flow like the sap in the trees. Ideas and plans plotted over the winter now become implemented. Tackle and rigging, fixed and replaced over those long, cold months is now ready to go. Travel plans are close to fruition and the anticipation starts to build. Campers are de-winterized, washed, waxed, tuned up and inspected. Tires pumped and pressurized, batteries checked, propane filled, seals inspected, and supplies loaded. Spring Trip season had arrived.

The time to push off into the unknown is nigh. Food, fishing gear and photo equipment is gathered and squeezed into the camper. Clothing is packed, documents are checked and final calls are made and reservations are reviewed. The refrigerator is turned on and you are almost ready to go.

First you review the 3,000 items on the check list so as not to forget the things you missed. Of course, at our age that is imperative. It is impossible to remember everything, even if you are young and your brain functioning at 100 percent. I like to think of brain function like a basic stock market investment thesis. Take 100 and subtract your age. That is the amount you should have invested in the stock market and is probably close to your brain functioning level. At age 65, my estimate is that my mind is operating at about 35 percent of what it used to. Get the picture?

I forget everything and my house looks like it was built out of Sticky notes. I make up lists and Sticky notes for everything. Sticky notes cover my tables, the coffee pot, my bedside nightstand and my computer. The refrigerator looks like a giant yellow Sticky holder and I've even found some long lost ones in the bathroom and on the steering wheel of my car. All the places you think you will visit at least once in a day. I hope the scientist at 3M that invented them is living a long and happy life. Talk about making lemonade from lemons. The inventor was originally trying to develop super-adhesive glue. He accidentally came up with the minimally adhesive glue used on the sticky notes. For a few years they could not get anyone to buy them until they were given out as samples at a consumer product convention. They then began to take off and the inventor was eventually enlisted into the invention hall of fame. For those of us heading towards our twilight years and apt to wander in a tangled fog of vague things to do, I consider it one of the greatest inventions of all times.

Conjuring up a travel and camping list is a job unto itself. There are 100's of items: clothing, food supplies, dishes, condiments, pots and pans, wrapping supplies, refrigerator list, freezer list, equipment list, sundry list, medical supplies, outdoor gear, rain gear, maps, books, liquor, blankets, sheets, cleaning supplies, emergency gear, binoculars, fishing gear, photo equipment, CDs, movies, foot gear, hammocks, chairs, repair items, batteries, levelers, tools, money, wallet, glasses, sunglasses, hats, bath supplies, utensils, umbrellas, park pass, reservation receipts, insurance, license, roadway service papers, reading material, book light, and on and on and on. The list stops only when your brain can't handle anymore and is smoking like a late night campfire. We still forget stuff, but my quest is to someday have the perfect list. Of course it would look like one of my CT scan printouts, rolling out in waves across the floor.

As you get older, food plays a more important role in your life. I think I've told you before how we love to cook and hate buying prepared meals. Of course this means on a long trip, weeks are spent preparing food for the trip. We make pizza dough, tomato sauce, crab cakes, stew, pepper steak, soups, chicken paprikash, sandwiches, blueberry and corn muffins, cookies and pies, and zucchini bread. This along with various meats, chicken, shrimp and scallops, and finally ice cubes, means I usually need a giant pressurized clamp to close the freezer door. But Jo somehow fits it all in. I like to feel that if a nuclear war hits when we are camping, we could probably live for months in our little camper up in the woods. Now this is all a lot of work. But making all our meals this way saves us thousands of dollars, is much healthier, and is a lot of fun.

I am not embarrassed to say I share the kitchen with my wife. At one point, I would have been. But after all we've been through I am glad to help out where I can. You may laugh and sneer, but what do you do for your wife? Buy her some flowers? Impress her with your sexual prowess? She can get that anywhere. I go out in the woods and pick a fresh bouquet of flowers and then prepare her a nice meal, say, of crab-stuffed flounder roll-ups, maybe a side of clams casino and a good bottle of wine and "Wallah"! That is how you keep a good woman by your side for 40 years. This is just a bit of advice for my young, male, camping readers.

Anyway, the house has been checked three times, faucets, stove and water turned off and camper warmed up. We had made plans for a "plant-sitter' to come by a couple of times a week to check on the house and water the plants for us. We are ready to go. This spring we decided on one more long practice trip so we had made reservations for campgrounds in Vermont, Maine, and the New York Adirondacks. This would be our final "prep" trip and we planned on relaxing and taking it easy for the month.

Our first stop was to be Acadia National Park. This is one of our favorite parks in the east and we had been there before. When planning the trip, still floundering a bit with the reservation system, I had missed getting a site for our first night. But the next morning at one thousandth of one second after 10:00 A.M., I managed to nab the last site in the campground. Of course I could do like some people and book a week early and then cancel half the days later on, but to me that system is disgusting. I always believed in playing by the rules. Someone even bragged to me about doing that at one of the campgrounds we visited. What a loser.

So, off we went to our first overnight stop in Massachusetts.

CHAPTER 18

NEW ENGLAND RAMBLE

It was a decent site after a long drive up the New York Thruway and then east on Massachusetts 90. Being a little tight, we did lose our rain gutters in the branches, but we had a quiet night and a campfire and retired early to bed. Massachusetts overcharges for their no-hook-up state parks. I don't know why, but seeing that it was an expensive sort of ho-hum state park I probably won't return unless I have to. The next day, after a long drive up the Maine coast we arrived at Acadia National Park. For this trip we decided to stay off the island at a federal campground in an area called Schoodic Woods. The campground was laid out beautifully and the sites had plenty of privacy. We knew Acadia gets quite crowded and we wanted to be away from the throngs of people on the island when relaxing.

We think Acadia National Park is the most beautiful place in the eastern U.S.A. Opened in 1929, most of the Park's area was donated by some of our past illustrious industrial scions, including John Rockefeller Jr. who also had the system of carriage roads built throughout the island. Meandering through the woods on these 45 miles of roads, over stone archways and beneath the forest canopies leads you to scenic vistas and quiet wooded retreats. The trails are amazing. The Island itself offers many lakes and bays for fishing and kayaking, horse drawn carriage rides, trolleys and shuttle buses, and shopping and dining in downtown Bar Harbor, a small town on the northeast corner of the island. The best part of the park is the Park Loop Road, a 25 mile paved road that winds its way along the coast and then up and through the woods to the park headquarters. The sweeping vistas over the bays and harbors are the most beautiful I've ever seen. Large jagged rocks spill down to the ocean beneath towering pines. When you sit on the rock ledges you can hear the thundering waves beating the shoreline. The strong breeze cleanses your senses with the salty brine of the sea while uplifting your spirits. The cobwebs of stress and melancholy that burrow down in your being over a long winter are soon cleared. We felt refreshed and alive.

The Cliffs of Otter stand like giant stone monoliths to the south where you can watch rock climbers scale the granite peaks amidst the soaring gulls. Located between the cliffs is Sand Beach, a small protected beach for swimming and relaxing. Driving south, you wind your way along beautiful harbors until you turn your way north to the Bubble Mountains and the Jordan Pond House. Supposedly a beautiful rest stop to have lunch alongside Jordan Pond, we have yet to visit this coveted stop. When we were there, the line of cars parked alongside the Loop, extended for a least a quarter mile, so we decided to skip the luncheon and proceeded to find lunch somewhere else. There are many small restaurants on the island and we had a nice little bite of fish 'n chips and seafood chowder in a small restaurant tucked in on the side of a cove and overlooking a marina. It was a beautiful day with the sun shining and the gulls crying and wheeling overhead. Lobster boats bobbed in the harbor and colorful floats decorated the waterfront shacks. We then left for a drive along the "quiet" side of the island. There was hardly any traffic as we headed through Southwest Harbor and Bass Harbor and proceeded along the Seawall where the pounding surf roars and the seaweed lays strewn along the stony shore. Upon arriving in Somesville, I stopped to take a few pictures of a cute, little white bridge that spanned a stream, bedecked with bright red geraniums and a smattering of petunias.

Acadia is a photographers dream. Photographing the bays and sounds, the rugged coastline, the Porcupine Islands, Bass Harbor Head lighthouse, lobster boats and shacks, the quaint villages and last but not least, sunrise on Cadillac Mountain can keep you busy for days. Sunrise on Cadillac Mountain is a type of touristy cliché, but it is worth the 6:00 A.M. trip to the summit at least once. From your perch at the top you can see the whole of the island as the sun rises and begins to slant its way over the horizon and across the mountain top. A standing ovation from the small crowd saluted the amazing moment of the start of a new day on the continental USA. What a beautiful sight and amazing morning.

After some shopping and lunch we took a scenic ride on the schooner "Margaret Todd" which plied its way along the harbor, passing seals lying on the rocky outcrops while weaving between the omnipresent lobster boats. The Margaret Todd is a four-masted, 151 foot schooner that sails out of Bar Harbor. If you are inclined, you can volunteer to help raise and lower the sails as it makes its way around the bay. Returning to the marina, the skies were flooded with blood red colors as the sun set over the hills. We had an amazing day in one of the most beautiful spots in the country.

Of course there were a few flies in the ointment. For one, it was supposed to be the cool time of the year in Maine. During our visit the temperatures came close to hitting 100 degrees and it was sweltering. In addition, the island was mobbed with people. Every scenic spot was overrun with hordes of people and trying to find some quiet time was difficult. Lastly, my new nemesis – bridges, arose to challenge me yet again.

Driving south on the Park Loop road armed with a park RV brochure, we were informed that there was a 10'6" bridge at the bottom of the Loop and should proceed in a clockwise direction around the island to avoid it. Well, according to the ranger I talked with later, it is such a beautiful drive they don't like to clutter the surroundings with anything as trivial as a sign directing you which way to go. Ergo, I cruised past the turnoff and headed the wrong way on the Loop. Up and down the hills, the forest rose up on both sides of the road, which of course had no shoulder. As we dropped farther and farther down the mountainside surrounded by the towering pines, I realized we were getting close to the bridge and had no way to turn around or pull over. We were being sucked to our doom. My mind was filled with the picture of a 24 foot motor home blocking traffic for 10 miles back up the Loop road, as we waited for a police escort to back all the way up and over the mountain. I began to sweat as we got closer and closer to the bridge and I could not conceive of any way out of our dilemma. A line of cars followed us down into the steep valley as we approached the bridge. We slowed almost to a stop but God helped me out again. It seems that the bridge was 10'6" at the bottom of the archway above the road, but was plenty high in the middle.

"Whew", we lucked out again. We proceeded under the arch as my grip slowly relaxed and my beating heart retreated to its normal pace. This bridge stuff was going to kill me yet.

We eventually returned to quiet, laid-back Schoodic Woods, off the island, and relaxed by the campfire, staring up at the multitude of stars. The next day was for relaxing. After a late morning breakfast, we took a nice bike ride down the trail to a beautiful cove looking out over the rocky islands. Another photo-op presented itself. The wild flowers along the shoreline were bent in submission to the strong wind, framing the rocky island guarding the entrance to the harbor. The beautiful sight made my morning.

We then trudged and struggled back up the hills to the campground. It wasn't quite as beautiful on the way back up, as sweat filled our eyes and our 65 year old bodies struggled to make it back up the steep inclines. We did stop by a quiet stream and rested alongside for a moment and listened to the chuckle of the waters playing over the small rocks. The shade cooled us off and soon we were on our way again. We starting walking our bikes up the hill until we finally reached the flat part of the trail on top of the mountain, and then pedaled our way back to camp.

We relaxed until late afternoon when we took a little drive around the small town and stopped at a lobster pound to procure our dinner. Now I know I constantly explain how we don't eat out to save money, but there are exceptions: one of them being eating a buttery, steamed lobster on the coast of Maine. They are relatively affordable if you stop at one of the lobster pounds in the area. We could prepare them ourselves but neither of us relished the idea of killing the cute little buggers. Guilt filled my mind as I turned my head and gave the thumbs down to the server, signaling death to the poor crustaceans presented to us for our dinner selection. Their beady little eyes begged for mercy, but none was forthcoming. If I was rich I would have bought out all the poor little lobsters and released them back to the sea – smiling happily as they swam back to the murky depths. But alas, I am poor, we were hungry, and their time had come. Back at the campsite, with a side of 'slaw and fries and a bottle of wine, they did not die in vain. It was a sumptuous meal. After dinner I relaxed in a chair and proceeded to review our future, plotted journey while my beautiful wife Jo practiced her guitar beneath the setting sun. What a beautiful and busy visit to Acadia and special memories made.

Later in the evening, I relaxed to read a book in bed. It was called the "Road to Little Dribbling" by one of my favorite authors, Bill Bryson. Perusing some of the pages, I was somewhat taken aback when he criticized conservatives. I was hurt. I liked Mr. Bryson. Why did he not all of a sudden like me? Being a bit irked, I put the book aside and stared at the cover. What kind of name for a town was "Little Dribbling"? Those crazy British folks. Then again I realized that the British can never beat the U.S. in anything except for maybe their fascination with royalty or their penchant for crazy food dishes. I therefore started to look up crazy American town names. Rest assured we are crazier. There are so many strange names that I won't list them all but you will get my drift. Who would want to live in a town called "Hell", or "Half Hell" or "Hell for Certain"? What about "PeePee", "Buttsville" or "Greasy Corner"? Not me, but I could see myself living in "Carefree", "Normal", "Happy Valley", "Niceville", "Happyland" or "Little Heaven". I put together a list as a suggestion for a long and wild night on the towns. Your first destination could be a visit to "Romance". If that proved unproductive, you could stop to check out "Sweetlips", then, if things really got rolling you could head to "French Lick" before finishing up at "Intercourse", then "Climax" and then what? "Good Grief". Then it might be time to "Cut and Shoot" before reaching "Burnout". "Why"? "Why Not", as two other towns exclaim. The names I loved the most are the really crazy ones. I think I would love to live in the following towns. The people must have a hilarious sense of humor and I would look forward to living amongst them. How about living in "Bacon Level", "Two Egg", "Mud Lick", "Yum Yum", "No Where", or "Knockemstiff"? It sounds to me like it would be a blast living there unless they are over-run from an excess of residents that are living in "Ding Dong", "Asylum" or "Looneyville", in which case maybe you might fear for your life. My three favorites were "Scratch Ankle", "Chicken Bristle" and "Booger Hole". How could you not want to live in these towns? Imagine, every time you address an envelope with a home address, you would burst out laughing and laughing is good. They sound like my kind of towns. I think a person could write a whole book just on crazy town names – maybe next time.

These weighty thoughts I pondered as I turned off the light and snuggled down in my blankets. Thoughts of living in "Zzyzx" were putting me to sleep. Mr. Bryson's book lay unread for the moment but he had shunted me in the direction of humor and that is always a good thing. I love retirement – you get to spend time pondering the important things in life.

The next morning we packed up and regrettably said goodbye to Schoodic Woods. We were heading up into the wilds of northwestern Maine to Cathedral Pines Campground. I left with a smile on my face and some humor in my heart.

Cathedral Pines was also a beautiful campground. Nestled along the side of Flagstaff Lake in the Rangeley Lake area of Maine, we reached the campground after a 4 or 5 hour drive through the woods from Acadia. Situated approximately 25 miles from the Canadian border, this place was out there - trees and lakes in every direction and minimal people. The campground is operated by a non-profit and thereby relatively affordable. It has 119 sites, many with sewer and water. It has a private beach, canoe & kayak rentals and a boat ramp. Large spacious sites were shaded by the huge red pines that covered the ground with a thick bed of pine needles. At first we had a site across the road from the water, but noticing the site across the way was empty, we asked if we could move over alongside the lake. They agreed to our move and we had a huge site on the shores of the beautiful lake. Electric only, but it was worth it. What a view. As this place was in the middle of nowhere and this was supposed to be a relaxing vacation, we relaxed. We hung out at the site. Jo and I tried a little painting and we went for walks and rode our bikes around the campground. In the late afternoon a thunderstorm rolled over but it was gone in about an hour. As the sun broke out in patches, a beautiful rainbow crossed over the lake as the shadows of the clouds passed over the mountains. As evening fell, the lapping of the waves on the shore lulled us into a relaxed stupor. I finally got up and started a campfire as the loons began chortling and laughing hilariously out on the lake. Who doesn't love that crazy laugh of the loons? Their cries echoed over the quiet waters as the sun set behind the mountains and a dark curtain descended around our fire. The sizzle of the burning embers lulled us to sleep. That day will be burnt into my memory for a while. After a peaceful sleep we lounged around the campsite the whole next day and I plotted my route to our next stop on our journey to Vermont.

We headed south the next morning and then west on Route 2. We stopped for lunch at the historic Sunday River covered bridge and spent an hour alongside the stream eating our sandwiches and watching and listening to the water tumble and flow over the rocks. Continuing west, we crossed northern New Hampshire and entered northern Vermont. We headed west until we reached route 100 in Vermont. Route 100 is a beautiful road that bisects the middle of the state. It winds over the hills and dales through bucolic farm country. In late spring in Vermont, the trip suffuses your body with the fresh scents of the erupting, unbelievably green foliage of Vermont's rural hills. I think route 100 is one of the prettiest roads in the nation. Cows idled along the hillsides, rushing streams flowed alongside the roadway and every so often an old, weathered general store beckoned to the weary traveler. It was a beautiful and bucolic ride. After heading south a bit, I decided we had to take route 17 west over the mountains to reach Bristol, our destination.

The relaxed, bucolic ride was over. This twisting, turning, serpentine challenge had me once again gripping the wheel tightly and creeping along at 25 miles per hour. After downshifting to second gear and taking a turn that resembled the end of a paper clip we passed by a sign stating that trucks and trailers should not be on this route. Fine place to put the sign! How about at the beginning of the route? Well at this point we were almost over the mountain so I continued in low gear through the fog and mist that was now enveloping our rig and the mountaintop. As a novice camper, I was now learning that some of those "scenic" routes with the little dots on the map had to be investigated a bit before attempting to traverse their courses. We eventually made it over the top with a few prayers and slowly glided our way down into the valley to the town of Bristol - a pretty, quaint town, absent all the normal tourist attractions and mobs of people - our kind of town. The reason for camping in Bristol is that is was close to a nice bass lake and not too far from my brother, who lives in Vermont. We both love bass fishing and he was going to pick me up at the campground so we could spend a day or two fishing. We were staying at Green Mountain Family campground, a nice, quiet campground nestled alongside the mountains. We proceeded to check in and meet the friendly owners, Gary and Joann. Always seeking peace and quiet, we crept past the resident goats up and around the hill to a site hidden under the pine canopy. As Covid was now spreading up and down the east coast, there were few campers and minimal noise. We were close to the bath house, a short distance to the pool and had a beautiful mountain view as the sun rose.

The next morning we did a little bit of yoga outdoors under the pines and then made a big breakfast. We went for a ride around the campground, chatted with the owners for a bit and visited the cute trio of resident goats. In the afternoon, I surprised Jo with a new hammock. I set it up for her, made her a margarita, and told her to relax while I made dinner. She swayed back and forth in the hammock, pushed by the light breeze and relaxed under the late afternoon sun, its golden rays streaming through the trees. Since we are always working around our house, we have never really appreciated the calming effects of a hammock, never seeming to have the time to use one. After a few hours, when I was putting dinner on the table, Jo came over and pronounced that this was the best afternoon she had had in years. I topped off her day with some breaded seafood, a bottle of wine, a fresh salad and some wild rice. What a way to live!

We never appreciated the relaxation afforded by extended camping and were thoroughly enjoying ourselves. When you get out in the trees and fresh air and out of the house, all your troubles are forgotten and serenity reappears in your life. We had forgotten what serenity was and where it had gone. It is always there, you just have to give it a chance to come out.

Well, we did and now after a couple weeks we were finally, really relaxed. We forgot about bills, health problems, to-do lists, and societal worries. The yoga sessions seemed to flow smoother, my back stopped hurting for a change, and we were smiling at each other and really meaning it. No wonder campers are so happy! One of the owners, Joann, was sweet enough to give us some fresh picked greens from her garden for our salad and they were delicious. After dinner, we relaxed by the campfire and put on some good music. Joann the owner stopped by and we sat around chatting and sipping some wine under the starry skies. She had moved up to Vermont from Southern New Jersey. It seems to me that half the population of Vermont once lived in New Jersey. It was another beautiful day.

The next day there was a light rain, so we took a trip to town to buy a few supplies and do a bit of shopping. In the afternoon, the rain let up and we were invited to a campground dinner under the huge gazebo in the nearby field. We arrived with some potato salad we had made and got to meet most of the other campers. With the clang of horseshoes ringing in the background we chatted with our new neighbors and heard many interesting stories. One was about a young couple just getting married who planned to live off grid in their self-constructed log cabin in the nearby hills. Another interesting chat we had was with a young man who lived at the campground in an old trailer he purchased for $5,000 and fixed up. He ran ski clinics and guided ski tours in the winter in Vermont and piloted boats along the Maine shores in the summer. They were exciting plans and endeavors. I wished that I was young again.

The following morning my brother arrived for our fishing trip and we packed up and made ready to go. He had brought his wife along and the two girls set up for a day-long gabfest.

We arrived at the pond and launched our little skiff into the creek. It is a fairly large pond, situated at the end of a long stream lined with cattails and lily pads - a bass fisherman's delight. We put-putted up the placid creek just as the early morning sun was breaking through the mists hanging low over the water. I had a particular affection for this pond as I had caught my personal record bass here and looked forward to a good day.

Vermont has dozens and dozens of great bass ponds and lakes and I have been trying to explore all of them since I have been coming up here for the last 30 years. My favorites are the ones just large enough that you can spend a day fishing all of the lake, but small enough to be comfortable in a small boat or kayak. They all seem to hold a prodigious amount of nice bass. They are also relatively quiet and a busy day on some of the lakes means seeing one or two other fisherman. Many times we fish all alone, unlike New Jersey where a typical day brings dozens of fisherman and bass boats. Quietly gliding along a mountain lake, listening to the ripples of the water gurgling off behind you and placidly floating through a field of lily pads waiting for that small tug is enough to make a fisherman's heart purr, whether any fish are caught or not. On an especially nice day you might be startled by the slap of a beaver's tale as the sun is going down or be treated to the chortle of a pair of loons.

Kingfishers screech across the streams, and the soul-searching hooting of the owls can be heard in the distance. Occasionally you will hear a Pileated Woodpecker chopping large chunks of wood from the aged trees surrounding the lakes. Who needs fish? Then again if you're lucky enough to hook a nice slamming bass and fight him through the pads and the stumps, you will be making a memory to be treasured forever. I've caught quite a few nice ones over the years and my portfolio of bass fishing trips with my brother is forever tucked into my mind. I love Vermont lakes so much that I told my sweetie to one day spread my ashes along the banks of one of my favorites.

On this particular day, all we managed was a few smaller ones, but the day was beautiful as always and I gave them all a kiss and sent them on their ways. We put-putted our way back to the landing amidst the vibrant greens of the Vermont season. Beautiful Pink Lady Slippers lined the trails along the banks and bright blue Flag Irises glistened in the setting sun. Cattails swayed in the light breeze as the Red-winged Blackbirds chortled from their swaying perches. Bullfrogs hidden amongst the pads began their evening bellows as we headed to the dock. As the dull glow of the setting sun dropped behind a distant mountain, we loaded up the boat in the dark and headed back to camp where the girls were dishing up a nice dinner of barbequed chicken, potato salad and coleslaw. We sat around the campfire and reminisced for a while and then our visitor's took their leave. We were left alone, sitting in the quiet darkness, listening to the sizzle and pop of the burning pine.

We did manage to get out again the next day for a while towards evening but that day also wasn't very productive in the bass haul so we called it a wrap once again and returned to camp for some more chit-chat, with wine and family around the fire. That was it for the fishing and visits and we spent the rest of the week relaxing at the campsite and going for walks and bicycle rides. We were going to miss our Vermont stay and once again talked about moving there as we always have for the last 30 years. Once again we came to the conclusion that we just have to be content with our annual visits. In a way, maybe this is better, as I often think of our visits as a special treat and maybe living there would be too much, and the novelty and beauty would fade over time. Thoughts of dozens of feet of annual snow and pond ice thick enough to drive a car over never seem to help the decision-making process either.

We were soon off to our last stop - the Adirondacks of New York. Northampton Beach campground in the southern Adirondacks was another beautiful campground spread out on a peninsula along Sacandaga Lake. I could not believe my luck, as this campground was even more beautiful than the rest. I guess my hours of research paid off. Every campground we stayed in on the whole trip was beautiful. We had a gorgeous waterfront site beneath the tall pines. Mostly sunny, we spent the next three days super-relaxing at the site. We broke out the hammocks again and whiled away hours just slowly swinging by the waters edge. We painted, took strolls through the woods and just chilled for the remainder of our trip. I rued not having brought my kayak on this journey and vowed to take it in the future.

It would be a bit of a pain, not having any type of contraption for mounting it on the camper, but after a couple of sarcastic comments from the co-navigator I have since discovered that with a bit of twisting and turning and shoving I can fit it into the motor home. It takes up most of the living area, but hey, what's more important, living space or kayak? Well, we know the answer to that.

I tried a few half-hearted casts from the bank of the lake, but nothing was biting close to shore. At least I once again saved myself the cost of a non-resident New York fishing license. We will return to that beautiful campground in the future. It was one of our favorites. There are quite a few things to do in the Adirondacks, such as hiking and kayaking, float planes and boat rides. There is also the beautiful Adirondack museum which is well worth a visit, as well as many quaint, small towns. But we had done most of that in the past, I did not have my kayak, and we were quite a distance from the museum, so we elected to just relax for the end of our trip and take it easy. The next day we got up early and headed south. After the normal horrendous trip through New York and New Jersey we made it home safely.

It was a fantastic trip, the RV performed perfectly, and we had a great time. We had tasted a bit of that solace that we were seeking, but it was not enough. Once more engaged in everyday life with its bills and chores and health concerns, our store of relaxation began to slowly dissipate, but I was already plotting and planning our next trip, which was coming up soon. After having plenty of practice, we figured now was the time for our first "bigger" trip and we set our sights on Michigan and Minnesota.

Moss Glen Falls, Vermont

Sunday River Covered Bridge, Maine

Porcupine Islands, Maine

Acadia National Park, Maine

Loon on Little Tunk Lake, Maine

Vermont countryside

Somesville, Mt. Desert Island, Maine

CHAPTER 19

THE GREAT NORTH WOODS

I spent the summer months plotting and reserving our sites for our visit to Michigan and Minnesota. We wanted to spend a maximum of one month on the trip as we were still not sure how long we could happily exist in our little 24 foot box. If you are not a full time RV traveler, planning a trip like this is walking a fine line between how many sights you want to fit into the trip and how many days you would like to spend at each spot. Since our grand plan is to see most of the sights in the country in four or five years, we have to opt for quicker stops at more places rather than leisurely, weekly stays here or there. Most of our stops are only for 2 or 3 days at a time. Calculating about seven days to get out and back, that left us approximately 23 days for sightseeing. On the way back I did want to take part of the River Road down along the Mississippi River, so we were left with about 18 days to visit the two states. Narrowing down our choices we opted to stop at Sleeping Bear Dunes National Park, Mackinac Island, and Pictured Rocks national seashore in Michigan, spend a couple days in northern Wisconsin, and then stop at Ely and Lake Itasca, the headwaters of the Mississippi in Minnesota.

We were excited about our first big trip with Bea and spent the summer packing, plotting and getting ready for our Labor Day weekend lift off. I was also excited because this trip was finally the excuse for me to buy a new camera. I am a fairly serious photographer but had always used slide film in my shooting. I never switched over to digital because of the costs involved and the fact that I consider digital photography more of a technical experience and less artsy. But, with all this traveling planned, I knew I had to do something, so Mr. frugal laid out $1700 bucks for a new Canon 6d digital camera and lens. Labor Day soon rolled around and with our refrigerator and freezer bursting at the seams, we left home and headed for the far north – the land of fur traders, voyageurs, and wolves.

After a 7 hour drive, we spent our first overnight stop at Bush Mountain Recreation Area, a COE campground northeast of Pittsburg, Pa. It was nice enough and after an uneventful night, we left and drove most of the way across Ohio. We were planning on staying at one of the rest stops on the Ohio Turnpike as they have over-night RV parking, but after seeing a desolate parking lot in a field with no other travelers, we opted to head to the nearest state park. Not a good move, since it was Labor Day weekend and we had no reservation. We ended up crunched into a tiny grass site alongside a road surrounded by campers. At each end of our camper, tents were set up. One tent was populated with screaming children and the other with ersatz hippies, strumming their guitars and singing while the wafting odors of campfires and cannabis streamed through our camper. Now everyone likes a little guitar playing around the campfire but after a few hours of out-of-tune strumming and wailing, it gets to you. The campground was mobbed and after a quick dinner and walk, we hit the sack. Half stoned from the smoke clouds around our camper we nodded off to the sounds of screaming kids, fireworks, howling dogs and some kind of off-key screeching from the site next door, which steadily increased as the presumed amount of cannabis inhaled also increased.

We awoke early, went for a bike ride and then left for the first official site on our journey: Sleeping Bear Dunes National Park. The name is derived from an Ojibwa Indian legend in which a mother bear and her two cubs swam across the lake to escape a forest fire. The cubs drowned and became the islands to the south and the spot where the mother sadly waited for them was named Sleeping Bear Dunes. The campground was beautiful and became one of our favorites of the year. The sites were large and situated beneath huge tall pines that wavered in the breeze. It was extremely quiet and peaceful. We had a quick dinner and sat by the campfire for the evening. A storm was coming so we headed to bed early. We awoke in the middle of the night amidst howling winds and pounding hail. Praying that our camper would not be crushed by the towering pines or dented beyond recognition by the hail storms, we fitfully went back to sleep and awoke to a beautiful morning.

In the morning, I found no dents in the RV, no fallen trees and life was good again. After a late breakfast, we took a ride around Sleeping Bear Dunes Park. It was quite beautiful. Towering dunes, 500 feet high, dropped precipitously to the lake below. The sun glinted off the beautiful aquamarine waters of Lake Michigan as large, puffy, cumulus clouds drifted over the sail boats and fishing vessels on the lake. A small wooden pier projected off the top of the dunes to allow visitors a view of the coastline from high above. You could also look down at the few crazy people who opted to go down to the bottom of the dunes, by the shoreline, and who now had to march almost straight up in the deep sands back to the top. I almost had a heart attack just watching them and after a couple of hours they made it back to the top where they collapsed in the sands. It seems that they had ignored the warning signs about the potential 2 hour trip back up or the $3,000 rescue fee charged if you couldn't make it back on your own. Oh, to be young again. I got a few great shots with the new camera, and we finished up our sojourn with a pleasant drive around the hilly shoreline and wound our way back to camp. We only planned on a one day stop here, but seeing how beautiful it was, we now wished we had a few more days to spend in the area. Maybe a return visit on a future trip? It would definitely be worth it. So after a nice walk around the campground and a seat by the campfire for a while, we turned in for the night. The next morning after a hearty breakfast and early start we headed for Mackinac Island.

Mackinac Island is a popular tourist area of approximately 4 square miles located between Michigan's upper and lower peninsulas and Lake Michigan and Lake Huron.

Originally settled by Native Americans at least 700 years before the Europeans arrived, it was considered to be the home of the "Great Spirit" and according to legend was the first land to appear after the "Great Flood". In 1670, the first mission was founded on the island by French

Jesuits and it later became an important fur trading post. Eventually the fur trading and fishing industries turned the island into an important center of commerce and tourism began to flourish with the building of hotels and shops along the island. In 1875, most of Mackinac Island was dedicated as our country's second National Park. You might not ever heard of it as being a National Park and that is because it was transferred to the State of Michigan after 20 years and it was delisted as a National Park. Motor vehicles have always been restricted on the island.

We arrived at Mackinaw Mill Creek campground in the late afternoon and proceeded to search for our site. Mackinaw Mill Creek campground is a huge campground located on the shores of Lake Huron with nice beaches and a great view of the Mackinac Bridge, the only northern route to the upper peninsula of Michigan. It has cabin and cottage rentals and over 600 sites for camping sprawled out over 200 acres. It actually took us a while to find our site but eventually we made it. Don't try it without a map. We usually eschew staying in commercial campgrounds but this one was quite nice with trees and shrubs separating the sites and nice views of the lake. The main attraction though, was that it had a shuttle to the ferry which is the only way to get to Mackinac Island and therefore would save us some driving and parking with the motor home. We once again had only scheduled one day for the visit and therefore did not partake of any of the campground amenities and hit the sack early so we could catch the early shuttle and ferry to the Island.

We got up early and made our way to the shuttle stop for an 8:30 departure. It was nice as very few people were on the early shuttle and in a little while we were on our way across the lake on a crowded ferry. Where did all the people come from? It was a bit chilly and windy as we bounced and jerked our way along and the ferry made a little detour to go under the Mackinac Bridge on the way to the island. There were still some remnants of the rays from the sunrise glaring off the huge bridge spanning the Mackinac Straits where Lake Michigan and Lake Huron meet. It was quite an intimidating sight, knowing that the following day I would have to drive over it. As you can tell, my fear of bridges seems to be increasing on our travels as we have to cross some of these crazy structures in our journeys. High bridges, long bridges, bridges with minimal railings, bridges with no pavement, or metal grating you can see through. Skinny bridges, windy bridges- the list can go on and on for those of us a bit leery of crossing bridges, especially in a motor home. Well this bridge had it all.

Built in 1957, this bridge spans the 5 mile stretch of the Mackinac Straits, connecting the Upper and Lower peninsulas of Michigan. The bridge deck is 200 ft. high and in a part of the span you can see below through the grated metal decking. Citing the Mackinac Bridge Authority, the towers rise 552 feet high and the bridge consists of 42,000 miles of cable holding the whole thing together on piers that extend 250 feet below the waters' surface. It is the longest suspension bridge in the western hemisphere and can sway up to 30 feet in high winds. When riding up in a motor home, the railings look like little curbs, as you peer down to the waters below. If you look up, you get vertigo and feel like driving right over the edge. If you look around all you see in the vast expanses of water as far as the eye can see to the right or left. Was it intimidating? You bet. It scared the crap out of me just looking up at it from the ferry. The vehicles on top looked like ants marching to their doom on a small stick in the middle of the sky.

We proceeded on our ferry ride and docked on the island. I was hoping for that nice bucolic feeling of being on a beautiful island and wandering the small villages. It was beautiful, but it was your typical tourist trap. Thousands of people roamed the small village, with kids screaming, cell phones flashing and every "quaint" store filled to bursting with large crowds of sweating, yapping, pushy tourists. Piles of horse manure littered the streets and smelled awful. Covid was also rampant at this point in time and we were petrified of catching it. To get away from the mobs, we decided to take a horse and buggy ride around the island. This was a little better and the ride went up into the hills for some scenic sights and somewhat less people. The relaxing ride wound its way through the forest and up along the hills on the coast. We also stopped at the Butterfly House and walked amongst the hundreds of butterflies flitting around the greenhouse. They landed on our heads, our hands and our shoulders. It was like being in a little tropical paradise and was quite entertaining.

I felt sorry for the horses, though. Even though they are big Percherons and Belgiums, the thought of them hauling around 50 to 75 people all day, in the heat, up and down the steep hills, was a little disconcerting. The poor fellows really had to work for their "pay". Hopefully in the future they will have a nice relaxing retirement somewhere on some beautiful meadow in the hills. They earned it.

It was a nice ride. We toured the old fort and enjoyed the old Victorian homes and the Grand Hotel. Would I do it again? Probably not, but it was worth a one day look around the island. As the day wound down, we enjoyed a sandwich on the hills overlooking the harbor. We could not find a restaurant we could even get into, but it was a nice scenic view and as the day came to an end, a nice breeze blew in from the lakes. It is probably very beautiful and quiet in the off season, but the crush of people, the heat and limited time made for a somewhat unpleasant visit. But I guess it is what it is, and you try to make the best of your travels. Everywhere we go seems to be overrun with people. Doesn't anyone work anymore?

We jumped on the ferry for a ride back to the campground and turned in pretty early. We had only scheduled one day here. We had gotten lucky, one day at Sleeping Bear Dunes and one day at Mackinac Island and we managed to visit both as planned. I tossed and turned all night worrying about my upcoming jaunt over the "BRIDGE". They only allow you to go 30 or 40 mph over the bridge as it is, and in windy conditions, they won't allow you over at all. It was October and it was a bit windy. Seeing how this is the only connection between the Upper Peninsula and the Lower, our chances of crossing seemed to be "blowing in the wind", as they say. It seemed a bit moronic to me, but hey, I don't live here, I just wanted to cross the bridge. Well to make a long story short, we made it over and the views were spectacular. Of course I prayed the whole time that one of those 42,000 miles of cable didn't decide to snap on this given day. It wasn't very windy and before you know it we were a hundred miles or so up the road and we stopped at Tahquamenon Falls for the view and a lunch break. We just stopped for a quick visit as we still had to go a hundred or so miles to the west to our camp site. The Falls were beautiful and there were nice trails to walk. We had lunch in the falls area and then headed to our campground on Indian Lake. I had reserved a nice spot along the shore of the lake and we were treated to a spectacular sunset. As the beautiful red and orange hues diffused across the horizon and reflected in the calm waters of the lake, I started a campfire and we relaxed for a bit until dark and then headed in for an early sleep. The next morning we treated ourselves to a large breakfast of pancakes and eggs and took our time getting ready for our next trip.

I had booked a 5:00 p.m. reservation on a catamaran to view the Pictured Rocks scenic outcroppings and cliffs. It was going to be somewhat of a hectic ride as the wind was blowing in excess of 30 mph. Our tour guide announced that anyone susceptible to sea sickness should probably not take the trip and they would refund their money. We decided to go ahead since we have a sailboat and assumed we would be okay on the rough water. The trip was spectacular. Was it a little bumpy? Yes, but beautiful. We bounced around all over the place as the catamaran broached the 6 foot waves, but it was quite exhilarating. To even walk around you had to hold onto the walls or railings and I laughed as some people came down the stairs on their butts. But it was fun and as we got closer to the cliffs, the waves calmed down a little and the ride became better. The late day sun glowed along the 15 miles of sandstone cliffs until we reached Spray Falls and turned around. It was quite beautiful and we probably took 50 pictures of the spectacular cliffs that can reach upwards of 200 feet and drop precipitously into the lake. Small caves and outcroppings line the shoreline. It was beautiful and we enjoyed it immensely. Someday, a longer, return trip seems to be in order as we had only scratched the surface of this beautiful area. Beautiful views, beaches, waterfalls, trails and tours and picturesque small towns - what's not to like?

The Upper Peninsula was fantastic and we vowed a return trip. You could definitely spend a couple weeks up there exploring and having a fantastic time. Being somewhat limited in the time available, I figured we could add a longer exploration of Upper Michigan to our future Northwestern Trip and it would definitely be worth it. So far, out of our few journeys, we are already planning to return for longer periods to upper coastal Maine, the Adirondacks and the Upper Peninsula of Michigan. I don't know if my 4 year plan can stand up to the beauty of this great country, but we will push forward and hopefully be in good enough shape a few years from now to continue travelling. We were delighted we got to see all those wonderful places at least once.

The next day we relaxed after our hectic 5 days of travelling. I made a pizza for dinner and Jo made 'smores for the campfire and we had a quiet, relaxing day.

We woke up refreshed, packed up and headed to Torch Lake in

Wisconsin. Another beautiful area, especially if you are a fisherman. Just in the county we were camping in, there are literally thousands of lakes. Unbelievable! Coming from South Jersey, I am limited to barely a dozen lakes to fish within a 50 mile radius. Here there were thousands. I almost decided to relocate on the spot. No matter which direction you went there were lakes. There were big lakes, small ponds, grassy lakes, stumpy lakes, windblown huge lakes and quiet, idyllic little lakes. I could spend the rest of my life fishing here and probably wouldn't live long enough to fish every lake in the county. It must be like heaven for a fisherman. But I decided it would be like having Halloween every day as a kid. You would eventually get sick of all the candy and would end up hating candy. So we more or less drove around starry-eyed looking at all the water and woods. Our campsite was quite nice and secluded, and looked magnificent as the trees were beginning to explode in colors and a nice autumn quiet descended over the forests. I even found a couple of my mushrooms that I hunt for back in Jersey and that made my day. Being the planner that I am, we had brought along our dehydrator and I smiled as I sliced up the mushrooms and dried them out for my annual harvest, since I was not at home to collect them. I only know one type of mushroom to pick, so my collecting is somewhat limited, but I hope to expand my knowledge in the future. There is nothing better than roaming through the woods on a fall day, a slight crispness in the air, and spying a little brown top peaking out from the brown grasses. I think they are beautiful and thanked God for the privilege of being able to collect them on that beautiful fall day. Fall is my favorite time of year, and if I could find a place that had fall weather year round I would move there in a snap (as long as it had some bass lakes in the vicinity and mushrooms for picking). What is ironic is that I don't even like to eat mushrooms. I just think they are beautiful and love harvesting them. Many of my friends and family are grateful for my jars of dried mushrooms that I pass out over the winter depending on how many I get. I love harvesting them.

There was nothing to really get "excited" about in the area, especially if you don't have a boat to fish from. So we spent two days relaxing and just soaking up the natural beauty. Jo practiced her guitar a bit and we went for a couple bike rides and walks. It was a beautiful relaxing spot.

We were soon packing up again and headed towards the last major destination of our journey to upper Minnesota. It was a beautiful drive through the hundreds of miles of forests and lakes and we finally arrived at Big Bear Lake near Ely, Minnesota. I always dreamed of checking out this area, imagining the fur trappers, exploration of distant lakes, Paul Bunyan, and the howling of the wolves in the wild. Well, the only fur trappers we saw were recreated in the visitor centers, Paul Bunyan was a statue and the only wolves we saw and heard were at the International Wolf Center. But it was still beautiful and exciting and we loved driving around the area. As for the lakes – please reference chapter one of this book. Yes I almost drowned, yes I lost approx. $2,000 in photo gear and fishing equipment, and yes I was scared shitless. But it was still worth it. At our ages and after our battles with cancer, enjoying life and making sweet memories is all that counts. Even if I knew what was going to happen, I would do it again in a heartbeat. I spent a few beautiful hours on a beautiful northern lake, got a bit of fishing in, watched a bald eagle soaring atop the pines, and condensed 5 years of physical conditioning into treading water for an hour on a beautiful fall afternoon in the wilds of northern Minnesota. I didn't die, and now have a great story to pass along to friends and family. If I do die soon, I have one more great memory to take with me. I will try to be more careful in the future – we are not getting any younger or more agile. Do I want to commit suicide by falling off a cliff on Angel Trail in Zion or get eaten by a bear in Glacier? No. But I trust in God that he will manage our lives to his end, and when you're time is up, you're time is up. So I am going to try to enjoy these retirement years as much as possible.

Now picking up from page one, after completing my physical stress test, I relaxed for a bit under the warm blankets in our RV. My numb legs did not function for a while, but soon I was up and around and whipped up a nice dinner of breaded cod and wild rice with asparagus. What a way to finish up a beautiful, exciting day. We crashed into our bed early and the next morning we were on our way to the Bear and Wolf centers. It was very interesting and the animals were beautiful. I did feel a bit of angst knowing they were somewhat enclosed and were not free to spend their lives roaming the mountains, but they were taken care of, had plenty to eat, and generally lived carefree lives as opposed to struggling in the wilds. Which is better? Who knows, but we as humans have to make the same decisions for ourselves. It was a nice day and we finished off with a scenic drive around the area and visited Ely, a little too big of a town for our tastes, but it was a nice town and we enjoyed ourselves. We headed back to camp and turned in early, pondering our trip for the next day to Bemidji State park and our visit to the Headwaters of the Mississippi.

Visiting the headwaters of the Mississippi has always been on my bucket list of travel destinations. Now maybe it's not really eye-popping or incredibly majestic, but the idea of seeing this mighty river start as a small stream up in the great north woods was something that struck my fancy as an interesting destination. Soon after setting up camp we took a ride up to the headwaters area. The river is so small at this point that you can jump over it. I found that amazing. According to the National Park Service, as this river flows south on its 2,300 mile journey through the states it attains a width of over 11 miles and discharges 593,000 cubic feet of water per second into the Gulf of Mexico. A million tons of goods are shipped through its ports annually. Standing here, watching the small stream course its way through the grasses, one would think they happened upon some small gem of a stream chuckling its way through the vast woods. The wind was blowing in off the lake and eagles soared overhead. It was fairly awe-inspiring to actually see the humble beginnings of this great river and the source of its birth. We headed back to camp and snuggled by the campfire for the evening before turning in early. It was October now, and getting a bit chilly. The next day, as part of our "get back in shape" program, we bicycled the 6 miles back to the headwaters. It was a nice ride through the forest up and down some hills to our destination. We stopped at a couple scenic areas and wound our way back to camp after passing a family of raccoons scampering across the trail. It was beautiful. At this point, the fall colors were amazing in the north woods. Crisp dark green backdrops interspersed with blazing reds and oranges sprinkled with the slashing whites and yellows of the birches. A vast pallet of colors was served up on a daily basis.

We decided to relax around the campground the next day and as Jo was practicing her guitar and I was relaxing in the hammock, a curious incident took place. Another RV drove up to our site, and the individual got out and was staring at us and the site number. Uh-oh......Slowly a tingle developed up my spine as it seemed this guy was implying this was his site. I told my wife he was some kind of screwball and proceeded to retrieve my trip itinerary list from the camper. I was chuckling, what an idiot, as I read the dates and destinations. OH MY GOD! We were supposed to be arriving at our site in south eastern Minnesota by now at Interstate Campground. I thought I was going to have a heart attack as my mind quickly exploded into a giant snarl of problems. We were only supposed to stop at Interstate overnight and continue another 7 hour drive the next day. The inner alarms went off, we ran around trying to pack up and I profusely apologized to the poor gentleman waiting to get into his site. We went from total relaxation to hyper drive in 5 minutes. What a shock to the system. We were packed and pulling out in 10 minutes, while feelings of dread took hold in my mind. It was now around 4:00 pm and we were looking at a 6 or 7 hour drive down to our next destination.

Now most retirees don't even like to drive more than 5 or 6 hours a day maximum, let alone at night. When you are our age, wear glasses and have a tendency to nod off in the evening, this was not a good scenario. As we drove off into the darkness, we were looking for a place to grab something to eat for the journey.

How does a certain national hoagie chain stay in business? We found this decrepit ramshackle eatery attached to a gas station in a little town we passed through. That was it for miles, and miles, and miles. Driving through the vast north woods might be beautiful and idyllic and quiet, but if you are hungry you have a problem. The food in the place looked like it was there since the building's construction, probably sometime around the turn of the century: shriveled up lettuce, dried out tomatoes and roast beef that looked like it was locally harvested road kill. The place smelled, was deserted, and it seemed that I had awoken the server from his drug induced coma. It was prepared without a word, slopped together on a stale role and handed over without comment. I went back to the RV and as we drove off down the highway I was half gagging over eating this excuse for food. I never did finish it, but I assumed the small bite of beef and bacteria would hold off any napping tendencies as I would be forced to stay awake from stomach cramps.

We eventually arrived at our no-hook-up site on the banks of the St.

Croix River at 11:30 p.m., and as I hesitantly backed into the dark, crooked site, I took out the site number pole in the process. We turned on our little lantern and collapsed into bed. I will never live this down with the copilot, but mistakes do happen....especially at my age and mental maturation. The next morning I caught a beautiful sunrise along the river and the cliffs as I tried to mentally prepare for another long drive down to Wabasha and the Eagle Center. I had tried to plan a nice little meander down the Mississippi as part of our return trip and that was our first destination.

We stopped at the Eagle Center in Wabasha, Minnesota on our trip for the day. We went in and viewed a couple of eagles in a small enclosure. That was it. It was a nice enough town, but maybe the time of year was wrong or something else, but we saw no eagles in flight, none in the surrounding trees and none along the river. It was actually quite boring. I am starting to realize that unless you see animals out in the wild, it's somewhat boring to see them in enclosures. I was disappointed with the eagle center, the bear center and the wolf center. They were all a bit interesting, but in my opinion not worth a lengthy drive to go see. What got me the most excited was being in Wabasha, the supposed town where they filmed "Grumpy Old Men", one of my favorite movies. Nothing too exciting about that either but at least when I watch the movie in the future I can better envision the area in which it is taking place.

We slowly made our way down the Mississippi toward Wyalusing State Park, our next destination. The upper Mississippi was quite scenic but as we went down lower and lower, it was somewhat disappointing. Major traffic jams and road construction left for a less than awesome drive. I had envisioned sweeping vistas and small quaint towns. When reading the blogs and literature I was pretty excited about driving along the Mississippi and was planning on traversing various sections of the river on our future trips. Now I am not so sure it is worth it. As mentioned before, it seemed like every few miles we were running into road construction and traffic jams. The roads were horrible - bumpy and full of potholes and the hoped for scenic views didn't really materialize for any extended period. The small quaint towns were mostly run down and sad looking and we came away with a pretty disappointing view of this segment of the trip. I thought it was going to be one of the highlights. Maybe I was on the wrong side of the river – who knows? Maybe we were just getting tired from all the driving.

Wyalusing state park was very scenic when we eventually reached our destination. The sites were spread out over hilly cliffs overlooking the Mississippi valley. We enjoyed very pretty views from up on the hills as the sun set and the lights came on in the valley below.

We only stayed one day to relax and then turned back eastward on our long trip home. Our next stop was Starved Rock State park in Illinois. I always try to plan our stops at parks that are interesting so that if we are just too tired to get out and about, we can at least enjoy our time at one of our beautiful state parks. Starved Rock for the most part didn't disappoint. We only had one day here, so we trekked along a few different trails throughout the day. We climbed our way up the stairs and walkways up to the cliff tops and were rewarded with a grand view overlooking the Illinois River. It was quite beautiful. The trails to the cliffs and canyons were beautiful also, except this time of year all the streams were dried up. I expected to see rushing little streams cascading down in all the nooks and crannies of the sandstone, but instead all we saw was the stained sandstone cliffs with nary a drop of water. It was disappointing. You had to use your imagination to envision the streams dropping into the chasms and make believe you heard the rush of the falling waters. Oh well, it was a pretty area and I am sure quite beautiful in the spring. Hopefully in our future continental crossings we can stop here again at a better time.

Early the next morning we pulled out and headed to our next destination in southwestern Ohio – Paint Creek State Park. This was to be a 2 day stopover as I had planned a little break from all the driving and was hoping to maybe get in a bit of fishing. Paint Creek was a nice campground. I had tried to select a site with a view of the lake, but at that time of year with all the trees leafed out, you really didn't see the lake. In addition, in the area with views, it was quite crowded. After pushing my way through the foliage, I watched in envy as the bass boats zipped around the lake.

I am still trying to figure out how to bring a kayak on our extended trips as I love kayaking and fishing. I haven't quite figured it out yet. I was too cheap to spring for a rack for the back of the camper. They can cost in the thousands of dollars which I was not prepared to pay for a couple pieces of bent pipe that hook on your bumper. Did I complain yet about the cost of everything nowadays? The rack is probably $25 worth of pipe structured into a skeleton that connects to your bumper, and into which you place your kayak. What is the other $1500 for? I have to erect and attach it. For that much money they should give you concierge service where they come out every time you use it and attach your kayak for you. Anyway, as an alternative, I tried fitting the kayak in the camper and actually made it, after my wife chuckled that it would be impossible. It takes up the whole floor space from the dashboard to the rear bed – but I got it in there. I might have dented one of our cabinets in the process but I love a challenge. After a bit of fruitful thought and a few snide and threatening remarks from Jo, I sadly decided that traveling cross-country with a kayak taking up all the living space in the RV would not be conducive to my physical well being or my 40 years of marriage.

I am currently in the process of reviewing blow-up kayaks. I am also considering bringing my $25 worth of pipe to a local welder who could probably put the whole thing together for a couple hundred bucks. Anyway, I refuse to crisscross this great country of ours for the next 5 years without my trusty kayak and a few wonderful fishing expeditions. For some odd reason, all the parks in the country that rent canoes and kayaks plant them 5 miles from your campsite. In addition they are usually the smallest pieces of junk made and you risk your life taking them out in any body of water larger than a bathtub (reference my opening page of almost drowning). There was a beautiful campground in South Carolina that was the one exception to these rules and I will write about that in the next few chapters. I always figured I could just go campground to campground and rent kayaks but I could see this plan was not going to work.

Did I mention to you how expensive everything is nowadays? I know, ha-ha, but I will give another example. A lot of places charge up to $30 to rent a canoe or kayak for half a day. Are you kidding me? The pieces of junk were probably bought for $500 and they get up to $60/day for renting them out. They pay them off in one or two week's rentals and for the next 5 or 10 years it is all profit. I can see that from your little capitalistic pig, private campground, but this is our government's state and federal parks. They are not supposed to rip off their citizens. What about the manufacturers themselves? Years ago we bought a beautiful 16 foot canoe made out of fiberglass with inlaid cedar strips and hand-made cane seating. It is a beautiful piece of workmanship and cost me $300. Made to last, I still have it 25 years later and it is in beautiful shape. What can you buy now for 2 or 3 times the price - a machine blown piece of junk plastic with piece of junk, plastic seats with a couple holes in each end and maybe a bottle holder. Are you kidding me again? Its probably $50 worth of plastic with no labor involved except for screwing down the seats and they charge $600? I still say we need a good old depression to straighten the prices out in this country.

Anyway, that's enough ranting. We spent the two days hanging around the campsite and I tried a few uninspiring casts from shore. My nights were filled with dreams of catching huge, lunker bass while fishing from my kayak.

The next day we moved on to western Maryland, the last destination of our trip. We stayed at Rocky Gap State Park. It was a nice enough campground and we had a nice quiet site in the woods. We made a campfire for our last night of camping and I prepared a pizza to go along with some red wine. It was a nice end to a really beautiful trip.

The following day we were headed home. Home? After five weeks and all of our stops and destinations, I could hardly remember it, but it was calling. We had been cramped up in Bea for so long, and after thousands of miles of driving, spending thousands of dollars and worrying about the traffic and the camper and the schedule, we looked forward to an extended break. It would be nice to get back to our homestead - with its 5 acres and 11 rooms to spread out in.

Well, we made it safely home. The first thing I did upon our arrival was to pull my lounge chair out to the front yard. I began discussing our trip with the local birds, squirrels and chipmunks while sipping a margarita. It was nice to be home. They were quite attentive as they rightly perceived that the daily feedings would now be back on track.

Was the trip worth it? Sure. We loved it and since winter was now approaching I looked forward to planning many more great trips over the winter. I might have almost drowned, lost all my camera and fishing gear, spent half of my IRA, got lost a million times (I hate GPS and only use maps), ran over a site number post, and spent an hour treading freezing waters in the great north woods, but the trip all-in-all was fantastic and I couldn't wait until our next one. We had no medical issues, Beatrice ran fantastically, and we returned home safe and sound. What more could you ask for? We saw some beautiful parts of the country that we had never seen before. Solace seemed to be getting closer and closer.

We spent the next few weeks getting the camper in shape for the winter, cutting and splitting wood, and taking care of the normal chores before winter set in. I did manage to get home early enough so that I could spend two weeks wandering the beautiful Pine Barrens picking and drying my mushrooms. It was a great fall and a great trip and we thanked our God for the privilege. I also whispered to him as an aside that we still had many wonderful places to visit and if he could just hold off with the clock for a while, we would greatly appreciate it.

Something interesting we noticed while travelling is the huge amount of farmland in this country. Once you get off the east coast, it seems like there is farmland everywhere. Across Western Pennsylvania, Ohio, Indiana, Illinois, Iowa, Minnesota, Michigan and Wisconsin we saw huge swaths of land devoted to agriculture and animal farming. We still haven't even reached the huge farmlands of Nebraska, South Dakota, or North Dakota. It is absolutely amazing how much is grown and raised in this country.

Now, we are traveling in order to see the sights of this country. What we didn't realize is that just seeing the vast amount of crop land in this country is a fantastic sight in and of itself. It is like the eighth wonder of the world and you can begin to understand why most of the people in the center of this country live and think differently than we do.

Some interesting government statistics that I've read are that there are approximately 2,000,000 small farms in the country. The U.S. exports over $135 billion dollars worth of food and grain every year. There are over 900 million acres of land farmed in the U.S. worth over 2 trillion dollars. Agriculture is a large part of this country's output and I think that it doesn't get the credit it deserves. All of us with our financial, analytical, sales, and management skills would be up s#*!'s creek without a paddle if our agricultural economy ever imploded. When you think that the basic necessities of our lives are food and water and that we only spend approximately 12% of our incomes on those items, you realize that living in America is a gift. When we drove out west many years ago, we passed corn, wheat, soybean and sunflower fields for days. Morning 'til night, we passed hundreds and hundreds of miles of farms. We all benefit from it. Looking out over the seemingly endless sunflower fields as the sun was glinting off their petals or seeing those waves and waves of grain dancing in the winds for days on end, one can't help but get a very patriotic feeling of what a great country we live in. Thank God for our farmers and ranchers and what they contribute to our well being and security.

Sleeping Bear Dunes, Michigan

Mackinac Island, Michigan

Mackinac Bridge, Michigan

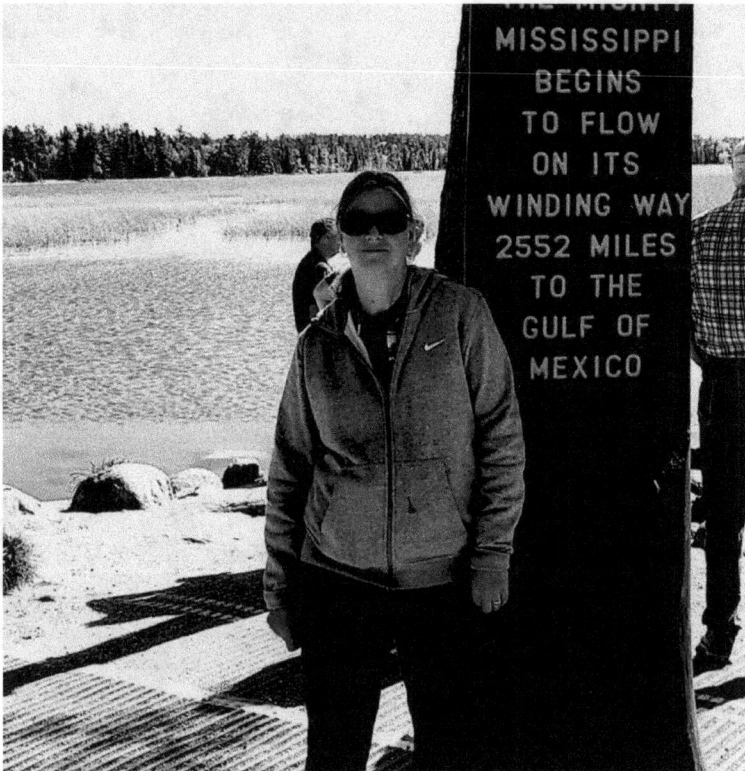

THE MIGHTY
MISSISSIPPI
BEGINS
TO FLOW
ON ITS
WINDING WAY
2552 MILES
TO THE
GULF OF
MEXICO

Headwaters of the Mississippi, Minnesota

CHAPTER 20

MID-ATLANTIC SWOON

We slogged our way through another dreary, wet, cold and damp South Jersey winter. In the fall we had decided to do a loop around some of the southern states for our spring trip. Since I still do some accounting and tax work in the spring, it is not possible for us at this time to plan an early Florida or southwest trip. By the time the end of April rolls around, it is pretty late to be heading to those destinations as it is already in the 90's, temperature wise. We haven't done much in the southern states to date, except for some wandering along the Skyline drive in Virginia and parts of the Blue Ridge Parkway. We were hoping to expand our scope a bit while experiencing some pleasant weather a little earlier than usual.

We were planning a trip down along the coast, travelling through Maryland, Virginia, the outer banks of N. Carolina, and the coast of S. Carolina down to Charleston. After that, we would swing around in a loop through Georgia, Tennessee and up along the southern Blue Ridge Parkway and across southern Virginia and home. It sounded like a fun plan. Most of these areas we had not visited, the weather should be real nice in May and we could make it a more "relaxing" trip as we did not expect many awe inspiring, fantastic sights to fill up our days with running around and photography. Instead we would mosey along, spend many days relaxing at the campsites and hopefully see some interesting places along the way. We had planned approximately 5 weeks for the trip.

Spring was now here and our departure date was soon beckoning. I slogged my way through another dull and boring tax season, putting aside a few bucks for our travels and my basic spending needs. Now, don't get me wrong. I love my clients and appreciate their support as it allows for some of my travel and hobby expenses. Without their support I would probably be sitting at home figuring out how to get by on my social security as opposed to seeing the country. So I am forever in their gratitude. However, after 40 years of calculating numbers in my head, trying to work with the ever changing IRS regulations, portfolio management and financial planning, I would hope that you can understand why my brain is fried, stress hormones run rampant through my body, and I am totally looking forward to that day when I can just worry about living my life on a day to day simple basis. It is not quite here yet and I am champing at the bit, but we "gotta" do what we "gotta" do.

The first week of May soon arrived and after cleaning up my tax season procrastinators, we were getting ready to go. We had previously dropped Bea off at the mechanics and she was ready to go also. We had cleaned her up, inside and outside and she was happy. Oil change, lube job, all hoses and fluids checked, tire pressure right on, and all systems seemed to be working fine. We were just about ready to go and spent the last week reviewing our travel plan, pre-cooking some dinners for our meals, and packing up all our clothes and gear. During the week, some ominous weather reports were filtering in for the upcoming week, but in this day and age of pre-booking everything, you have to go regardless of the weather. The night before we left, they were projecting 40 to 50 mph winds along the east coast from some off-shore system that seemed to be determined to wreck a little havoc on our east coast travelling plans.

The first part of our plan was to head south, take the Cape May ferry to Delaware, camp in Maryland for 2 nights and than hit the Outer Banks of North Carolina for about 5 days. Well you know what they say about the best laid plans......When we set out, the winds were howling and the rain was coming down – not quite the inspiration for the beginning of our trip. I had called ahead for a reservation on the ferry and "yes, they were running today". After waiting in line for a while we finally boarded and set off on our trip.

Usually, the ferry ride is a beautiful, bucolic, glide across the 17 mile bay, with sea gulls gliding by and porpoises cavorting in the glistening waters. Not today. Neither man nor beast should have been out cavorting today and the beasts, as usual, were the smart ones as nary a one was sighted. We, however, were out and were paying the price. These boats are quite large, longer than a football field and capable of carrying up to 100 vehicles. How bad could it be? Well it felt like we were on a large dinghy. The ferry lurched and rolled its way across the bay, as the gray, leaden-colored waters whipped into a frenzy of huge rolling swells. The six foot white caps threw off a constant blast of water, spraying hundreds of feet in the air. Just sitting in our camper was a challenge. It too was rocking, rolling, and swaying in the tightly packed vehicle area. Strange groans, thumps, and shrieks were heard as we roller-coasted our way across the bay.

I began to feel a bit sick so I lay in our bed and tried to read a book to distract myself from the uneasy feeling in my gut. That did not quite work, so I decided to get some air and headed outside. After struggling to hold onto the swaying walls of the ship, I reached the stairway and gamely proceeded to climb the stairs. I staggered my way up between the pitching walls, crawling hand over hand up the railing while my old knees and joints tried to cushion the one and two foot drops the stairs were experiencing. I made it to the upper walkway and staggered to the deck railing. At this point, everything was bouncing: my body, the ship, and the skies, and I was blasted with spray from the swells and drenched from the rain. I could not see anything. The seas and the sky seemed to meld together in a swirling gray tempo. The thought came into my mind, that in any given minute I could be hurled into the sea, never to be seen again. So, opting for reason over valor, I sucked in a few great gulps of fresh air and proceeded back to the RV. After slipping and sliding my way back down the stairwell, and lurching back to Bea, I crawled back into our bed as my sweetheart, with a wry smile, asked me how my walk was. I stuck my head under a pillow and tried to go unconscious for the rest of the trip.

Eventually we made it to the docking area and proceeded out into the rain-drenched roads of Delaware. After a long, wet ride, we settled into our campsite at Pokomoke State Park. It was raining, cold and damp, so we called it an early night and hit the sack at around 9:00 pm, hoping for a better tomorrow. How long could the rain and wind last? Well, actually they can last quite a while. Even though the rain subsided into intermittent showers, the winds howled all week. We were supposed to leave on the third day to travel to the outer banks of North Carolina. I kept checking the forecast every few hours hoping for the weather to clear, as we had to traverse the Chesapeake Bay Bridge and Tunnel to reach our destination. The Bridge is an eighteen mile span that crosses the Chesapeake Bay. With my fear of bridges, and the still howling 40 mph winds, there was no way I was going to cross that bridge anytime soon and it did not look like the winds were projected to drop for days. So, we mostly hung out at the campsite, fitting in some walks and rides in between the rain drops. I took some time to photograph the beautiful mountain laurel that was now exploding with glistening white flowers throughout the forest. We had been hoping for beautiful weather on this trip but it was not to be.

Weather forecasting for a trip six months in advance can be precarious. We actually had to use the heater the first couple nights – not what we were planning.

We did try one foray to Assateague National Seashore, but it did not work out. The morning of our attempt, the wind was gusting to 50 mph and as we sat at the visitor center trying to decide whether to cross the bridge onto the island, we were watching the low lying trees and grasses seemingly being ripped from the ground by the fury of the winds. No, I decided not to try the crossing attempt. Anyone foolish enough to cross a tall bridge in a 12ft high veritable fiberglass box when the wind was howling, either suffered from suicidal tendencies or was much closer to a one on one relationship with their God than I was. So we returned to camp and waited out the weather. The bridge still had a level 1 advisory out, meaning campers, trailers and trucks should not attempt a crossing. We had to extend our visit at Pokomoke for another 3 days until the winds and rain calmed down. In the meantime, the outer banks were getting flooded and the ferries were also closed down. You could not get on or off the islands. It was disappointing but we had to cancel our Outer Banks visit. Since all our trips are pre-booked, we could not change our itinerary to accommodate the weather setback.

One thing I did come away with from this trip is the idea that being a campground host can be quite advantageous if you are looking forward to extensive travel on a very limited budget. Our friendly host at the park was a congenial fellow from Louisiana who was camping in a tent. It seems that when it is sweltering in the south in the summer, he travels to northern campgrounds where he spends most of the rest of the year, living mostly for free in exchange for a few days work at the campground. Having no shelter or utility bills could cut ones annual budget quite a bit. With only food, auto and miscellaneous expenses, I would guess you could get by quite comfortably on $15,000 to $20,000/yr and live in some of the most scenic spots in the country. Food for thought, as the market was currently down 20% and my travel budget was slowly disappearing into the hands of those greedy Wall Street traders and bankers who will not stop stealing from us until everyone in the country is either broke or dead from jumping out their respective windows.

We proceeded to head down the coast to Charleston, our next destination. Charleston is supposedly a city full of natural beauty, romantic appeal, effusive charm, friendly people, and the number one small city in America. Now I don't know where some of these ideas originate, but obviously it is not a poll of small town, American people. I live in a small town of probably a few thousand individuals and as far as I am concerned, it is already too crowded and going downhill. Whoever calls Charleston, with 150,000 people, a small town with charm, obviously doesn't understand the definition of small, but hey, you can't fight the media. After being swept into the city on one of the major highways with bumper to bumper traffic and then disgorged into a riot of people, cars, noise and crazy streets and signs, my butt hole was beginning to pucker, and the muscles in my neck were stiffening as we searched for our campground – James Island County Park. After dodging low hanging tree limbs and negotiating the traffic, we finally made it. It was a decent park, but very crowded with giant class "A" campers and it was stifling hot. We had gone from freezing with our heat on a week ago, to now sweltering in the mid 90 temperatures. We planned on relaxing and calming our nerves for a day and decided to take a short trip to one of the beautiful plantations located outside of the city on the following day.

After a somewhat late start and getting lost for an hour, we made it to Magnolia Plantation. It was quite beautiful even though we had missed the blooming of the azaleas and rhododendrons. Shaded walkways led you around the gardens and through the trees drooping with Spanish moss. It was like being in a different world than South Jersey. It is one of the most renowned plantations in the country and has been owned by the same family for over 15 generations. Of course they all held onto it for so long because they are probably getting rich from it. After paying the general admission fee of $29, you could then add on the $10 fee to tour the historic site, the $10 fee for the nature tram, the $10 fee for the boat ride, the $10 fee for the historic garden walk and the $10 fee for the Audubon swamp trail. Assuming tens of thousands of visitors every year – you do the math. Being a staunch capitalist, I am not denouncing them for the amount of money they make every year, I am just jealous. However, the gardens were absolutely beautiful, even though we took the "cheap" route and did our own personal tour armed with a map and a couple bottles of water. We saw our first 10 foot alligator as it swam down one of the channels of water and I took some beautiful shots of egrets perched on the arched white bridges that spanned the canals. It was as if they were employed to perch in the beautiful setting just to enable the tourists in their picture taking. The historic home was being renovated at the time we were there, so we did not go in. It seems to be our luck, that every time we go some place, a portion is either closed off, or being renovated, and we never get to see it. As I write this, a fire is currently raging in Mariposa Grove in Yosemite National Park – it might be closed down when we plan to visit in two months. But that's the breaks and you take your travels as they come.

After touring the gardens we also purchased a ticket to enable us to walk the swamp trail, which I thought would be the most interesting. Being an avid photographer, I was hoping to get some really good wildlife shots in the swamp. There was a great tree in the middle of a pond loaded with nesting herons and egrets, but that was about it. As we plodded our way through the tall grasses, mostly what I saw were the beads of sweat dripping from my brow, the low water levels in our remaining bottles and Jo looking like she was going to drop from heat exhaustion. Was it worth it? Sure, it was beautiful and charming and was a delightful way to spend most of the day. But when we got back to the camper, we turned up the a/c full blast and cooled off with a cold water rinse before heading back to the campsite. How can people live down here in this heat?

The next day we had planned to take one of the tours of the city of Charleston. Due to the overheating the prior day, Jo was not feeling well and had a severe headache. So we bagged our plans for the day and luxuriated in the a/c from the camper, watching classic movies, eating and reading until the sun went down. Then we had a scrumptious shrimp dinner at our picnic table and sat by the campfire until we retired to bed. Pretty underwhelming, but fun never the less. I was already planning to revisit the city on our "Florida Trip" in the future as I suspect there were still many sights to see. We had only two days here because we lost a few from our weather delays of the previous week.

The next day we packed up and headed to Hamilton Branch campground on Strom Thurman reservoir in western South Carolina. Now our original plan was to rest here a few days after our hectic tours of the Outer Banks and Charleston. Obviously our trip up to now had been a bit less than hectic, but what the heck, you can never have too much relaxation after working for 40 years, fighting cancer, and constantly worrying about your health. So that is what we did. We really didn't have any choice as the place is pretty far in the boondocks. This place made it to my now annual top five lists of great campgrounds. My one big regret up until now was not figuring how to somehow bring along my best buddy - my kayak. Most of the places we camp have lakes or ponds to fish in and I still have not figured out how to take my kayak on my trips. But guess what? At this campground you could rent kayaks and they would deliver them to your site! Then they pick them up when you are done. This must have been what the Garden of Eden was like. Imagine a huge site at least a couple hundred feet in any direction from your neighbors, under the towering pines, with electric to run all your goodies, on the shore of a huge beautiful lake and a delivered kayak at your site. Oh my God. Nirvana.

I spent the first day hanging out as I sipped a margarita from the hammock whilst my beautiful wife strummed her guitar beneath the trees. We treated ourselves to another sumptuous meal of Steve's famous homemade pizza with some wine and then retired early to watch a movie classic on our DVD player.

Most of our visual entertainment at home comes from watching classic movies on our DVD. The world of modems and slingshots and streaming, etc. are way over our heads at our age and none of our technically proficient, loving nephews or nieces has yet blessed us with their help to set up all that crap. The TV programming sucks and our local cable purveyor seems to only have 5 movies in their entire collection. They play the same 5 movies over and over and over again until you get excited just reading the credits because that is the only new thing to watch – and they charge you $120/month for the privilege. What to do? I decided to start my own collection of DVD's and do my own programming for $0 per month. It was a bit expensive at first - I spent a whopping couple hundred dollars in the process, but it is worth it.

I have realized that to successfully get through life without spending a fortune, I just have to position myself adversely to all the latest gizmos and fads. A lot of people just give away or junk their old DVD's or you can also pick most of them up for a few bucks at yard sales, etc. A good friend of ours gave us her DVD player for nothing as ours gave out just as I was beginning my collection. Hey, for a couple hundred bucks we get to watch great movies a few nights every week for a relative pittance. That might last for the rest of our lives. What a deal. What would it cost the both of us to go to the movies a couple of times a week - $60? That's $3,000 a year. By skipping the movies for a couple of months, we now have a lifetime collection of great films. We don't have to get dressed, spend $5 for a 50 cent bucket of popcorn, or sit in uncomfortable seats for 2 hours while trying to watch a movie amidst the general din of a theater. We also miss all the stupid reruns, advertisements, and sitcoms that we are forced to watch on cable TV. Now we actually look forward to movie night. I am not talking the junk, one and two star movies that fill your local TV Guide. I am talking classics such as "On Golden Pond", "Stand By Me", "African Queen", or "Lilies of the Field" - all the while being comfortably ensconced on your couch, sipping wine in your underwear. You get the idea. Soon you have a couple hundred great movies that you can watch over and over, every few months for the rest of your life, for a few dollars a year vs. watching your local cable movies over and over again for $120/month. If any new "great" movies come out, you just add to your collection. Just keep following my advice, and by the end of the book you will be able to save up enough to camp for free! I will let you know how it works out.

The next day I paddled out on my "delivered" kayak and spent the morning fishing the lake. The fishing wasn't good, as I didn't catch anything. However, it was still a good day. I saw a couple "big" ones and that is almost as good, because any fisherman worth his salt can imagine catching one of them and the terrific fight that ensued. It was still a nice outing. I went out pretty early, so I caught the shimmering morning light as it radiated across the placid green waters. With that as a setting and the staccato screech of the Kingfishers as they darted across the waters, my anticipation was high. A few fish splashed here and there and I intently watched the waves undulate through the shoreline brush. The anticipation, that's all that really matters. That adrenaline rush you get as your muscles tense, your mind's singular focus on the rod tip, and the increasing rush of blood as it courses through your veins. Would it have been nice to hook into a nice lunker? Sure. But a nice calm early morning paddle on a placid pond is really what it's all about. As far as I am concerned the day was a success and in the early afternoon I pulled back into the campsite as happy and relaxed as I'd been in a long time.

The following day thunderstorms were rolling around so we were content with a bike ride, some good meals, and some serious reading to finish out the day. Once again our activities were cut a bit short due to the weather. Weather wise, it was not a great trip so far. We had hurricane force winds and rain for the first 5 days, 97 degree temperatures for the next 5 days, and rain and thunderstorms for the next 4 days. But do you know what? We were still having a great time, and if the weather ever cooperated it would get even better. Anything is better than sitting home and worrying about chores, bills, neighbors, and to-do lists.

Early the next morning, we packed it in and headed to our next stop at Cloudland Canyon in northwestern Georgia, but not before I got to say "Y'all" to the clerk at the checkout desk. I have been waiting all my life to say that to a Southerner. Jo didn't quite appreciate the gesture and mumbled something about my being an idiot, but she doesn't seem to appreciate the small things in life like I do.

Guess what? It rained for three more days! But again we made the best of it. It was a nice site, somewhat crowded but plenty of greenery for that feeling of seclusion and peace. We managed to squeeze in a few walks and bike rides in between the showers. The good news was that the temperatures finally backed off into the 80's and it was getting cooler out. We also squeaked in a moderate hike along the rim trail to take in the scenic vistas of the forest-covered canyon walls from the various overlooks. It was quite a nice hike. There are also trails throughout the park that run down into the canyon where you can view a couple of waterfalls. Alas, reality triumphed over valor again. The thought of taking a 2 mile hike down and back up from the canyon, in the rain, over slick wet rocks, was not appealing. I had learned my lesson from Minnesota, and did not want to risk life and limb for a scenic vista. I'm sure there will be 100's more to come and I wanted to stay alive to see the west coast, the southwest and eventually Alaska. After our long battles with cancer, our stamina was shot, our joints and limbs were stiff from the chemo and our muscles were weak. It is a slow rebuilding process and hopefully our strength and health will improve over the next couple years.

In the meantime, we were enjoying ourselves immensely. We feasted on a great Slavic treat for dinner - Kielbasa, cabbage, potatoes, and pumpernickel bread and then retired for the evening. I popped in another movie classic and slowly dozed off to the sound of soft rain on the roof.... I popped up a few hours later, to turn off the DVD, only to realize we had left the hatches open on the roof to air out the RV for a bit. The bed was soaking wet and I stepped off into a puddle on the floor. Hey, we're still new at this. Note to self – remember to shut the roof hatches when it is raining. After swabbing up the floor and checking all the windows, I jumped back into the wet bed and went back to sleep.

The next day the bedding was changed and we were back to "Happyville". It was still raining, so we cooked up a late, large breakfast of bacon and eggs with some fried potatoes and toast. Life was good. We moseyed about the afternoon, relaxed under the awning and practiced our painting as the ever present rain drops pitter-pattered around and over us. We had a nice dinner of pepper steak and a couple of glasses of wine and retired out to the veranda. We spent the evening jamming to some country music as Jo practiced her strumming on the guitar. It was her birthday, but since I could not fit a cake into the fridge, I bought two small individual apple pies and stuck a couple of candles in them. We celebrated a quiet birthday evening along the ridge of Cloudland Canyon – what could be better than that? The next day the rain finally stopped and after checking the tire pressure and fluids and cleaning up the site, we headed out to Lake Powhatan campground and recreation area near Ashville, North Carolina.

Well, we arrived at Lake Powhatan in the pouring rain. We also had a no hook-up site for three days to boot. It seems that when I was booking the sites on my list, I inadvertently overlooked Lake Powhatan and only remembered to book it a few weeks later. Of course this is a busy campground near Ashville, and all the sites with hook-ups were now gone. I tried to convince Jo we needed to practice staying in no-hook-up sites for our future travels, but she wasn't buying it, and mumbled something about my screwing up again. I interpreted the mumbling as a sign of affection and blew her a kiss. The older we get, the more she loves me.

We had a quiet first night reading by lantern light and listening to the now normal sound of rain bouncing off the roof. Can you believe it? The sun finally peaked out the next morning, so we decided to get out-and-about before it started to rain again. We had been down in this area before and had already experienced some of the natural beauty of the surrounding countryside. One thing I had wanted to do in the past but had never gotten around to doing was to visit the Biltmore Estate. So, off we went to check it out.

Now let me tell you this is a very impressive place. According to the "Guide to the Biltmore", the chateau-styled mansion built by George Vanderbilt in the late 1800's is sited on 8,000 hilly acres nestled amidst the beautiful surrounding hills. It is the largest privately owned house in the U.S. and contains approximately 178,000 sq. feet of living space. How many square foot of living space in your house – 1,000 to 2,000 square feet? This place is only about 100 times larger than your average house. The 250 rooms in the house consist of 35 bedrooms, 43 bathrooms, 65 fireplaces, three kitchens, a pantry room, laundry, and a myriad of other special rooms. It has a banquet hall, music room, winter garden, tapestry room, library, living hall, billiard room, gun room, basement gym and pool, bowling alley, smoking room and ….you get the picture. There is a room for everything. It blows your mind that someone could have this much money.

Anyway, after parking in the lot we took a shuttle to the entrance of the grounds. The estate is fronted by a large lawn, in the center of which is a beautiful fountain. The center tower of the home is situated between two projecting wings topped by steeply pitched turrets and sculptural ornamentation. Gargoyles gaze down at you from the heights. Carved statues, massive stone blocks, copper roof flashing, 16 chimneys; I could go on and on but words don't do it justice – you have to see it. Looking at the stone masterpiece I remarked to Jo that we could not even afford the steps. We had signed up for a later tour, so we opted to take a walk around the gardens. Stone walkways meandered about the trees and shrubs to a stone terrace overlooking acres and acres of formal gardens and the conservatory. Dozens of different flowers and fountains were laid out like a carpet at our feet. We wandered amongst the walkways and took a peek in the conservatory. As it was getting hot, we took a break on one of the small benches in the gardens and I snapped away for some beautiful flower photos. The acres of blooms were resplendent. We then strolled back along the garden wall, gawking at the beautiful fish ponds and statuary. Proceeding to the other side of the grounds we entered the stables and carriage house which have been converted to gift shops, a restaurant and bathrooms. We wandered around the gift shop, passing up the long restaurant line and finally settled on a gift we could afford – a couple bottles of wine from the estate's winery. After waiting in line for 20 minutes, we were informed that they do not accept cash! Really? I thought it was illegal in this country not to accept legal tender. Am I that old fashioned, preferring to limit my purchases to cash on hand? Well after realizing that my wallet was back in the RV which was about 3 miles away, we put our selections back and the Vanderbilt's were $30 poorer. Of course they did get us for the $160 entrance fee, of which I will be mumbling about for the next decade. Did I say things were getting crazy expensive in this country? But, I personally consider this place one of the wonders of the world, so I guess it was worth it. (???)

We then started our tour of the inside, greeted first with the beautiful sunken winter garden which glistened under the sun shining through the decorated skylights. After climbing the spiral grand staircase, we viewed paintings, tapestries, painted and etched marble ceilings, damask draped four-poster beds, gilt-edged china, and more statuary. Well, you get the picture. The opulence was overwhelming and I actually felt like throwing up after trying to take it all in. Even though I am poor, I am a capitalist and almost felt like apologizing to all the surrounding hordes of tourists. The fact that this great wealth, along with all the 100's of other estates of the scions of industry and finance, is not spread a little more evenly amongst the masses, is somewhat despicable. It is a shame, really, when you think of all the good this money could accomplish in the world. Generations and generations of wealth so massive that mathematically it is almost impossible to use up in the future.

Income re-distribution anyone? I believe that if you make it you should be allowed to keep it, but once you pass away, a severe estate tax should be imposed. It is the only way to fight severe income inequality. We peons would have a little better life, inequality would be restricted, and future generations of spoiled children would actually have some incentive to be productive and useful.

We skipped the visit to the winery, the lodge, or the restaurant. We did get lost exiting the grounds, but hey, you try to navigate various driveways that wind amongst the 8,000 acres. Did you know they also raised commercial timber and started the first Biltmore Forestry School? I opined about the amount of dollars the Magnolia plantation was making. What about this place? There must have been a thousand people there on that day. At $80 a head, and adding in the gift store, winery, lodge and restaurant receipts the estate must pull in at least $100,000 a day. Times how many days a year - 200 or 250 or 300? You do the math. They are making an easy 25 million a year and none of the descendents working for any of it, and this is just a small part of the total estate left by Mr. Vanderbilt. I think that a member of the Vanderbilt family was a member in the Jekyll Island Club, "the richest, most exclusive, most inaccessible club in the world". Isn't that where the Federal Reserve System was imagined and implemented? It seems that being a member of that club obviously paid off. Is the "Game" rigged?

Well we headed back to the campsite and called it a day after our long, hot march around the estate. I guess I wouldn't want an 8,000 acre estate because I wouldn't even have the energy to walk the grounds. Our five acres is plenty. I would, however, like to receive a small percentage of the estate receipts – something to be said for income re-distribution. I just had a great idea! The government should take a small percentage of the 400 billion they collect in tax revenue and give it directly to the people. That way instead of them pissing it away on some crap programs, the people would directly benefit from the government's taxation. This idea, along with the estate tax reconfiguration would make everyone happier and add a bit to their income. I think I should run for Congress.

The next morning we awoke to a beautiful, sunny day. How did we celebrate? Jo spent most of the day cleaning out the camper as it was becoming a tad slovenly after three weeks of travel in the rain and mud. I spent the day making some travel notes and checking over the camper systems and equipment. It had to be done, but we relaxed in the late afternoon with a couple glasses of wine and a nice lasagna dinner. Up the next morning, bright and early (about 9:30 am in retired camper speak), we got going for our visit to Chimney Rock which is located east of Ashville. Not too impressive? Well actually it was quite impressive. The "Rock" juts out like a thumb over the Lake and is reached by climbing a steep stairway. Sitting on the skinny peak of a mountain top overlooking Hickory Gorge and Lake Lure, the "Rock" enabled impressive, expansive views of the surrounding Blue Ridge Mountains rolling away to the horizon. Of course hundreds of other people wanted to see the same sights and we struggled along with the mob trying to get to the top. People with a fear of heights probably should not venture to the top, but we did and stood in the exact center of the viewing area, all the while scared that some little kid or his parent would accidentally push one of us off. There is a fence around the area, but if you are standing on the rocks in the center, the fence is almost below your feet. An incessant feeling of vertigo crept into my mind as I stared out into the clouds over the lake. The mob pressed in from all sides. It was an impressive view, but after a few minutes I was feeling a bit uncomfortable and we hiked our way back down and over to the shuttle in the now sunny, 90 degree afternoon. We made our way passed the village and the lake which were incredibly packed with people. We tried to get to a craft fair by the lake, but trying to park a 25 foot motor home in a small mountain village on Memorial Day weekend is nigh impossible. So we headed home to the campsite and called it a day. I would never risk damaging, scratching, or terrorizing my sweet little "Bea" who had up to this point performed admirably.

The next day we packed it in again, as we were now heading to Philpott Lake in Virginia. My route directed us approximately 100 miles to the east on highway 40 and then another 100 miles to the north on highway 77. Scanning the map, I now realized that the Blue Ridge Parkway actually bisected the box I was planning to drive and we could actually take a more scenic drive through the mountains and shave off 50 miles or so from the trip (I excelled in honors geometry in high school) if we followed the Parkway.

So off we went on our new route through the hills. I had previously checked to make sure we could fit under all the bridges along this part of the Parkway. It wasn't long before my neck muscles were tight again and my hands gripped to the wheel, as we roller-coasted and swayed our way around the mountains. Most of the road had no shoulder and I sweated as we careened around the tight, twisting corners. Now when I say "careened" I do not mean recklessly speeding. I only was doing between 20 and 25 mph, but at some points it felt like we might tip over. I wanted this drive to give me a little mountain driving experience for our upcoming Western trip and boy did I get it.

Now our motor home, like most somewhat newer vehicles is equipped with a "tow mode" for driving through the hills or hauling trailers. In my research I still could not come up with the answer of whether it is better to use tow mode or just manually shift your way through the mountains. Being the easier option, I put it in tow mode and drove on. I thought the transmission was going to explode! Powering up the hills and screaming down the hills, Jo was insistent I was going to blow up poor Bea while I kept assuring her that this is how they are made: with engine breaking, the transmissions are built to handle it and are smarter than we are. I began to have my doubts and suffered in agony as Bea screamed and howled her way through the hills. I could envision sparks and engine parts flying out the back of poor Bea onto the cars of the ass@#!!'s tail-gating me over the hills. Well, if nothing else, that would teach them. The road finally leveled out and I putted along to give Bea a break. I could see nothing - fog all around and nary a view. Eventually we made it to a lake alongside the road and pulled in for lunch and a break. While trying to relax my trembling nerves, we ate and I perused the map. We still had hundreds of miles to go and it was already after 2 o'clock in the afternoon - so much for a leisurely trip and an early site arrival! Let's see, 25 mph for over a hundred miles.....I was now projecting a 6 or 7 pm arrival as opposed to 3 o'clock. Not good, as I had just armed my co-pilot with another arrow for her to sling at me, alongside the snide remarks that questioned my planning abilities.

Once again humbled, I yelled "Lets Go", and off we went careening through the hills. They eventually flattened out a bit and I pushed my sweet Bea up towards 35 and 40 mph. It seemed like the trees and grasses were flying by as we swept along the narrow roadway. I prayed that a deer or even a chipmunk would dare not cross our path as trying to slow a 5 ton motor home packed to the gills is not an easy task and the result would probably not have been a pretty picture.

Time was of the essence. 60 year olds promptly eat around 5:00 pm everyday like clockwork. Eating an hour or two later could result in massive stomach and bowel problems, lack of sleep or even intestinal hemorrhaging from the bodily clock being thrown off its schedule! On we pressed. Finally we reached the exit and proceeded to scream down another 5 mile hill to the valley below and our eventual site.

What a beautiful site - lakefront, with water and electric, it was almost worth the death-defying trip. We crashed early and I fell into a deep slumber while my body trembled and my mind careened about like a firecracker. We relaxed the whole next day, giving ourselves and Bea a much deserved rest. The weather was finally cooperating and we spent the day exploring the campground and swaying in the hammocks. The following morning we planned to go to Mabry Mill and the Music Center for some photos and, hopefully, some blue grass music.

Mabry Mill is an old restored grist mill in the hills alongside the Blue Ridge Parkway near the Virginia border. It makes for an iconic photo shot and the site includes a restored sawmill, blacksmith shop and a rustic cabin. Nestled beneath the towering sycamores and poplars, the 1905 Mill was once the center of activity in the surrounding area, and now, amidst the spring rhododendrons, a riot of color and cool shade greeted the visitors. The exceptionally friendly park service girls explained how weaving was done with the old looms and showed us some handmade brooms that they had crafted. They were very interesting and impressive. We wandered the area and took a couple of the "iconic" photo shots of the Mill and pond - the water wheel spewing a glistening cascade amidst the beautiful flowers. We took a break for lunch beneath the shaded trees and then headed for our next stop at the Blue Ridge Music Center.

The Music center consisted of an outdoor amphitheater, visitor center, gift shop and museum. It was very interesting. They showcase daily musical performances by local musicians in the outdoor amphitheater for free. They play a variety of blue grass and country music. Bill and Maggie Anderson, an elderly couple, were playing when we arrived, and they impressed us with their musical prowess and sweet demeanors. We bought one of their CD's and Jo and Bill spent some time discussing the craftsmanship employed in creating the guitars he hand-crafted as a side job. What an interesting couple. The best thing was that on this weekday there were only 4 other people at the concert. In the age of mobs of people and the spread of Covid, this was a real treat and we enjoyed ourselves immensely. Listening to them play while sitting in the cool shade and watching the swallows pirouette amongst the rafters with the green mountains as a backdrop, was a wonderful experience. If I lived in the area, I think I would visit almost every day. After a few delightful hours we moved further down the road to the Blue Ridge Folk Art center and became awed by the artisan crafts that were exhibited. Beautiful wooden carvings and bowls, jewelry, pottery and other hand crafted treasures were on display beneath the upstairs banisters that were draped with quilts. Quoted as the finest hand crafted items from the Appalachian area, I could believe it if you went by the prices. Did I say before that things are too expensive now-a-days? I looked into buying a small, hand-crafted broom about a foot long for a gift, but was dissuaded by the $90 price tag on the item. I also was interested in a nice hand-crafted walking stick, but the $120 price tag for a lacquered tree branch was a bit too much. Appalachia is often depicted as a run down, desperately poor area of the country, but if these people were getting these prices, they must have been doing ok. After checking out a $35 coffee mug we decided we probably had enough gifts as frugality triumphed over our temporary insanity. So off we went, gift-less, but nevertheless greatly impressed with the art.

Our last stop of the day was to be in the town of Mt. Airy, which was situated along our return route. Now Mt. Airy might not ring any particular bells as to its famous name or delightful restaurants or impressive scenery, but if you are a fan of the Andy Griffith show, you will know that the town was used as the backdrop for the show and now includes reproductions of the famous jail, the courthouse and the gas station. The town also has erected a museum and statues depicting the characters and the story. Of course by now it was getting late, so I raced my way towards "Mayberry" seeking to enjoy a few moments of nostalgia in one of America's famous small towns. Well, after getting lost again, we pulled into the parking lot of the museum at exactly 5:00 pm which is when they closed. I was very disappointed, snapped a couple shots of the statues and proceeded to wander about town looking for the other noted establishments. My lovely personal assistant (and wife) does not quite enjoy the show as much as me and refused to wander any further in the 85 degree heat after a 7 hour day of travelling about. So I continued on alone, wandering the streets and determined to meet with success. I finally did find a few of the buildings, but by then, they had also closed and my clothes were sticking to me like spandex from the heat of the day. I felt like I was going to have a heart attack after walking a couples miles in my heat induced delirium. I took a few photos, and after finishing off my small bottle of water, staggered back a mile to the camper and air conditioning. I was greeted by a wry smile and comment, something to the effect of: "how was your stroll"? I proceeded to scrape my sticky clothes off and guzzle a gallon of water while sitting perched in front of the a/c. Driving back to the campground while intermittently dozing off as the sun set over the hills, we finally made it back for our extremely late dinner, the effects of which I have discussed previously. After a quick couple of hot dogs, into the sack we went after an extremely long but beautiful and interesting day – one of the highlights of our trip. We relaxed in the heat and thunderstorms the whole next day. My weary bones were aching, my stomach was crying out for large portions of sustainable meals, and my mind was more or less shut down from all the heat and excitement. I know, I'm going a bit overboard for one day's sightseeing, but for this out of shape old man, a day's walking in the heat on my creaking old joints and bones was enough, and I needed a day's rest. Thank god for retirement.

We lounged about camp the whole next day.

The next morning we packed up and headed for our last three day stop at North Bend campground on Kerr Lake in Virginia. We arrived early at our site after a 4 hour drive and pitched our "camp" on the lakeside lot with the electricity plugged in, the a/c running and the breaded crab cakes ready for the pan. This place was a little tight, but I think we had the best site in the campground (as noted by our fellow travelers). Every evening we were treated to a beautiful sunset over the far end of the lake. This place was really out in the boonies also, and as I could find nowhere interesting to go, we had another relaxing 3 days.

Now, I know you're thinking how many relaxing days do these people want? The answer from these two sexagenarians is plenty! After 40 years of working 5 or 6 days a week, working on our house on weekends and vacations, battling various medical anomalies and working our five acres- WE NEEDED ALL THE RELAXATION YOU CAN GET. Don't chuckle too much because some day you will be in the same boat. Besides, by relaxation I do not mean do nothing. Yoga in the morning followed by a big breakfast, followed by a quick bike ride, a snack at lunch and a long walk in the afternoon is not "nothing"! A few hours spent in the hammock reading a book while exercising my wrist with a wine glass is also part of my personal fitness plan and it seems to be working well.

So that's what we did for the next three days and let me tell you it was worth it. We were feeling ready to go again, our brains were back to functioning level, and everything was stretched, pulled, and back into shape. We enjoyed our stay at the campground. It is a Corp of Engineer campground and you should check them out as a viable alternative if you can't get into or don't like a certain state park while still wanting to eschew the private campgrounds. They are usually all located on beautiful lakes, have power and are extremely clean and manicured. Some can be a bit tighter than your average state park, but for the money, they are a steal. If you have a Senior National Park Pass, some of these beautiful sites can be had for as little as $10 or $11 dollars a night - only in America. That comes out to around $4,000 dollars for a whole years' vacationing in some of the most scenic spots in America. Food for thought as the real estate taxes on my house cost me more than that.

We wrapped it up after day 3 and headed for Martinak State Park in Maryland. As we travelled north, we once again had to go over the Chesapeake Bay Bridge and Tunnel. I had to fight the wind and the steering all the way across. However, there was no fog this time and the view was gorgeous. Glistening waves as far as the eye can see and soaring gulls - enough to satisfy any seashore aficionado's vision of the perfect day. We crossed over and headed northwest up into Maryland, this time opting for a ride along the bay shore as opposed to the ocean shore. I had heard nice things about the quaint little Chesapeake Bay towns and wanted to check them out.

We arrived at Martinak State Park in the late afternoon and cruised around the campground looking for our site. The Park itself was somewhat underwhelming. There was no one in the office and it took me about 15 minutes to angle my way between the trees so that I could hook up to the rusty old water pipe sticking out of the ground. The sites were decent enough, but the grass was not cut and there was trash in the fire ring. The campground was almost deserted and of course we took to wondering why, as all the previous campgrounds had been packed. We eventually found out that there was construction taking place along the river bank and it was strewn with pilings and construction equipment and red tape. In addition, bless their souls, they forgot to mention on their website that the pump-out station was closed. It was our last campsite before heading home and it had no pump-out. We were off to an inauspicious start, but I tried to think positive and make the best of it. One of the good points was that it was quiet – no kids screaming, no dogs barking, and no radios blaring. That was nice, but somewhat spooky and I made sure everything was locked up tight when we went to bed. Sitting outside as the night approached, I remembered a favorite quote of one of my favorite authors, Mr. Steinbeck: "We can populate the dark with horrors". I could not get rid of a nagging feeling that maybe unsuspecting, naïve tourists had been getting hacked to death here lately. It was a dark, silent night and nary another camper in sight. I know, a little crazy, but when you're on vacation and your mind is emptied of everyday garbage, it has the freedom to roam and some times not for the best. It would be great if the nation's governors would someday realize that everyone does not travel with a security detail and that when you're out in the boonies and the local crazy, wild-eyed, drunk, mental cases wander into the campground looking for some fun, it would be nice to have something to protect yourself with, other than water bottles or frying pans.

Anyway, we awoke to a beautiful, quiet morning, had a big breakfast, and pushed off to the local town of St. Michaels, about 30 miles away. It was a pretty little town, albeit a bit touristy. We toured the Chesapeake Bay Maritime Museum. The admission price was a steal at only $30 for both of us and we got to see numerous historic bay boats, a fowling piece collection, hand-carved decoys, sail making, various maritime historical artifacts, and watch the construction of the Maryland Dove, a representative 17th century sailing ship.

The museum is dedicated to focusing on the history and traditions of the Chesapeake Bay area. There were very few people about and we had a pleasant stroll. We were able to chat with some of the workers about their jobs and duties. We had a pleasant discussion with the sail maker about the materials and traditions involved with making sails and also got some practical advice concerning repairs to the boat dodger and bimini on our sailboat.

It seems that the older and sturdier sewing machines were indeed capable of sewing through the thick material of our boat canvas using the proper needles and thread. Word to the wise – never throw away "old, outdated" equipment if it still works because it will probably last longer and require less maintenance than anything you can buy new. Well, guess what, someone had given Jo an old "White" sewing machine that still worked. Since Jo has three different machines, she had not used the White yet. However, after our chat and a few minor adjustments to the machine, she was later able to sew a couple zippers into the boat canvas. In the fall she is planning to order some plastic for the dodger. We figure it will cost us about $60 to repair both pieces and maybe a day or two's worth of labor. This will save us the quoted estimate of $1500 from the local canvas repair man. That will be great as I really don't appreciate paying brain surgeon fees to the local canvas guy while I am trying to survive on social security. Jo amazes me with her crafting ability. Over the years she has sewn shirts, dresses, repaired and mended tons of clothing and has completely outfitted our house with new window coverings for the 20 plus windows it contains. Of course I now suggested that she get into the canvas repair and boat cover business, but she was having none of it as she is enjoying her retirement too much. Oh well, I might not become the next scion of boat canvas repairs, but at least I get my buttons sewn on and my torn pants repaired for nothing. Every little bit helps!

Okay, back to the story. We visited the museum store, but once again could find nothing really compelling to buy at the prices quoted and headed back to the camper. Crossing the lot, we wandered by the marina restaurant with its outdoor seating and wonderful aromas now wafted across our noses. The beautiful views, along with the arresting aromas, must have made me temporarily insane because I talked my lovely wife into finally splurging on a restaurant meal.

Now one would think, in the crab capital of the world, that their fare would either be very reasonably priced or that they would even give you some crab just for showing up and visiting their establishment. Not to be. It seems that tourists are prey for any capitalistic pig that decides to go into business. I should have been forewarned when the menu mentioned something about "market price". I realize that those are scary words on a restaurant menu, but I had read somewhere that the Chesapeake Bay harvests approximately 55 million blue claw crabs annually. How high could the "market" be? Oh, stupid, foolish, tourist. We both ordered crab sandwiches which came with slaw and French fries. I had an ice tea and Jo had a beer. The cost of the two sandwiches and drinks was $82. I almost regurgitated my sandwich for a refund.

Now I know that buying crab meat can be expensive. I occasionally splurge at home and buy this special treat. I know that a 16 ounce container can be bought for around $30. I also know that I can make 10 crab cakes out of the contents of that container. Assuming our friendly restaurateur pays a wholesale price of approximately $20 per can, it means that their cost is around $2 per crab cake. Unless the ice in my tea was imported from some pristine waters in the far reaches of Antarctica or Jo's beer was produced at some little brewery in the mountains of distant Nepal, I couldn't, for the life of me, figure out how our bill could be so high. I stumbled in shock out into the parking lot and was once again reminded as to why we never eat out. I disconsolately pondered the idea for the rest of the day that we were the biggest rubes in America. Maybe they were "magic" crab cakes. The sad thing was that the crab cakes weren't any better than what we could have whipped up in the camper in an hour.

After almost choking on my lunch bill, we took a walk downtown to view the myriad shops and stopped in the winery. Now these prices were much more reasonable and we picked up 2 bottles of very fine tasting wine for 30 bucks. We headed back to the camper and I was surprised once again at all the farmland in these United States. We passed by miles and miles of farms. Some, interestingly enough, contained old seafaring homes with their square Victorian look and walkways on the roof for looking out to sea. I guess they come in handy when looking out over the farm, but they did look a bit out of place. Either they are homes for retired sailors or the owners are getting ready for the rising sea levels.

I would like to mention a safety tip to my readers. On the ride home I pulled into some small town hoping to take a nice, cool, break in the local park. Of course I could not find it, having gotten lost again. When I came to a halt at a stoplight, the copilot decided to get up and get a drink from the fridge. The light turned green and I ever so slightly accelerated out onto the highway. I heard a big boom and cursing and turned around to see my sweet other half on her butt on the floor and legs akimbo in the air. Water dripped from her hair as she struggled to regain her footing. I couldn't hold back a little chuckle. Well, at least Bea was alright, but the copilot was not happy and proceeded to yell and berate me all the way back to the campground as, according to her "I gunned it out onto the road, maybe on purpose". Now, of course I beg to differ, but it does show that it is best not to walk around the camper when travelling. Due to the forces of inertia, when in motion, you can become exceedingly unbalanced at any given moment. It was just a shame that I didn't have my camera at the ready – I would have had a priceless memento of our trip.

We packed up the next day and happily (yeah sure) proceeded to a distant campground in order to dump our waste tanks. Once on the road, we pounded along in the seething traffic of Interstate 95 as it goes from Maryland towards Philadelphia until we gratefully crossed over the Delaware Memorial Bridge. We exited and then passed over the bucolic countryside towards home. Were we glad to be home? Yes. Did we wish to head out camping again? Yes. Sometimes the choices in life are just too difficult. We unpacked all the "stuff", I washed and cleaned up Bea, and made an appointment for her for a little pampering and a tune up as she had treated us so well on our journey.

I now sit at my desk, wrapping up the reservations and plans for our upcoming West Coast trip while also starting on our next year's Southwest trip. Since state reservation windows open anywhere between 2 months or 13 months, you have the joy of trying to nail down two different vacations in two different years. When we leave on this year's trip in late August, I will have to be booking sites for next years fall trip. I just hope the campgrounds have cell service or we will be up sh!#'s creek trying to find good sites for next year. We shall see.

All together this was a good trip. Not spectacular or grandiose, but the places we visited were very beautiful, very interesting, and we got to practice living in a small box for 5 weeks while still staying married. I learned to be scared shitless when driving up and down mountainous terrain, and learned it's ok to spend a lot of money when you are retired and travelling, even if you don't have much to begin with. The clock is ticking – on we go.

Smokey Mountain Vista

Mabry Mill, Blue Ridge Parkway

Magnolia Plantation, South Carolina

The Biltmore Estate, North Carolina

Smokey Mountain Visitor

CHAPTER 21

GO WEST OLD MAN

Inspired by the admonitions of the orators of the past, we had planned our first big trip since our travel plan inceptions. We planned a large loop across the United States to California, up the Oregon coast, back down and across the Columbia River Gorge, through the Black Hills and then back home. It was, from my perspective, a vast undertaking. I was feeling a bit of trepidation. Due to the brilliance of certain elected/non-elected officials, gas is currently $4.75/ gallon. Based on my estimate of at least 10,000 miles, that projects to a $4,750 gas bill for our travels. Adding up all the other expenses, I projected that our total outlay for the trip would be around $8,000 - so much for travelling on the cheap.

In addition, the country currently sits under a massive heat dome with temperatures exceeding 100 degrees in many places in the country. Rivers and lakes are running low and hundreds of fires are breaking out around the country. Things are looking a little bleak. I have booked all our sites at either national or state parks. Usually this is a great idea. However, watching the temperatures climb, I worried about our stays in California and Nevada. It seems that these states can't afford to install utility hook-ups in their state parks.

I can see that, in Nevada's case, since all it has are abandoned mines and a few aliens roaming about, their tax revenue might not be able to fully support its campgrounds. But what is the problem with California? They have more money than God. Doesn't anyone in California own an RV or camp? We plan on being in California and Nevada approximately three weeks. We will die if this heat does not dissipate. We couldn't change our plans now. I told Jo that they might find us somewhere on the "Loneliest Highway", dead in our 24ft. oven. Right now it is 115 degrees in Las Vegas. I don't know what the temperature would be in our motor home, but suffice it to say it would probably not be pretty. From what I understand, there is little to no cell service on the way. If anything were to happen, say for instance, like a flat tire, we would be goners! Not a nice thought.......stumbling our way across the Nevada desert trying to get to Reno, sharing our last bottle of water while our skin melts off like wax on a candle. I could picture the buzzards picking at our sun bleached bones....

Oh well, if nothing else, I can now eat all I want as I am sure I will be sweating off pounds and pounds of fat as we traverse the west.

We have been running around trying to finish all our home projects as well as getting things ready for the trip. I made an appointment at the local mechanic shop to get Bea some tender loving care before we leave. I had to wait 2 months for an appointment - unbelievable. We are starting to plan our menus and pre-make our usual culinary treats. If you remember, I lost my camera and some gear on our wonderful trip to Michigan and Minnesota. So, since we were still expecting to do our longest and best trips in the future, I once again ordered another new camera and lens and a few filters - another $2,000 down the drain. This retirement stuff was getting expensive.

Has anyone ordered a new camera lately? Thank God for high tech – yeah, sure. My old camera had a couple buttons and was very simple to use if you had any basic photographic skills. Not this new one. It came with an instruction booklet that looked like a NASA rocket manual – hundreds of pages of technical specs and directives. It took me all day just to figure out how to turn it on and try a few different procedures. Every little thing you do has 25 options and buttons and wheels and stuff I don't even understand. You should not have to be an electrical engineer in order to operate your camera. Sadly, photography as an art is gone. It is now a technical endeavor. It is no longer about taking the "perfectly lighted shot". Now you take any old shot, download it to your photography software and then adjust the lighting, the white balance, the highlights, the colors, and you can even insert or delete subjects. The end result is a photo that doesn't even remotely resemble the original.

Photographic skills are no longer required – only technical expertise.

Like everything else in the tech world, they are making our lives "simpler". Yeah, right. Since I have decided to make the grand leap from the Stone Age up to the current millennium, I have purchased a cell phone, a new camera and a Wi-Fi modem. I have had the cell phone for two years and still can't figure out how to operate it effectively. My Wi-Fi blinks constantly, like a crazed animal and drops our calls and internet connections faster than a call girl drops her drawers.

I am currently perusing the job wanted ads looking for an unemployed nuclear physicist to help me with my camera. Last night I was trying to book a site for our trip next year but couldn't because our brand new, state of the art 5g phones could not download the site information from a state's campground listings. Oh, the joy of progress. I am beginning to understand the mass shootings and why 16 percent of our teenagers now need psychiatric help. It is really not funny.

Technological progress is making everyone crazy. Just think of their grand vision – a totally wired world where all you have to do is flip a few switches and have all your wants and needs easily taken care of. I'm sure I can't wait. Obviously the job of the future is psychiatry because we are all going to go nuts.

But that is okay because tech has an answer for that too – the "Metaverse". After freezing in the winter because our solar panels generate no heat, eating our bugs for dinner and walking to the nearest store 20 miles away because we can no longer afford our vehicles, we can escape to the Metaverse – the utopian heaven where everything is wonderful and all our problems are gone. Our economy and GDP will be collapsing, and the real world will be dissolving into crappola while we spend our days gleefully roaming the shores of the Metaverse. We will all be indebted to the great institutions of Government, Tech, and the Media for allowing us to die such a happy and pain free death. Some people wonder why we older folk long for the days past, of simplicity and dependability.

I read the other day that a battery died in someone's electric car. It cost more to replace the battery than the cost of the whole car! I can't wait for the future – we will have to take out a home equity loan just to replace the battery in our vehicles. What the tech companies don't tell you is their plan to have everything in the country running on software in the future. Then all they have to do is change the software every few years to make you buy all new "stuff": new phones, new computers, new appliances, new autos, and new everything else. As you can see, their plan is predicated on draining every last dollar from every last person on the planet. Don't fall for their ruse. We still have a 30 year old refrigerator that runs great. Now maybe Jo has to paint it every few years so it doesn't look like a giant rust box in our kitchen, but it works great, runs perfectly and cost us a grand total of $300 many decades ago. Are you in a rush to keep up with the neighbors with all their new stuff? Don't be. We are all being led down the primrose path like lemmings to the sea.

Well, that is my rant for the day, probably because I am in a bad mood from worrying about our up coming safari across the deserts and the fact that I have to make a dental appointment. I really do try to think of the good things, but things being as they are, it is hard. I am trying. I will try to concentrate on the more mundane aspects of retirement travel – how to pay for all this travel, whether I will die wandering the vast western deserts, or how to keep my house from being robbed as we travel this great country of ours. Yes, things are looking up already.

CHAPTER 22

INTO THE GREAT UNKNOWN

After a short break at home from our Southern trip, the summer flew by and we were ready for our first "BIG TRIP". We were leaving for California and the west coast in mid-august and planning to travel up the coast to the top of Oregon before turning east and heading home again. It was to be a nine week trip. We planned to leave by August 15th so that we could be home before it started getting too cold and of course so I could get in the last two weeks of mushroom picking season. It was a surprisingly cool August so far in New Jersey and I was glad because I didn't want to be roasting my way around the country. It seems that the "heat domes" had dissipated. When you have to book your sites months in advance you just have to take the weather the way it comes and it was looking to be beautiful. It was also looking to be expensive due to the gas prices and the extensive amount of time we would be on the road.

We spent the two weeks prior to our departure loading up Bea, as usual. This was a big trip. We stuffed her until every cabinet, hole, shelf, crevice and orifice was filled. We had enough food, water, medicinal supplies, tools and clothes to survive, by my estimation, at least six months in the barren deserts or mountainous wilds that we would encounter on our trip. Everything was checked over on Bea and she was ready to roll. So were we. On August 15th, off we went.

In a few days we quickly traversed the states of Pennsylvania, Ohio, Indiana and Illinois and now my sights were set on the great Mississippi River. As we crossed over it my heart began to beat a little harder. As an east coast resident of New Jersey, I don't consider a trip really exciting until you cross over the mighty Mississippi and head out into the wilds of the central and western states. We had done quite a bit of travelling up and down the east coast and after a while it was a bit boring. Now we were entering new lands with exciting new discoveries to be had. Crossing the brown, throbbing waters of "Old Miss" opened up vast unknown territories, with new cities and wild lands to explore. Over we went and new doors were now opened.

One of my favorite books growing up was "The Adventures of Tom Sawyer" by Mark Twain. His description of the exciting explorations of Tom, along with Becky and Huck Finn in the town of St. Petersburg (which is based on Hannibal, Missouri) sounded idyllic to this old man: exploring the caves, rafting and fishing the Mississippi – what a way to grow up. I had always wanted to check out the area and here we were.

I envisioned a quaint little town with bicycles traversing the dirt lanes amidst the pretty houses surrounded by tall elms. Of course it's never like that. Now it was a large city with swirling interstates and streams of humanity being directed around detours and horrible road construction.

Is every road in America under construction? It seemed like our whole trip was a matter of dodging orange cones and detouring around bridge construction, road tarring and ramp erection. If they ever get finished, half the population of the country is going to be out of work. I would also love to have the contract for cone placement on the roads of this country. Every road construction project we have passed through has about 500 yards of construction going on while 15 miles of cones have been laid in either direction. I don't know who has the contracts, but he must be a billionaire.

Anyway, I had picked a site at Indian Creek campground, a Corp of Engineers facility. The campground was neat as a pin, as usual. The site was beautiful, up on a high hill overlooking Mark Twain Lake. It was also surprisingly un-crowded. There were only 4 or 5 campers anywhere near us and peace and quiet reined. After 3 long days of driving, we had an early dinner of homemade pizza, jumped in the showers and hit the sack early after watching a movie, and listened to the rain pitter-patter on the roof.

Later that night we were awakened to a different pitter-patter on the roof. Only this was quite a bit louder. I jumped up and banged on the ceiling and could hear a scrambling towards the rear of the coach roof. After waiting a minute I heard the bikes on the back of the camper moving and was scared that some burglar was trying to make off with them. I lifted up the rear curtain and pointed the flashlight out the rear window. It was a burglar alright, but not the human kind – the fuzzy kind with the black mask and 5 fingers hanging onto our roof ladder. They are famous break-in artists and thieves and nothing is safe from their prying little fingers. They have been known to break into coolers, open latches and doors, break through screens and can climb anywhere. After staring at his cherubic smile for a moment, I ran outside while grabbing the gun and proceeded to put a bullet in his cherubic ass.

Not really – just kidding. But I did yell at him and told him to move on to the next camper and off he scampered into the dark. Back to sleep we went with the calming rain drops dancing on Bea's roof.

The next morning the rain stopped, the sun came out and after a hearty breakfast, off to Hannibal we went. It had a fairly cute downtown and we wandered by the shops and stopped for an ice cream. We visited the Tom Sawyer and Becky Thatcher houses and stopped in a few of the stores. We walked down by the waterfront and were considering a ride on the sternwheeler anchored there, but the departure times were not conducive to our visit so we sadly passed up the ride. Of course everyone wants to take a paddle boat ride on the Mississippi, but it was not to be.

So off we went to find the famous caves. Of course they also had a winery, campground and city truck tours to suck a little more money out of you, but we stuck with the caves only. Even though privately owned, the cave is now a National Natural Landmark. Originally called McDougal's Cave, it was renamed in 1880 as Mark Twain Cave, in honor of Samuel Clemens, the author of "The Adventures of Tom Sawyer". The labyrinth consists of over 490 passageways that slither their way through the limestone rocks.

After forging our way through the large gift shop, we got our tickets for the tour, waited a few minutes and off we went, following the cute little tour guide down through the underground chambers. It was very interesting and exciting. We saw Jesse James' hideout and Injun Joe's Lair.

As we scampered, slithered, and wandered our way among the limestone rocks, an eerie silence descended, broken only by the chatter of our fellow visitors as it echoed its way down the hundreds of passage ways. The tour was quite long and the chambers had hundreds of signatures up along the rocks. I'm sure Becky's and Tom's were up there somewhere. After winding our way up and down and through the skinny rock passageways, we entered a larger chamber and here our cute little guide tried to freak us out a bit by turning off the lights. Wow. We were in a total, inky black cavern and you could not even see the person standing next to you. It was total silence, except for the squeaks of the bats and plops of the dripping water. I could hear myself breathing. All of a sudden I felt the tons of rock pressing down on me and being somewhat claustrophobic, I began to feel a bit uneasy. My anxiety was rising as I stood in the inky blackness and listened to the hushed, belabored breathing of my fellow explorers. I quickly went into my fantasy mode to escape the uneasiness and that is when I imagined exploring the caves with only Becky and myself. Becky was Tom Sawyer's sweetheart in one of my favorite books, "The Adventures of Tom Sawyer" by Mark Twain.

We were totally lost. It was black, so black that I couldn't even see Becky's hand. Our candle had burnt out long ago and we now stooped, crawled and felt our way along the porous rock passageways. Have you ever been in a place so dark that your eyes cannot adjust because there is no light? We were engulfed with total blackness and total silence. I could hear my heart pounding as fear gripped me. I could hear the rustle and squeaks of the thousands of bats in the upper chambers. I could hear the plops of the dripping water as is leaked and fell from the rock shelves above and the occasional splashes as we stepped into the frequent puddles. It was cold. I could hear Becky quietly whimpering and held on tight to her hand lest we become separated. What started out as a beautiful day had now turned into a disastrous frolic.

We had been playing and picnicking among the hills stretching along the Mississippi River during our annual school picnic outing. School was ending soon and I had decided that I had to make my play on Becky before we all dispersed for the summer months.

She was a beautiful girl. Long golden tresses tumbled down around her shoulders, light brown freckles splayed across her nose and cheeks like sprinkles on a cookie, and those pretty blue eyes were enough to melt their way into any boy's heart. She had a smile like an angel and was gentle as a doe. Of course like all the young girls, she could sew and cook, but Becky could also gut a fish and would spend time with us shooting marbles and climbing trees. In short – a young man's dream and I was determined to make her "my girl" before anyone else could. After lolling around the picnic area for a while I asked her if she would like to take a walk up to the caves along the hillside for something exciting to do. She readily agreed and off we went. Now everyone knows that children were not allowed to play in the caves as they were considered somewhat mysterious and dangerous, but I assured her I was experienced in exploring the tunnels and she would be safe with me. Wanting to impress her with my bravery and daring, I led the way farther and farther back into the caves until the silence engulfed us. We wandered about for a bit and I began to realize that we were lost. The candle we had carried for lighting had now burned out.

We were in a fix as our cries for help echoed hopelessly through the hundreds of cold, black chambers. We stumbled in the pitch dark for hours until we eventually crawled and wriggled our way into what felt like a deep round stone enclosure. We decided to take a rest before moving on. Feeling my way around the stones, I discovered a couple of discarded cans and a pile of sticks and ashes. Someone had been here and had made a fire not too long ago – the ashes were still warm.

I heard a scuffling noise and peered down the passageway toward where the noise had come from. I saw a faint light – was help on the way?

I strained to see through the darkness and a small ray of hope rose in my chest. Now I could see a faint image of dirty, oil stained workpants, a ripped and torn shirt and a dark, shaggy mane of hair. OH MY GOD! IT WAS INJUN JOE! His red eyes and the knife he held in his hand reflected the dim light of the lantern he was carrying in those scarred and crooked fingers. The town had been on the lookout for that evil, heinous Joe as he had been implicated in a recent murder. He was obviously hiding out in the caves. Becky screamed and I held her hand tight as I tried to race out of the chamber entrance but Joe had now heard us and was headed our way. We plunged back into the chamber and I desperately felt around for any type of weapon to defend ourselves. As I felt around in the pitch dark, my hand found an opening in the far back corner of the chamber where we were huddling in fear. I could hear Joe cursing now as he got closer. I detected a small breeze on my fingertips and pulled Becky along behind me as we crawled through a skinny crevice. Somewhat submerged in a large puddle of water, we scooted our way through the rocks, banging and scratching our arms and legs until I could see a faint ray of light in the distance. I quickly dragged Becky along behind me knowing that if Injun Joe got a hold of us that would be the end of our lives. The chamber slowly got wider and we raced along trying to distance ourselves from the murderous madman who we could hear not far behind. Suddenly, my foot slipped into a crevice along the edge of the wall and I started to fall. I grasped Becky tighter and we plunged and rolled down into a black cavern. We lay there gasping for breath as Becky sobbed into my shoulder and a searing pain screamed up the side of my leg. We lay there in the blackness trembling from fear and pain. Then we saw a faint glimmer of light as Joe passed by our small chamber, which was hidden in the dark. We could hear his curses and oaths as they echoed off the limestone walls, receding further and further. We stumbled and felt our way through the chambers for a while longer and finally made our way through a small opening in the side of the hill. Had we escaped? At first, I might have played the fool, but now the thought entered my mind that I could be the hero. I pulled Becky closer and vowed to always protect and love her. I was rewarded with a shy cherubic smile and my heart skipped a beat. I leaned closer for my first tentative smooch…..

Something began to jab my shoulder repeatedly. I rejoined reality with a start and could see the exit sign to the caves in the distance.

"Hurry up, they're leaving us behind."

I groggily stumbled out into the light, tightly grasping Jo's hand.

"What were you doing back there?" she said..

"You almost broke my hand you were squeezing it so hard and fumbling all around. I know you're claustrophobic, but you really went crazy when she turned the lights out."

I mumbled something in return as we exited into the parking lot, and while I returned to the RV, Jo went into the gift shop with the parting statement that "I really think you are losing it sometimes."

I didn't try to explain as I knew she would not understand a young man's arduous passions or an old man's fantasies of being young again.

She would just think I was crazy.

Jo returned with a few of the required mementos and we decided to call it a day.

They also had another cave tour, with flashlights only, but I did not want to test the limits of my claustrophobia, so off we went, back to the campground. It was a beautiful and exciting day and after getting back to the campsite we took a hike along the cliffs of the lake as the sun slowly started sinking in the west. I whipped up a chicken parm and pasta dinner and we relaxed at the picnic table eating and sipping our wine while the sun sank over the lake.

The next day we arose and pulled out early (that's around 9:30 in retired camper time), heading for Lincoln, Nebraska. After 350 miles of corn and soybean fields we made it. This was just an overnight stop, so we had a quick meal, took a little rest, and hit the sack. The campground was not very impressive –very tightly packed sites in an open field with no shade.

Up and out early again the next morning we had a 400 mile ride to our next destination: Scott's Bluff. We had reserved a site at Lake View campground on Lake Minatare in Nebraska. Lake Minatare was about 30 miles from the Bluff. It was not a great site. The campground sat alongside the huge lake basin. It was difficult to find and we circled the lake 2 times and had to call the office before we found the entrance. The sites were very tight and our "lakefront premium" site backed up to an almost dry lake bed - not very impressive. What was impressive were the huge cottonwood trees interspersed among the campsites and along the "lake". I didn't realize they grew so big.

Something was now beginning to irk me and I'm sure it bothers other campers as well. Some states now list their campground fee and then when you get there they charge a "visitor's fee" or "park fee". It's a sneaky way of extorting more money out of the campers when it is the end of the day and they are 30 miles out in the middle of nowhere. So we had to pay an additional $20 fee to be able to set up our site. I was now not too impressed with Nebraska State campgrounds - overpriced, tight, and pretty boring. I am therefore throwing Nebraska State parks into the bin with Massachusetts State parks as really not being worth the visit. The site did have shade though, and since the temperature was now starting to climb, a welcome relief. Another irk was the fact that we paid $3.10/gal. for gas on the east side of the state and $4.00/gal. on the west side. How can the gas vary by $1.00/gal. in the same state?

The ride had been pretty. We were finally breaking out into the west and we drove through rolling hills of light green sagebrush and beautiful blue skies. The farmland was finally petering out and we started passing through range land. Since we were entering cowboy country, we had a quick dinner of the cowpokes favorite - hot dogs and beans. I was starting to walk a little bowl-legged and wished I had a cowboy hat. I could picture Jo and me riding our trusty steeds over the sage-covered hills into the sunset. The campground was very peaceful, so we hit the sack early.

The next morning we were up and out very early (this is around 9:00 a.m. for retired campers) in order to beat the heat which was projected to climb into the 90's. Our destination was Scott's Bluff, about 25 miles away.

Scott's Bluff is a towering 800 ft. sandstone bluff seemingly out in the middle of nowhere that travelers along the Oregon Trail used for a landmark. After travelling hundreds and hundreds of miles across the relatively flat, dry, grass prairie and rugged badlands, they used the Bluff to ensure that they were still on the trail. The National Park Service protects over 3,000 acres and historical overland trail remnants within the Park. You can actually hike and see the ruts made by the wagons as they drove toward their western destinations. Over 250,000 western migrants passed by Scott's Bluff in the mid-1800's. It is the largest of several bluffs in the area and was called "Me-a-pa-te"- meaning "the hill that is hard to go around", by the local Indians - something to be said for the local Indian's astute observations.

There was a very nice visitor center and I bought a couple of books about the Oregon Trail. They are very interesting and detailed the hardships and adventures of our first overland migrants. During the early 1800's, the U.S. government wanted to populate the lands out west that the British government had recently ceded title to. To encourage this settlement, the government offered free plots of a hundred acres or so to prospective settlers. This, along with a gold rush that started in California persuaded thousands of individuals to pack up, leave home and head west. Saying good-bye to extended family and friends, they travelled west, leaving most of their belongings behind. As many as 500 wagons passed along the trail in a single day. The books described the hardships and perils faced by the settlers on their journeys.

The first book, "The Oregon Trail, Yesterday and Today" was written by William E. Hill and describes the ordeals the settlers encountered. Livestock and humans suffered from thirst, starvation, heat, cold, swollen rivers and horrific storms. Many people and their livestock died on the trek. The trail was littered with dead carcasses and the stench could be horrific. As the livestock died off, the travelers had to discard many of their personal items – furniture, clothes, keepsakes, trunks, stoves and even the wagons themselves and all this stuff lay alongside the trail. Wood was almost nonexistent for campfires and they had to use buffalo chips to fuel their campfires. Grass, game and water was sparse. Since most of the families were of poor means, many only owned 1 wagon at best and minimal livestock. Many were forced to walk the 2,000 mile trek, some without shoes. Some very poor people went only with pushcarts or wheelbarrows. Many that would survive the lack of food and water died from diseases that were rampant on the trails, drowned or were killed in accidents.

The second book was a compilation of excerpts from diaries of children and was titled "Stories of Young Pioneers in Their Own Words", written by Violet Kimball. It depicted the children's everyday life on the trail, the ordeals that they faced, what they did for fun and recreation, their chores and responsibilities. Even pre-teens cooked, hunted for game and drove the livestock. One paragraph describes how the alkaline dust and water made the children's hands and faces bleed after the caustic solution burned their dry skin. Another paragraph described swallowing mouthfuls of mosquitoes.

Both books were extremely interesting and I was greatly impressed with the strength and bravery showcased by the settler's and their families in conquering these great lands.

After chatting with the ranger, we decided that taking the drive to the top of the bluff would be a bit risky in the RV, so we parked Bea and strolled and hiked the immediate area. It was a beautiful area for pictures. The seemingly endless grass and sage, the huge bluffs lighted by the sun and the covered wagons displayed by the Park Service along the trail made for a memorable sight. It let you feel what the migrants saw on the westward travels. The temperature was soon hitting 100 degrees and it was hot and dry. We were in rattlesnake territory now so we were quite careful where we stepped. We wandered into the "Legacy of the Plains" museum to cool off a bit and enjoyed our meanderings through the exhibits. They showcased antique tractors, farm implements, wagons and autos and displayed historic artifacts and memorabilia from the day. It was a beautiful finish to a beautiful day.

Back at camp, after lolling a bit in the shade, we had a couple of quick sausage, pepper, and potato sandwiches (also known as "Jimmy Buffs" in New Jersey) and retired to watch a movie.

So far we had hit a few of the somewhat interesting places on our journey across the country but now we were headed for one of the big ones – Rocky Mountain National Park in Colorado.

Rocky Mountain National Park is located near Estes Park, Colorado. According to the National Park Service, the Park consists of 415 square miles of mountains, alpine lakes, tundra and wooded forests. The area was deemed a park in 1915 by President Woodrow Wilson and is the third most visited park in the country. It welcomes almost 5 million tourists every year. Visitors might encounter bears, deer, mountain lions, bighorn sheep, moose, elk, coyotes, and bobcats all the way down to marmots and pica. Wildlife viewing is one of the major attractions of the park. Some of the other activities include hiking some of the 350 miles of trails, photography, rock climbing, fishing, camping, horseback riding and back country skiing. In the nearby town of Estes, plenty of shopping is available and you can rent condos and cabins or can stay in various B & B's or motels. The Park itself has 5 established campgrounds for campers to select from, some nicer than others.

We had about a 200 mile ride from Scott's Bluff, so we departed the flat lands after a big breakfast and headed to the mountains. Mid-afternoon, after crawling our way through the throngs of people and cars in Estes Park and waiting out a torrential downpour, we wound our way through a beautiful canyon and arrived at our destination - Glacier campground. The campground was pretty poor: sites were crammed together in a small valley between the hills and was also jam packed with people. I scraped Bea on a branch backing in and no matter where I stepped outside of the RV I was surrounded with people and picnic tables. I did take a beautiful short hike on a trail up above the campsite and when resting on a rock, taking photos, I watched a bunch of horseback riders ambling by. It looked like fun, so maybe one of these days.......

My only previous attempt at horse back riding was in my early teens at a stable not far from home. Everyone seemed to have a grand time except for me. From the moment I mounted up, my horse acted as though his mind was gone and it was now occupied by some evil spirit. He trotted around in circles, refused to listen to commands or follow his buddies and eventually charged down the wrong trail into an area of low pine trees. I think he was trying to rip my head off on the limbs and scar me for life from the smaller branches raking my face and arms. He almost succeeded. I dismounted, a bloody mess, and walked back to the stables. Well, that was it for the horseback riding for this guy. But watching them now did present a beautiful image as they ambled their way along the mountainous hillside. That beautiful image is still in my mind, and maybe someday in the future I will give it another try - if I find out that I am going to die shortly anyway.

After the hiking and photography we had a nice meal and proceeded to chit-chat by lantern light, as of course, this 3rd most visited Park in the country had no hook-ups – no water and no electric. One might ponder why is this so? Is it because as a nation we contribute approximately 50 billion dollars to foreign aid, or maybe the 1 trillion dollars we spend on welfare – and now we are broke? Now I am sure all of that money goes to good causes but you think they could squeak out a few million dollars to connect the national parks with water and electric. I think as taxpayers, maybe we should get just a little bit back, as opposed to them spending all our tax dollars on stuff that doesn't help the average taxpayer.

Maybe it is because they don't want to ruin the pristine landscapes with underground pipes and electric wires. I'm sure there is some "Ranger Rick" somewhere in Washington preaching the value of enjoying the rugged wilds in your tent while heating your oatmeal over a Bunsen burner. That's fine and dandy, but for those of us who have had to work all our lives to pay the taxes to support these parks and can't retire until our sixties, it can be a bit of a challenge. My body can't take those 20 degree nights in a tent anymore and reading by candlelight would probably finish off the rest of my fading vision. The government leases land to ranchers so their insatiable livestock can clear to the dirt millions of acres of grasslands, leases land to miners and oil companies who happily make money while killing us with their pollution and leases land to logging companies who merrily proceed to clear cut hundreds of thousands of acres of forested hillsides. So one agency of the government allows the legal pillaging and ruination of our land and resources, while another agency doesn't even want to dig up and cover over a little bit of dirt. Theoretically there might possibly be some logic to as to how the various branches of government operate in disparate ways, but damned if I can figure it out. I'm just one of those stupid rednecks who can't handle his own money and needs the government to do it for him.

Anyway, we hit the sack soon after dark (due to our fading lantern) and woke up bright and early the next day to brilliant sunshine. We decided to take a ride up to Sprague Lake to check out any possible local wildlife. Well, what do you know? There was two mother moose in the lake with their babies. After watching them meander about, one of the calves actually came up on shore about twenty feet away to feed on the shoreline vegetation. I was going crazy trying to get some good photos as I crawled over the fallen timbers and peeked through the brush. What a beautiful and exciting start to the trip. After a couple dozen photos, we started to amble around the lake for a pleasant short hike. It presented a gorgeous picture. Huge boulders and rocks lined the shores of the lake and a nice trail weaved its way along the green, glistening waters. Of course, half way around it started pouring, so we hustled back to Bea and had a late lunch.

Very interesting weather here as it seemed that every morning the sun came out and every afternoon rain and thunderstorms swept over the hills. We eventually learned to sightsee and hike in the mornings and head back to camp in the afternoons. Then in the early evenings, the rain passed on and we were treated to spectacular sunsets. What more could you ask for?

The next day we headed over to Moraine Campground, a couple miles down the road for the balance of our stay. This campground was much nicer. The sites were more spread out and the back of our camper faced a little hill, which when climbed, gave a beautiful view of a little rock and grass-strewn valley surrounded by massive peaks. Colorful lichens covered the rocks and small wild flowers peeked out from the tall grasses. Mule deer wandered in and out of our site and the chipmunks and magpies would eat sunflower seeds and peanuts from our hands. I could watch the fly fisherman casting their silken loops in the small stream meandering across the meadow. It was a peaceful and bucolic sight. The next day was our big ride up Trail Ridge Road so we went to bed early in anticipation and to keep warm in the 40 degree temp's.

So far the weather had been kind of crazy. We left home in the 70's, crossed Nebraska in the high 90's, and were now shivering in the 40's. If only we had electric. I'm one of those people who do not like to run their generators if possible, because it ruins the peace and quiet and beauty of an area and drives nearby campers crazy.

The next morning was again bright and sunny and after a hearty breakfast we packed up and headed up the Trail Ridge Road. Considered Colorado's "Highway to the Sky", it runs for 48 miles between the east and west side of the park. The highest part is an 11 mile stretch that runs above the tree line at approximately 12,000 feet and according to Horace Albright, the director of the 1931 National Park Service "it is hard to describe what a sensation this new road is going to make". It made a sensation all right. At first it was a beautiful winding road up through the hills amidst the pine forests and rocky ridges. Slowly, it got tighter and steeper and a little scarier. Eventually it was a tight, steep, narrow ribbon of tar with hairpin turns overlooking the valleys with no shoulder and minimal guard rails. We felt like eagles soaring up in the clouds with the valleys so far below you could barely see the bottom. What views: 12,000 foot granite peaks rising up into the clouds as far as you could see. We were on the top of the world and the views were majestic.

Of course, after a while we also started to feel a little "sensation", like Horace had mentioned, but it was not the good kind. Remember, we're from South Jersey where the point of highest altitude is Apple Pie Hill, which soars a grandiose 200 feet above sea level and houses an old fire tower in the Pine Barrens. At 12,000 feet there is a lot less oxygen and after a while we began to feel a bit disconcerted as the nausea, lightheadedness, and strange tingling sensations began to kick in. We were both breathing heavily. After stopping to sightsee at an overlook near the top of the road I walked back to Bea and noticed the wan look on Jo's face.

"Are you ok? I asked.

"I'm feeling a little funny".

"Me too" I said.

As we continued on our way swooping and spiraling up the Trail towards the rim we both started feeling a bit dizzy. My brain was feeling detached from the rest of my body and my sense of equilibrium was quickly dissipating as we made our way up the mountainside.

"We better turn around before it gets worse" Jo stated as the effects began to strengthen.

So, just before reaching the top, I found a small pull-off to turn Bea around. The tail end of Bea hung out over the 12,000 ft. precipice as I performed my "K" turn on the cliff-side ridge with my butthole puckering, then down we went. I didn't want it to get so bad that I couldn't drive anymore and we were stranded up there in the clouds. After dropping a few thousand feet we began to feel better, but it was quite an exhilarating and mind blowing experience, and we didn't even have to use any illegal drugs – a natural high. Sorry to say we did not make it to the top but it was fun never-the-less. I didn't think I would make it that far being a 40 year smoker but my lungs held in there pretty good. I had heard horror stories of smokers going up in the Rockies and actually passing out from lack of oxygen, but I made it, albeit a bit worse for wear..

We drove back to the campsite and relaxed for an hour. I was reading about a meadow where big horn sheep could be spotted in the evening, so later in the day, after the inevitable rain shower, we took a ride back up the mountain, but to a lower altitude. We stayed at the viewing area for a couple hours and made ourselves some stew for dinner while waiting for the sheep to show up - one of the benefits of owning an RV. Of course the sheep never showed up. I did manage to get one picture of a lone, regal elk trotting across the meadow about a quarter mile away, but that was it. We headed back to camp in the dark, somewhat disappointed but it was a beautiful and exhilarating day none the less. The next day we took it easy and lounged around the camp and took a few short hikes into the surrounding hills. We had the inevitable afternoon rain, but the sun soon came out and we enjoyed another beautiful sunset. After dinner we sat by the campfire and talked about the trip highlights that we had experienced so far.

We hit the sack early and planned to do a bit more sightseeing the next morning before leaving. I got up at sunrise and took a couple of beautiful early morning photos with the mists dancing across the valley and then we took a ride down to the meadow near the stream. We sat alongside the stream for a bit and listened to the rippling waters in the total silence. A few geese were honking in the muted morning light and a few elk were bugling somewhere in the mountains. It was great. We took a short hike up into the hills and on the way back I got a nice photo of a fat little marmot lounging atop a large rock. We relaxed for a bit by the stream again while trying to imprint the postcard picture into our memories. Then we said farewell to Rocky Mountain National Park.

We now had a 300 mile ride to our next destination: Rifle Gap Falls State Park, on the other side of the Rockies.

Now we came to the scary part of the trip that I had been dreading since planning began last fall - traversing the continental divide to get to western Colorado. The camping blogs were full of stories of brake failures, overheating engines and runaway truck ramps. Thankfully our trip to the southern Smokies in the spring prepared me a bit for mountain travel. I wondered if Bea could handle it.

Up, up, up we went and Bea labored at 25 mph for miles on end. I purposefully snuck in amongst the tractor trailers so that inpatient travelers would not be riding my ass and laying on their horns for me to speed up or get out of the way. Bea was huffing and puffing and was not used to the altitudes either. Finally, after quite a while, we went up and over the Rockies through the Eisenhower tunnel at 11,158 feet, located at the peak of the Continental Divide. It is the highest tunnel in the United States and was considered an engineering marvel when it was built. The views of the mountains, cliffs, rushing waterfalls and alpine meadows were a sight to behold and we felt like we were soaring in an airplane. It was breathtaking and exhilarating. Now came the scary part – going down.

Before leaving on our trip I searched the blogs for my question as to whether it was okay to traverse these mountains in tow gear or would we have to use manual shifting. The responses seemed to be equally divided as to what to use and I couldn't get a definitive answer. Well I now have the definitive answer: trying to use tow gear when coming down the

Rockies is like trying to conquer the Roman Army with a slingshot. The engine constantly up shifts into a higher and higher gear as you plunge down the mountainsides going faster and faster. I was frequently riding the brakes and I was beginning to get scared that I was overworking them. After trying out tow gear for a few miles, I realized the only way we were going to survive was to manual shift in 2nd and 3rd gear for the next 20 miles or so. Remember to practice your manual shifting before you attempt crossing the Rockies or travelling the west coast.

The trip was fantastic. I didn't see that much as I tightly grasped the wheel, watched my speedometer and tach and pumped the brakes, but what I did see was gorgeous: endless miles of mountain peaks, sweeping vistas, gorges, and canyons as we made our way through the Colorado National Monument, down through Glenwood Canyon and on into the foothills of the Rockies. As you enter the Canyon area you cross over multiple bridges and viaducts alongside and over the Colorado River, some cantilevered over the river and suspended from the cliff side. That beautiful and amazing ride was in itself worth our trip out west. Like a roller coaster ride in a theme park, it was exhilarating. Don't be scared to go – just take it easy, be careful and enjoy the ride.

We eventually arrived at Rifle Gap State Park after a long day of driving. I had underestimated the ride, forgetting to take into account the hours of driving at 25 mph across the Rockies. It was a nice enough campground. Somewhat tight and minimal shade – but we did have the best site alongside the lake. Of course, as with all the other lakes out here in the west, it was pretty dried up and mostly offered up a sight of lakebed vegetation, grass and mud. It was only an overnight stop though, so it was nice enough.

Jo cooked up a nice roasted chicken dinner and then we took showers to cool off from the heat. We mostly just sat around in the evening trying to grasp the beautiful scenery we had just experienced while crossing those majestic mountains and valleys. The next day we were on our way to Utah, but before leaving, we took a trip up to Rifle Falls State Park, just up the road. It was quite scenic. Like a little tropical paradise, three distinct falls drop from the rock ledges spraying their mists about the lush foliage at the bottom. Beautiful trails wove through the flowered walkways and along the limestone caves at the bottom of the falls. It was very scenic and offered a cool respite from the heat of the day. After a couple hours we were on our way to Yuba Lake State Park in Utah.

We drove 300 plus miles of scenic road through the western part of Colorado, across the San Rafael Swell and across Utah. We passed through gorgeous red canyons, escarpments and valleys dotted with sage brush. Now maybe if you lived out here for a while it is just a vast wasteland to you, but to us east coast flatlanders, we thought it was exceptionally beautiful. I was stopping at almost every pull-off to take pictures and every one kept getting more and more beautiful. It was just a little tease for the southwestern trip we were planning for next year. Already I am running out of descriptions for the scenery on this trip. Ever since western Nebraska the scenery had been magnificent. The trip was worth it just for the views we had this far - and we still had thousands of miles to go. Sometimes I envy those full timers who have months and months to visit all these special scenic areas. Maybe someday….

We finally arrived at Yuba Lake and made a big mistake – we took the wrong road (not the first time, of course). Some of these parks must think it's hilarious that all the out-of-towners get lost looking for their campgrounds. It happens all the time. Their signage is horrible. We got off the highway exit ramp and saw a sign to the "Painted Hills", which was where our campground was located. So I followed the signs down a dirt road. We even passed a bunch of campers up on a hill so I assumed we were going the right way. Well after about 3 miles of vicious washboard road when I thought the whole camper might disintegrate, it turned into a single lane track through the sand. As we navigated around the intermittent puddles, the sand got deeper and deeper and the road skinnier and skinnier until I felt like we were in the Baja 500. We started going up and down some hills with rocks the size of boulders littering the road while taking 90 degree turns through the sand dunes. I didn't think we were going to make it. Bea was creaking, squealing, and groaning as we trekked along at 5 mph. I was scared to go too fast and scared to go too slow as we might get stuck in the sand. It was impossible to back up or turn around and we had no cell service. I really thought we were not going to make it and they would find our bleached bones somewhere out in the sage-covered hills a few months hence.

It seems that we had gone the wrong way around the mountain on a four-wheeler dirt track with my poor Bea. I am still amazed that we somehow made it. In fact, a few days later my filling fell out and I blame it on that road. After about two hours we finally came to a tar road and guess what? 50ft down the road was the campground. I was spitting by the time the camp host came over to say hello and am embarrassed to say that I really let the poor guy have it about "how we could have died, probably ruined my camper, lack of signage, etc." So he more or less gave me my site directions and walked off mumbling something about how we should not use GPS for directions. As I was yelling at him about not using GPS, he went into his camper and shut the door.

We made it to our site which was on the mountainside and had a beautiful view of the valley below. Of course our "lake view" site did not have a view of a lake as it was dried into a little puddle way down below, but the view was pretty. A pastel kaleidoscope of muted pink, green, blue, purple and tan hills and grasses unfolded like a carpet to the horizon. The site was very nice with a concrete pad, water and electric, and a covered picnic area. As the sun was setting I made a pizza and we had a couple of drinks in the shade of the picnic area, while we tried to cool off - both physically and mentally. It was a beautiful sunset with the rays bouncing off the big, white, drifting clouds and I spent the evening pondering roadside signs and dried up lakes.

Mississippi Sternwheeler

Scott's Bluff, Nebraska

Sprague Lake, Rocky Mountain National Park

Rifle Gap Reservoir, Colorado

Rocky Mountain Silhouette

Big Thompson River, Rocky Mountain National Park

Mule Deer

Campsite Visitor

CHAPTER 23

SAGE BRUSH & TUMBLEWEEDS

The next morning, bright and early we were on our way to Nevada and "the Loneliest Road". In 1986 Life magazine named highway 50 through Nevada the "Loneliest Road in America" and claimed there were no points of interest along the route and warned readers to not travel the road unless they were confident in their survival skills. You can imagine the "look" I got from the assistant navigator when I repeated this interesting fact to her.

Maybe the quote was a bit of an overstatement, but I got the idea and liked it. After thousands of miles of cramped and crowded cities and highways we were ready for a bit of "real lonely". All you need to enjoy the road is plenty of gas, a couple of spare tires, plenty of water and a great imagination. The road passes by old ghost towns, mines, pony express and Indian lore sites and cute, "little" towns – very little. There were hundreds and hundreds of miles of nothing, in between tiny little towns of almost nothing, with nothing to distract you. I drove along, somewhat mesmerized by the openness. A seemingly endless river of tar passed beneath big white puffy clouds that rolled over the vast, open hills and sage covered sand. I thought it was quite beautiful and could finally relax driving, occasionally passing a car every 20 miles or so. I don't know how people get around out here. By the time you drive to the gas station 200 miles away to get gas and then come home, you are out of gas again. Thankfully, Bea has a 55 gallon fuel tank. After one long stretch of a couple hundred miles of nothing we passed a little "town" of a couple trailers, a café and 5 mailboxes - a regular "Walkabout Creek". I'll tell you what, if anyone is ever looking to find you, this is the place to go if you don't want to be found.

Soon after starting our passage across Nevada we came to Great Basin National Park. I had wanted to stop here because it is one of the least visited National Parks and was supposedly very beautiful. I had originally had a site reserved here but in the great wisdom of the government I received an e-mail three days before we started our trip that let me know that they had made a mistake and my 26 foot site was actually a 16 foot site. Well guess what? Trying to reserve a new site in a National Park a week before your arrival is impossible anywhere in these United States. So I was forced to make a reservation at Ward Mountain campground around 50 miles further down the road and I did not want to go 100 miles out of our direction to visit the park the next day. We stopped just for the afternoon.

Created in 1922, the Park is situated up in the mountains and features great hikes up amongst the Bristlecone pines, Wheeler Peak and its glacier, Lehmann Caves, and supposedly has fantastic night sky viewing. The roads are quite steep and high so we ditched the idea of a cruise to the top of the mountain, and since we did not have a lot of time for a hike, we decided to just view the visitor's area and take a tour of the caves. When we went to sign up for the cave hike, the longer, more interesting hike was all booked up so we had to settle for the little hike of around an hour.

Now as you know I like to take opportunities in this book to vent my little frustrations about life in general and the U.S. government in particular. Wait 'til you hear this one. The teenage government employee asked if we had been in any other caves recently, because of the danger of some fungus that could be transported between caves on clothing or hair, etc. I said yes because we had been in the Mark Twain caves a few weeks prior. He then proceeded to tell us that if we had not changed our clothes or taken a shower since then, we were not allowed in the caves. Now, I might not be the cleanest guy in the world since being retired but I think I could safely say that yes, I had taken a shower and changed my clothes since two weeks ago. He then proceeded to say that the rule goes all the way back 10 years, so in case you are planning a visit and have visited any other cave within the last 10 years and have not taken a shower or changed your clothes since then, you will not be let in. Wait until the left hears about this law as it sounds very prejudicial to me regarding the homeless. Be that as it may, is every one that writes laws in this country an imbecile? After laughing for a bit, I was going to ask him if he was in fact an imbecile but since he had that "Clint Eastwood" look in his eyes and a side arm strapped to his hip, I demurred. If the federal government thinks that the people in this country go for weeks and months and years without showers or changing clothes they have a lot more pressing things to worry about then cave fungus. Bubonic Plague anyone?

Anyway the cave tour was very pretty but very short. Upon exiting we had an ice cream and then watched in disbelief as a horrific hail storm came over the mountain and proceeded to beat to near death every human or machine that was in the parking lot. What did I say about crazy weather on this trip? I was now glad that we did not have the time for that scenic ramble up through the bristlecone pines. That's probably why they have those short, stubby branches. We would have been pelted to death.

After a while the sun came back out as though nothing happened and we said good-bye to Great Basin and headed to our site at Ward Mountain - another very interesting day.

Ward Mountain campground was quite nice, but it was a U.S. government campground, therefore it also had no water or electric. It was very scenic, being up on the hillside with views of the surrounding mountains. The sites were spacious enough and cuddled within the surrounding pinion pines, junipers and sagebrush. Someone dressed like a bum came walking up towards our camper and I immediately began looking for a big rock that I could use for protection. It turned out that he was the camp host. Some of the camp hosts on these far out campgrounds in the west are a bit dodgy looking, but after a chat with the fellow he seemed very nice and filled me in on his modus operandi. He said he hosts at Ward Mountain for the summer and early fall and during the late fall he heads to Quartzsite, Arizona where he gets a site for $1,500 for the winter season: once again, how to live cheaply in America. For $1,500 he covers his yearly housing expenses. Not a bad deal. In addition, if he hosted down south somewhere for the winter season, his housing expense would be exactly zero! Can't make it in

America? I don't want to hear it. My thoughts rambled about as I considered living full time on the road in Bea, parked in fantastically beautiful spots around the country with gasoline and food as our only expenses. Sometimes it sounds like Nirvana to me.

Of course there is always the opposite example. The couple across from us had one of those $350,000, forty-foot units with slide-outs and cable antenna and they were pulling a Jeep. They had owned a smaller unit, but she just "needed that washer and dryer and fireplace", so therefore they purchased the largest, most lavish class A they could afford. I guess "to each his own", so we tried to settle in for a peaceful night reading by lantern light. Our neighbors ran their generator all night with the lights blazing while they sat outside watching their big screen TV: so much for the peaceful sigh of the breeze through the trees and listening to the coyotes howl. Oh well, unless you want to camp in a tent, some times you are forced to put up with the rude neighbors. Thankfully they were gone the next morning - must have been too rustic for them as there was no pool available.

We relaxed for the whole next day as there was literally no place to go. Guess what? It was our 40th anniversary! Now Jo has had the privilege of living with the greatest, sweetest, hardest working, most considerate, best lover on the planet for the last 40 years. I couldn't imagine she would want for anything else so I had not purchased any gifts. However, just to put a cherry on top of her exciting day, I decided to search the area for any small natural gift to give her. I managed to come up with a couple of wild flowers, a few cute stones (does every woman camper in America collect stones?) and an old elk jawbone I found on the trail. She smiled with love and eternal gratitude as she accepted my special gifts. Yes, she is one lucky girl I thought to myself.

Sipping our wine as the sun set, we exchanged our big smooches and hit the sack early. The next morning we left for Bob Scott campground, approximately half way across Nevada - with the elk jawbone prominently displayed on the dashboard. It was a beautiful, calm, relaxing drive across the Nevada desert. All day long, every 20 miles or so, we would rise up over the surrounding hills only to see another 20 mile valley to cross. Disappointingly we saw no wildlife. While I thought it was quite beautiful, they must have thought it was quite inhospitable - no antelope, no coyotes, no roadrunners, nothing. Our entertainment was watching the dirt devils and tumbleweeds blow across the road and watching the clouds as they drew varying shadowy shapes across the hillsides. We were sailing a vast sea of sand and scrub, as far as the eye could see.

For the first time in my life, after weeks and weeks of driving, I actually got a cramp in my foot and it was becoming somewhat painful to drive. By my quick calculations, I had probably pressed on the accelerator and brake approximately 15,000 times in the last month (surprisingly couldn't find the answer on the internet) so Jo took over for a while to hone her hill-driving skills. It made for a somewhat tense afternoon. Not appreciating my back-seat driving tutelage, a few tense words might have been exchanged.

Now, like most men, I fear for my life when driving as a passenger with my wife. It seemed to me she was going 80 mph while gabbing about the beautiful scenery as we swerved our way down the highway. Like the scene from "Planes, Trains and Automobiles", my fingertips were jammed into the dashboard, my feet were pressed up against the front of the passenger seating area and my bulging eyes were locked straight ahead as I contemplated a horrifying death. After an hour or so of terror, I managed to wrest back control of the steering wheel from my sweetness – all the while listening to a few expletives and mumblings about "back-seat drivers, never going to drive with you again, pain in the ass, driving me crazy", etc.,etc.,etc. So, yes the cramp in my foot was back but the cramps in my neck, back, fingers and legs were now gone – a decent trade off as far as I was concerned.

After a while, we were copacetically situated back in happy travel mode, our marriage still intact, and on we soared across the vast open spaces of Nevada. 200 miles out in the middle of nowhere we arrived late in the afternoon at Bob Scott campground. It was another U.S. government site with no hook-ups once again, but it too was situated with a pretty view of the surrounding hills.

There were only 2 other campers when we arrived - 2 single gentlemen that looked like they lived there – tents, awnings, supplies, food and gear were splayed in disarray around their sites. Where did they get their groceries and water? I was silently praying that they did not make their living by robbing unsuspecting senior campers out in the middle of nowhere. The place only had about 12 sites of varying sizes and slopes, but since we got there early, we got one of the best sites with a little shade and nice flat parking area. Dogs and beans on the prairie that night as we sat outside in the evening to cool off and watch the flights of a new bird to us – I think they were Nighthawks but am not sure. They swooped and pirouetted in the darkening skies as we lay back in our recliners. I remembered a title from one of my favorite bands, Pink Floyd, and began to "breathe in the air". We listened, for the first time, to the howl of the nearby coyotes. Now this is what it's all about! A feeling of solace was beginning to sink in. Finally, I was beginning to get into the rhythm of the day, the night and the wind as we sat in our quiet spot on the sage-covered hills. It took a few weeks but we were finally relaxed and our minds at peace. As the night sky darkened, a brilliant Milky Way explosion of colorful stars and gases spread out from horizon to horizon and draped down to the ground in every direction. I could smell the soft scent of the sage and the burning of the wood as it sizzled and crackled behind us and could feel the cool breeze on my face as I watched the tiny glowing embers slowly rise into the night sky. I was experiencing an unbelievable natural high. All my senses were alive and in tune with the present. I felt as if I was one with the natural world.

After relaxing for a while, I practiced taking some night photos, but was not too successful. I think I needed a faster lens. After loosing all my photo gear last year while trying to drown in a Minnesota lake, I didn't quite have the funds to refurbish with all top of the line equipment. You need a fast, wide-angle lens to take good star photos and they can cost thousands and thousands of dollars. It seems my cheapo wide angle lens is too slow and my cheapo faster lens is not wide enough. So, I didn't get any grand photos, but the visions of that star-studded extravaganza will be etched in my memory forever.

The next morning we awoke to the sweet fragrant smell of the sage and the bawling of a few cows on the nearby hills as the night's dark shadows receded. As the glistening line of light crept up the rolling, tawny hills, they transcended into bright orange waves peppered with the shadows of small roving clouds and flecked with the glistening sage – a veritable kaleidoscope of colors. We loaded up our "Conestoga Wagon" and headed out for our final push across the western plains. The trip across Nevada on the "Loneliest Highway" was spectacular and we would miss its peace and serenity, but we had to move on. Our new destination was Lake Tahoe in California.

Campsite Serenade

"The Loneliest Road", Nevada

Approaching Hail Storm, Great Basin National Park

CHAPTER 24

THE GOLDEN
(SOMEWHAT TARNISHED) STATE

After the crystallized silence of the sage-covered plains we eventually arrived in Truckee, California, a short distance from Lake Tahoe. I planned our overnight stop here just to take a quick look at beautiful Lake Tahoe. It was indeed beautiful – crystalline blue waters nestled between the surrounding mountains. Our campsite at Granite Flat campground was also beautiful. It was snuggled alongside a meandering mountain stream with vertical mountainsides reaching up towards the clouds on the other side of the flowing stream. Tall pines and rocks festooned the craggy hills and the gurgling of the stream could be heard down close to the dark blue waters. But alas, when one turned around, the roar of the traffic 100ft. away fouled the bucolic site. Non-stop, all day and night, the traffic screamed by and destroyed the potential beauty of the site. What a shame.

We fell asleep to the incessant roar of the passing cars as they whined their way up and down the hill with music blasting, gears revving and throttles gunning. Do people ever sleep in California? The cacophony lasted all night - the juxtaposition of heaven and hell.

The next day we went for a drive around the lake and our disappointment only grew. Hordes of tourists and traffic were encountered as we crept our way around the mountain. Finding no place to park, we headed our way up towards Inspiration Point and a possible hike. A beautiful hike and bike trail ran alongside the lake, but we couldn't get anywhere near it. The pull-offs were jam packed with cars and people and strollers. I finally squeezed into one of them, but no spaces were available and I scraped my hubcap trying to creep around the mobs of people while exiting between the low rock walls. We then proceeded up the steep mountainside to try to get to Inspiration Point and were stalled by groups of cars being intermittently waved along through the road construction. At this point, the road was extremely narrow and steep and the cliff alongside plunged vertically down to the Lake below. When again idling on one perilous incline, I pulled over, put on my parking break and cut my wheels in the hope that poor Bea would not begin rolling backwards down the mountain. Jumping out, I snapped a few gorgeous pictures from far up above the lake. I was forced to sit for a moment as a feeling of vertigo overwhelmed me. Standing at a 35 degree angle and looking straight down through a camera lens at the moving waters does not improve one's sense of balance. The snaking line of cars was now making its way forward, so I got back into Bea and managed to catch the rear of the slow progression moving up and over the mountain. A beautiful moment, yes, but ruined by the throngs of humanity. We proceeded around the lake, but after finding no place to park Bea, we headed back to the campsite. After a quick meal, Jo practiced on her guitar as I "glassed" the facing mountainside, hoping to maybe catch a glance of some Rocky Mountain sheep or a rambling bear. All the while we listened to the drone of traffic and overhead planes. Oh how we yearned for the tumbleweed highways and soulful silence of the plains.

The next morning we left bright and early for Yosemite National Park, another one of the "Big Boys" of the National Park System. We left with some trepidation because as we were crossing the States, a gigantic heat dome began settling in over the western U.S.A. Still trying to enjoy the sites at our federal campgrounds we were also still without hook-ups for the next 2 weeks at our reserved sites. California is not the place you want to be in the middle of a heat wave with no electric, trying to live in a 24ft. fiberglass box. I was not able to get a site in Yosemite Park even though I was on the computer at one second after 9:00 am six months prior. We had to settle for a site at Forks Landing at Bass Lake, approximately 30 miles away from the southern-most entrance to the Park. The campground itself was pretty disappointing. Online it looked like a beautiful shaded site overlooking the lake. In reality it was a site you had to be a camping contortionist to get into. Bea felt like she was going to overturn when I was trying to back into the site due to the severe angle of the hill. Once parked, we heard a car go by. Walking to the back of our campsite, we were surprised to see a well travelled road directly behind us and about 10 ft down the hill. You couldn't see it on the campground website, but there it was. There was also no shade. It seems that sometime between posting the photo of the site online and us arriving at the site, someone had cut the trees down. We were now roasting on a hillside with no shade or electric in the 100 degree temperatures.

After melting for a bit I decided to walk down across the road to the lake. No hope there either. From the top of the hill down to the lake, the state had covered the hillside with rock skree – those 8 inch chunks of rock that you will surely break your neck on if you decide to walk on them. I could picture my busted up body lying at the bottom of the hillside. Not wanting to risk my life, I climbed back up to the site and morosely pondered whether my skin would start peeling off in the stifling heat. I could hardly breathe and was roasting like a marshmallow. Not even considering the thought of a campfire in the heat of the night and not having any electric to put on the air, we retired early after reading by lantern light for a bit and drifted off into a sweat-induced coma.

The following morning, bright and early, I jumped out into the cool (75 degree) air and unhooked for our trip up to Yosemite National Park. I had previously had to make a reservation just to enter the park, as it is becoming so crowded these days. After a 40 minute ride up and down the mountains we arrived at the southern entrance to the Park. I was taking a chance going this way because according to the park literature, the tunnel into the park is only 10'ft 2" at the curb when entering the park. Bea is 11'ft 3". I figured I could squeak through somehow. Probably a stupid idea, but to go up and around to the western entrance of the park, it would have taken an additional 2 hours and with the heat rising we were in somewhat of a hurry. Well, it worked – no cars were coming out of the park at that early hour and I gunned it down the middle of the arched tunnel. We were now happily ensconced in the Park.

Our first stop was the Mariposa Grove of giant sequoias, which is located in the very southern portion of the Park. According to the National Park Service, giant sequoias are the most massive trees on earth. Large specimens can attain a mind numbing circumference of over 100 feet and reach a height of 300 feet. These orange colored trees are massive and take centuries to grow. The oldest of the trees have been dated at over 3,200 years old – almost 1,200 years before Christ was born. Trying to imagine a seed, which approximates the size of a small pebble growing into one of these behemoths, was enough to blow my mind. As a result of fires, drought and logging in the late 1800's, the remaining trees are now listed as endangered and protected. Their three foot thick bark and the tannic acid in their sap helps to protect them from fires, but they can still be damaged from intensely hot blazes. Fires had been raging in this area of California lately and I wanted to see them while the getting was good. Almost all of the remaining sequoias are located in the western Sierra Nevada Mountains and here we now sat, waiting for the shuttle that takes you to the grove arrival area. We opted to walk the moderate Grizzly Giant Loop Trail which was approximately 2 miles in length. Already sweltering, we started off on our trek to see the Bachelor, The Three Graces and the 2,000 year old Grizzly Giant, a few of the renowned trees located on the trail. We started out on the boardwalk and eventually huffed and puffed our way up the hillside, as it turned into a dirt track with a moderate elevation gain. The massive trees were a beautiful, light orange color and soared up into the blue skies. It is impossible to get a full picture of one in your photos unless you stand ½ mile away. If you could lean up against them and spread your arms, you would not reach even a tenth of the way around their massive trunks. The sad part was that you couldn't get up close to give them a hug as they were surrounded by wooden barriers. Some were scorched black from a fire that had recently swept through the park. The crowd ambled through the grove in a hushed whisper as the cathedral-like spires soared to the heavens around us. Deer meandered through the low brush and squirrels chattered at us as we ambled about their woodland homes. After sweating our way around the grove for a few hours, the crowds were beginning to thicken and our blood flow was beginning to thin. We were hot and tired and it was time to move on. We headed towards the shuttle, but as I looked back, staring at the magnificent giants, I could not help thanking the Lord for the beauty he has blessed us with.

We arrived back at Bea and headed for our next stop – Yosemite

Valley. Being later in the day, the Park was now swarming with automobiles and people. After a half hour ride through the Park, we managed to find a parking spot after exiting the Wawona Tunnel on highway 41. Before us lay that famous vista, often photographed by Ansel Adams, draped across the mountain valley. The view encompasses El Capitan, Half Dome, and Bridalveil Falls. If you could conjure up in your mind the most beautiful spot in the world, this panoramic vista would probably be close. Sheer granite walls rising thousands of feet framed the lush green valley snuggled in their rocky hands. It was the wrong time of day for photography, but I took dozens of photos anyway. You had to sit down a bit just to inhale a bit of the majestic surroundings. If you could infuse that vision into your mind and body, I feel as though you would never get old, never be sad, and live forever. That is what the majesty of our great parks does for you and that is why you should try to visit as many as possible. I pondered the fact that we all need a bit of majesty in our lives to cut through the cobwebs of clutter and the dust of time which slowly accumulates in us and kills and strangles our souls. We sat in silence as birds soared in the mountain drafts and the sun glistened off the sheer granite walls. Something was missing but I couldn't quite put my finger on it.

We then proceeded to drive east towards the Valley itself. The temperature was now in the 100's but amazingly after driving the loop a few times, we managed to snag a parking spot in the shade of the pines. We had originally planned to find an early parking spot and spend the day bicycling around the valley. In the blistering heat, that was now out of the question. Those magnificent, glistening sheer granite walls now trapped all the heat between the mountains and it was sweltering as I roamed about trying to take in all the awe-inspiring scenery. As I sweated and plodded my way around the parking area, I was trying to get a glimpse of Yosemite Falls – the iconic vision of Yosemite, supposedly located somewhere in the Valley.

Yosemite Falls, at approximately 2,500 feet high, is one of the tallest waterfalls in the country. Flowing off the North Rim of Yosemite Valley, the Falls plunge in 3 distinct cascades to the valley below. A little bell rang in my head – that's what was missing! Where were the falls? I thought maybe I was going blind from all the sweat in my eyes and asked a few of my fellow tourists. Their response: "THEY ARE DRIED UP"! Are you kidding me? I had driven across country to see this monumental vista and they dried up? It wasn't "summer", it was September. Why hadn't anyone warned me? How was that possible? It seems the blistering heat of the summer and the drought we had been experiencing since crossing the great Mississippi had dried up the falls in Yosemite. I thought I was going to cry. What a bummer. I ruefully stared up at the granite cliffs imagining the plumes of water spraying out from the cliff tops and plunging to the valley floor. Alas, there would be no photos. I dejectedly wandered back to Bea to find the doors and windows open and Jo lying on the bed with the battery powered fan going full tilt. It was hot. Rejecting the idea of a hike to the visitor center or museum in the throngs of tourists and heat of the day, we sadly decided to leave our spot and head back to camp as it was now too hot to do anything.

Driving the camper with the A/C on was our only relief and we soaked in the cool air as we wound our way back over the mountains to Bass Lake. I guess it was not hot enough yet for Californians because the restaurant we stopped in near the campground only had their doors and windows open and no air conditioning. Was there no escape from this heat? After a somewhat blasé meal, we wandered through the gift shop for a while, waiting for the sun to finally sink over the mountains. It eventually did and we made our way back to camp where we sat outside in the dark, trying to cool off while simultaneously waging a war with the local mosquitoes.

The next day, we took a ride to the nearby town of Coarsegold. We stumbled upon an art/flea market and spent a while perusing the various booths and piles of mostly used junk. Once again the heat was unbearable. As I stood in a veritable coma by one of the booths, I did play with the idea of purchasing a beautiful machete for protection on our travels. The ornamental handle holding the glinting steel had caught my eye for a second.

In America, only thugs, rapists, and murderers are allowed to carry firearms and travelers are always looking for ways to protect themselves. But, alas, my seared brain was not functioning and I ambled off into the heat waves. I did part with $2 for a DVD for my collection but that was about it. We grabbed lunch in a somewhat cooler restaurant located on the grounds and then headed "home" in the blazing sun.

On the way back to the campground we came upon one of those school fundraising car washes and I decided to splurge on poor Bea so that she could feel cool and all spiffy after a long journey. After thousands of miles of rain and hail, 12,000 ft. peaks, grime and dirt and blistering heat, she needed to be pampered. Greeted with somewhat wan smiles, the kids looked at us a bit warily when we pulled into the wash down area. After handing them a few extension poles for washing and a bit of cajoling, they valiantly undertook the project. A bit later, Bea was smiling, we were smiling and the kids were smiling after I handed them a $50 for their efforts. Off we went back to camp. After a cold dinner of shrimp, salad and wine I sat outside writing my log and Jo practiced her guitar while the sun set over the lake. Finally, late at night the temperature dipped into the high 70's and we uncomfortably fell asleep to the hum of the mosquitoes and the drone of the battery-powered fan.

Early the next morning I went for a walk around the campground. Do any of my fellow Americans take advantage of these beautiful National Parks? I greeted one woman with a "hello" and she promptly responded with a "good evening". Strangely enough, it seems that our campground was inhabited with a diverse population of Mexicans, Koreans, Philippines, Chinese, Germans, and other ethnic peoples that I couldn't categorize. They were all pleasant enough but I felt like I was in another country. All I could do was to smile and wave. I couldn't talk to any of them and headed back to camp amidst the aroma of foreign foods wafting through the air. It seems our parks are famous around the world.

Today we had to move to another site. Originally I was disappointed with the fact that we could only get our "beautiful" site for 2 days and then had to settle for a secondary site with no view, up the hill from the main campground. Now it was somewhat of a blessing. After driving up the hill on the skinniest campground road I had ever seen, we parked in a nice shady spot under the tall pines. The riotous noise and screaming near our old site faded into the distance and we settled in to a cooler, quieter spot up on the hillside. Foregoing any further attempts to sightsee in the blistering heat of southern California, we sadly elected to spend the day in the relative cool of our site for our final day in Yosemite. We were tired, sweaty, dehydrated and somewhat dizzy at this point and the heat was becoming a serious health concern.

To sum up our visit to Yosemite, it was somewhat disappointing. The Mariposa Grove was partially blackened by fire. Yosemite Falls was dried up. Glacier Point road was closed to traffic. Half the campgrounds in the Park were closed and we were forced to stay outside the Park. The heat was ungodly.

Other than that it was still a nice visit and we were astounded by the Park's beauty. It was definitely one of the prettiest parks we had ever visited and had a few things been different, the visit would have been momentous - maybe next time under better circumstances?

The next morning I gave Bea a quick check up and then off we headed to Clear Lake, California. This was only going to be an overnight stop on our way to visit the great California Redwoods.

My relationship with the state of California had, up until now, been somewhat strained, to say the least. Since entering California at Lake Tahoe a week ago, poor Bea had been struggling up and down the mountains in 2nd and 3rd gear almost the whole way. Fires were raging across the state, including a few near Lake Tahoe and around Yosemite. Smoke wafted through the air about charred black stumps and vegetation. The throngs of people had limited our ability to sightsee to a certain degree, and the lack of hook-ups at the state parks had made our trip through the state somewhat uncomfortable.

After chugging up and over the mountains again this morning, we eventually entered the Sacramento Valley area and were immediately swept up into a massive tidal wave of traffic. After bouncing along on the pothole-rutted "Freeway" for a few hours, we finally exited back off onto a relatively calm road crossing the Napa Valley. Yes, the miles and miles of vineyards were beautiful and maybe we should have stopped for a visit. Did we? Yes, but only for gas. Let me tell you why. First, the roadsides of California are littered with trash and garbage with intermittent homeless camps and rusty old RV's that people are trying to live in. This made my copilot Jo, an eco-friendly "neat-nik", somewhat flustered. After paying for my 50 gallons of gasoline at $5.90/gallon, I too was quite a bit flustered. Are they crazy out here in California? Oil is oil all across the country. Thousands of miles of pipeline direct it to every corner of this great country. This was approximately twice as much as I had paid per gallon on our previous yearly travels and $2 more per gallon than what I paid back in South Jersey. I therefore concluded that the difference in price must all be a result of taxes. Where does it all go? It's obviously not going towards trash pick up, road maintenance or utility installation in the campgrounds. Maybe it is used to support the millions of poor immigrants streaming across the state's southern borders. I was not a "happy camper".

We were still under what the weather reports were saying was a "heat dome". That was quite the understatement. It was more like hell's inferno. The temperature, late afternoon, was now 109 degrees under bright sunny skies with little wind. As I walked to the kiosk to pay my bill I thought I was going to die. Blast furnace heat was filling my eyes with sweat, I felt like I couldn't breath and my skin was sizzling like a steak on the grill. I probably lost 5 pounds just walking across the lot. I swear you could fry an egg on my forehead and I was petrified that the rubber soles on my sneakers would melt onto the molten-like tar surface of the parking lot and leave me forever standing there like Lot's wife in Sodom after fire rained down from heaven.

Eventually I made it back to the camper and we proceeded up and down the hills toward Clear Lake as our A/C unit fought a losing battle with the heat. From what I could see with my sweat filled eyes, it was quite pretty. The tall grasses danced and waved upon the tan and mauve colored hills. I was not looking forward to the evening at our campsite with no electrical outlets to plug into. What can I say? It was horrible. When we eventually tried to sleep the temperature dropped all the way down to a "cool" 89 degrees. The campground was almost deserted as it seemed we were the only people crazy enough to camp in 100 degree plus weather. How we made it that night, I do not know. Trying to sleep was like sticking your head in a plastic bag right after someone sucked all the air out. We slipped and slithered our way across the sheets every time one of us got up to get another bottle of water to keep from dying of dehydration. The pores of our skin made a funny little noise as the bodily fluids got sucked from our innards, like rotisserie chickens baking in a 24ft. oven.

At sunrise the next morning I crawled out to a relatively cool morning in the 80's. A slightly cooler breeze engulfed me as I slogged my way down to the lake and it presented a beautiful picture. The tawny brown hills across the water suffused the golden light of the early morning sunrise. Hundreds of seagulls, pelicans, egrets, ducks, cormorants, grebes and hawks soared and dove over the lake. The coves were jammed with various waterfowl species chattering and screeching as they exchanged their "good mornings". It was quite a sight. I took a few photos of the birds and then spent some time chasing the colorful dragonflies around as they darted through the rushes. I sat for a moment and infused the beautiful dawn into my mind.

After a while I returned to the RV, put the coffee on and woke my sweetheart from her sticky slumbers. Today we were headed up to Redwood country and the anticipation was beginning to build. I gave Bea a quick check-up, fired up the engine and we were soon on our way. The cool, dark Redwoods beckoned.

Seeing the great Redwoods was always number one on my bucket list of travel destinations. Some of the trees date back to the Jurassic period and they are the tallest living things on earth, potentially growing 400 feet in height. They are so tall, that due to the effects of gravity they are not able to suck water up to the tops of their dizzying heights but must rely on rainfall and fog to replenish their thirst. That is why their geographic dispersion is limited to the northern California coast and southern Oregon as the cool and foggy climate there suits their needs. Their roots do not run very deep but they intertwine with their neighbors, the result being that they brace each other against powerful storms and floods. Their thick bark protects them from fire and insects. As opposed to the relatively sparse, light and open groves of their Sequoia cousins, the Redwoods thrive in foggy, dark, dense groves overgrown with ferns, mosses, and mushrooms. I yearned to see their majesty.

As we approached Humboldt State Park, the temperatures were finally dropping and we eagerly looked forward to a refreshing few days in the coolness of the Redwood forests. We abruptly entered the "Avenue of the Giants" and the feeling was one of amazement. Indescribably huge, brown monoliths lined the road, encroaching on the lanes. Wider than Bea, their massive bodies blocked out the sunlight as we entered the grove. The roadway weaved and meandered like a ribbon through the understory amidst the dark giants. At the first pull-off we jumped out to take it all in. As we wandered between the massive trunks splayed with dark green fern leaves, we craned our necks upward toward the distant canopies flecked with the light of a bright blue sky. It looked like a scene from "Jurassic Park" and I expected to see a pterodactyl soaring through the dark, moss-laden limbs. A sense of somber awe engulfed us and we could not even speak as we crept around the behemoths. Our stunned senses could not absorb the reality. Now I know why everyone in California walks around shrieking like their minds are blown apart. It's not from drug use, it's the incredible scenery. It was like we stumbled upon a long lost treasure buried deep in the California forests - a massive, breathing fortress. Looking back at Bea, she looked like a tiny "Matchbox" toy cowering in the distant shadows. Hanging spider webs draped the spaces between the thick bark slabs and slugs and salamanders crept down below beneath the chest-high ferns. We tried to hug one of these symbols of God's immensity but together we could not even reach a quarter of the way around its massive trunk. We headed back to Bea and drove on to the campsite in silence. We were literally dumbfounded as we contemplated living among these giants for a few days.

We had a beautiful site tucked in the shadowed forest and I quickly jumped out to wander and stare some more. The silence was soon broken as I tripped over one of the Park's wooden posts that had, for whatever reason, been sprinkled about the campsites. I thought I broke my shin bone as the blood oozed down my leg and I hopped my way over to the picnic table, cursing and swearing. Jo soon came to my rescue with a bag of ice and a margarita as I sat, pondering once again, the stupidity of government. Maybe they thought it would be funny watching the tourists break their shins as they wandered about, staring up at the trees in the dark shadows. Why else would you scatter knee-high posts all around a campground?

While eating dinner, my filling fell out. "Damn". After almost breaking my shinbone, now I had a broken tooth. I headed out to enjoy the quiet evening while the disheartening thought of "bad things always happen in threes" flitted playfully about my mind. Later, while relaxing with an ice pack on my shinbone and a flask of wine by my side, I drifted off into a serene slumber. I awoke an hour later and got up to check on my sweetie-pie - "Crunch". What the hell was that? I couldn't see because

I had removed my glasses before slumbering. Oh crap, I thought, after realizing I had stepped on them. The day was deteriorating rapidly. I had gotten the filling replaced a week before we left on vacation and the glasses were only a few months old. I tripped over my wine flask while hobbling back to Bea, my vision skewed by the bent glasses. It was time to call it a day.

The heat wave looked to finally be over – we would survive. I spent the next morning trying to straighten out my glasses with a pair of pliers. They sort of worked after I was done, but it wasn't pretty. They sat at a 30 degree angle across my face – my left eyeball peaking beneath the lens while my right eyeball peaked above. If I averaged my vision between the two of them, I could manage. It was like floating in a lake with one eye above the waterline and one eye below. I had a new "outlook" on life.

After I was finished, we spent the rest of the day hiking around the forest on the myriad of trails and then went for a quick drive to the Visitor Center to pick up a few token remembrances. The next morning we would be leaving, but only up to the northwestern part of the Redwoods and Jedidiah Smith Redwoods State Park.

It was a nice drive down towards the coast and through the beautiful meadows along the Newton Drury Scenic Route. We were unlucky in that we didn't see any elk, but it was still quite warm out and they were probably still up in the mountains. On the way, we stopped for groceries in some type of food outlet and it was not very impressive. The parking lot was full of trash and bums and homeless people wandered about the area. California contains such beautiful and scenic areas and it broke my heart to see how the masses of humanity were destroying it. People have no respect for each other or nature and can be quite disgusting at times.

We arrived at Jedidiah Smith campground late in the afternoon and settled in to another beautiful site amongst the towering Redwoods. This site was more spacious and more secluded. It was great. One of the trails passed right behind the site and we spent some more time wandering amongst the behemoths. After a quick meal we sat by the campfire for the evening as it was now quite a bit cooler out. I stared up at the few stars twinkling amid the forest canopy and pondered the magnificence and beauty of our planet. You can't help it. After being awed by the majesty and beauty of the forest, you begin to feel humbled. I felt like a little flea sitting alongside the massive trunks and Bea looked like a little toy. So I pondered some more: the immensity of the universe, the thousands of years that had gone by since these monoliths were seedlings, the rhythm and pulse of nature and the infinitesimal specks of nothingness that we are in the grand scheme of things. It was a very thought provoking and humbling experience.

Every one should immerse one's self in majesty occasionally – it's good to keep our egos a bit in check. I know that's not a modern way of thinking. Now-a-days, it is taught that you should love yourself. Humility is for fools and if people don't agree with you, that is their problem. Always put yourself first – you are a beautiful person and deserve to live a happy and wonderful life, etc., etc., etc.

What a bunch of bullshit. We are here like any other species and don't deserve anything. You make your way through life as well as you can. You love and respect those around you. We are a communal society and as such you seek out help and guidance from the smarter folks you come in contact with. Yes, there are smarter folks than you. That's why we have progressed as much as we have. All those narcissistic fools running around out there make me want to vomit. Most of us strive to be better people but we are a hell of a long way from perfection and we don't deserve to love ourselves until we've earned it. I have a hard enough time liking myself sometimes let alone loving myself. I'll probably be getting a few calls from the psychologists, but that is how I feel. Maybe instead of loving ourselves first so that we can love others, we should love others first so that we can earn the right to begin to love ourselves.

That is the end of my preaching for a bit – one of my many imperfections.

We spent a few days hiking and biking Jedidiah Smith Redwoods. It was glorious. Riding out of the woods at one point we came to the Smith River - an absolutely beautiful, aquamarine stream winding its way through the giant trees. Wildflowers lined the banks of the rock strewn stream bed. The crystalline waters chattered and gurgled their way in a slow serpentine course through the giant pines. It was very peaceful and quiet as we sat watching a few kayakers slowly drifting atop the clear, rippling waters. Puffy white clouds floated above and Kingfishers roller-coasted and screeched between the canopied shallows. After spending a few days in the dark forest our eyes hurt from the blinding sunlight. Of course Jo picked up a few rocks and wildflowers that we then had to struggle with on our ride back to our site.

The next morning we enjoyed a few serene hours about the campsite and then headed off to the "Trees of Mystery". This is a unique park attraction located in the heart of the Redwoods near Klamath, California. A bit skeptical of it being the usual "tourist trap", we sauntered across the parking lot past the giant statue of Paul Bunyan and Babe, his trusty ox. It turned out to be quite a nice experience. Once we waded through the huge gift shop, we purchased our tickets and entered the forest. It contained a couple of huge specimens of the Redwoods. One, the Brotherhood Tree reached 297 feet up into the sky and had a circumference of 19 ft. Try to wrap your arms and your head around that. It was twice as tall as the Statue of Liberty and large enough to drive a truck through. It was a massive specimen. The second was the "Cathedral Tree" which consisted of nine trees growing shoulder to shoulder in a circle where they had sprung as saplings, subsisting off of their fallen parent. The site, a small clearing often used for weddings and church services was nestled between the huge tree trunks. Making our way up and down the somewhat strenuous, hilly, trail, we soon came upon the Canopy Trail. Arial, netted suspension bridges hung between platforms high in the trees. It looked amazing and up the steep stairs we climbed. It was beautiful being suspended up in the canopy above the lush foliage below, but also a bit scary. The bridges move and sway as you cross them and I found myself clutching the skinny railings a few times. The views were spectacular and looking way down at the people walking the trails below was exhilarating. After swaying across the various bridges and hanging out at the wooden platforms surrounding the trees for awhile, we approached the spiral staircase to descend. That was the real scary part. As I looked down the steep staircase, I could see the tiny steps dropping further and further down and around the massive trunk and, I'll admit that my legs began to shake a bit. Hanging on for dear life, we eventually made it back to terra firma and safety. It was a great, exhilarating feeling and I thought about constructing my own platform in the woods at home. I loved being up in the forest canopy.

We strode on along the trail and came to the Skytrail gondolas. We passed on that even though it promised spectacular views from the summit out towards the ocean. Our legs were still a bit shaky and we were a bit tired. Wandering down the mountainside towards the exit, we came across beautiful sculptures placed amidst the trees. First we were accosted by a giant mosquito with a six foot proboscis and then crept hurriedly past the menacing eyes of Sasquatch. Giant chain-sawed wooden sculptures lined the trail and led us down to the exit where a large collection of ancient Native American art and artifacts are displayed. It is one of the largest private collections in the world and was quite impressive. Upon exiting, we of course picked up a few items in the surprisingly nice and interesting gift shop and then headed back to camp.

After a tasty dinner of shrimp scampi, we retired with our wine glasses, out beneath the treed canopy overhead. We spent the night watching the crackling embers of the fire lazily float up into the quiet, darkened skies. Nearby, a pair of owls hooted a synchronized good night. This was, by far, the most special visit in our cross country journey. The next day we lounged around camp, taking a few short hikes and a bike ride. I was trying my best to infuse my body with some of the surrounding majesty. At the end of the day we did some yoga and meditation amidst our giant friends and gave them a few hugs good-bye. In the morning we would be off on our jaunt up the Oregon Coast. The Redwoods would not be forgotten.

Lake Tahoe, California

Yosemite Valley, California

California "Mosquito"

Clear Lake, California

Redwood Majesty

CHAPTER 25

FALLING IN LOVE WITH OREGON

The next morning, bright and early we were off on our journey to explore the rugged Oregon Coast. It wasn't long before I shouted to Jo -"Ocian in View! O! The Joy!" She looked at me a bit strangely, not recognizing my favorite quote from William Clark, who, when reaching the mouth of the Columbia River in 1805, uttered the same precious words. I couldn't contain my joy. He had accomplished an unparalleled feat, and though ours was some what lacking in the same magnitude, we had for the first time crossed the continental U.S.A. We had endured blistering heat and frozen sleet, had crossed vast deserts and rivers and had scaled the highest peaks of the Rockies on our trek to the Pacific Ocean. Beautiful sun-glinted waves tumbled along the beaches and swirled around the massive offshore rock formations which stood like giant sentinels guarding the shoreline. We had entered the Samuel Boardman State Scenic Corridor. Situated near Brookings, Oregon, the 12 mile highway features a multitude of picnic areas and viewpoints along Oregon's craggy headlands. We stopped at the Natural Bridges, an area that features several iconic, arched rocks and blow holes scattered along the shoreline. A beautiful trail meandered along the ridgeline beneath ancient Sitka spruce trees, then down to the rocky shores below. The views were fantastic. The thunder of the waves leaping up the stone sea stacks competed with the screeching gulls for our attention while the aquamarine waters glistened in the windows of the arched stones. Wow. Wow. Wow. We were amazed, agog, and blown away. I'm running out of adjectives to describe the beauty of this country. Our senses were temporarily overwhelmed. Compared to the flat sandy beaches of the East Coast, this was like an ongoing celebration of nature's beauty saluted with crescendos of liquid fireworks and dazzling displays of stone, trees, and the pulsing, oceanic waves. Traveling on along the coast, I searched for sun glasses for my eyes and for my sensory receptors as they were both overcome by the brilliance.

We stopped for a late lunch at a quiet beach alongside the highway. It was really strange – THERE WAS NO ONE ON THE BEACH! As opposed to the throngs of visitors along the east coast beaches, this one was deserted. What a great place for a quiet reverie or to walk your dog. I wandered down between the grass-covered dunes that were topped with little yellow wildflowers. The constant wind bent the grass into make-shift artisan brushes etching beautiful pictographs into the gray sands of the dunes. Piles of driftwood outlined the beach and Jo was in her collecting glory. As we rested eating our lunch, fishing boats broached the waves while gulls and terns skipped along the white wave crests. Nice.

After a scenic drive along the coast and through several picturesque small towns we arrived at J. Honeyman Memorial State Park, our new home for a couple of days. It was a nice campground situated at the southern end of the Oregon Dunes National Recreation Area where giant sand dunes wash across the hills and spill down to the coast. After a nice meal we relaxed for the evening and celebrated. We were finally back to electricity and the modern world. We spent the evening watching a movie classic and then reading by real light as opposed to dim lantern light. Since entering Nevada two weeks ago, we had been without hook-ups. No more worrying about battery usage, running the generator or reading by lantern light. We were back in the 21st century!

The next morning after a couple of long, warming showers in the coach, we headed up the highway to Haceta Head Lighthouse. A long climb up the mountainside resulted in spectacular vistas along the coast from the lighthouse grounds. The red and white tower is situated on a craggy mountainside perched along the seaside cliffs and can be seen from 20 miles out to sea. It was an iconic photo op. I scrambled here and there along the cliff-side trail trying to capture the perfect photo of the lighthouse, the craggy shoreline and the glistening waves, armed with my camera. After hiking back down, we headed on toward Cape Perpetua and its beautiful vistas, rocking and rolling up and down the steep mountains along the coast. After a few hours we headed back to the campground.

Following an energy-packed meal of lasagna, we hiked out to the dunes along a campground trail. I thought we would die trekking up the sand-laden hills. Maybe it was the lasagna weighing us down or, god forbid, our old out-of-shape physiques, but it took us about an hour to hike to the top of the small dunes as we sank ankle-deep in the sands. I kept telling Jo that there would be beautiful views from the top as we struggled and rested and struggled our way up the hill. We finally made it to the top and the views - of more sandy dunes. I had expected to see the ocean but we were too far away. We slumped down in the sand in disappointment. I tried to slow my racing heart by breathing in the salty breeze as it coursed over the dunes and through the grasses. We watched dune buggies race along the hills in the distance, spewing great rooster tails of sand. We had discussed taking a ride on one but Jo thought it might be too strenuous for us. After watching them for a bit, I was sorry we didn't try it. I felt like we missed a once-in-a-lifetime opportunity. But I am still here, alive and writing, so maybe it was the best decision.

Going down was a hell of a lot easier and took only 5 minutes. In the parking lot we emptied the gallon of sand out of our shoes and headed back to the campsite beneath the setting sun. A peaceful night was spent beneath the trees and we hit the sack early, hoping to still wake up the next morning after our arduous treks up the mountain and up into the dunes.

The next day we took a peaceful drive up the coast to the Oregon aquarium. Along the way, fog was rolling in off the sea and drifting up into the headlands where a colorful array of autumn-hued shrubs and flowers splashed down the mountain side, peeking out from the white mists. We finally reached the aquarium which housed colorful exhibits of various sea creatures: fish, anemones, jellyfish, crabs, otters and various denizens of the deep. We walked through an underwater tunnel with sharks and rays swimming above and around us. The bird life section was closed which was a shame because I had looked forward to viewing our coastal feathery friends. It was very nice and very interesting. We took a long, slow ride back to the campground, stopping at various viewpoints along the way. Fires were burning to the north so we were not allowed to have a campfire. Following a nice, baked sea-bass dinner, we retired to watch another movie classic for the evening. Our two allotted days were up and we would be moving on again the next morning.

Where to go in Oregon is a really hard decision. It is a big, beautiful, diverse state with dozens of beautiful scenic areas. Not having a month to visit, we had to carefully pick and choose where we wanted to stop. I had really wanted to see the southern coast, and having accomplished that, we now headed inland to Crater Lake.

It was a beautiful, scenic drive along the Umpqua River over hills and through tree-covered canyons. We passed beautiful small waterfalls and rapids as the waters coursed along the hills. We stopped at Toketee Falls along the way. The scenic Falls drop over 100 feet in two stages down into a dark pool along the river. A short trek through the old growth forest leads to a viewing platform high up above the roaring waters. It was quite pretty.

We ventured on to Crater Lake and entered the Park. We began to climb and went up and up and up. What happened to the campground? Bea was struggling as we climbed the steep mountainside. It seems we had entered the wrong end of the park. After quite a while we abruptly entered an open flat meadow and drove up to a scenic pull-off overlooking the nearby mountains peaks. Looking down - there she lay - a magnificent deep blue gem cradled between the pink-hued sides of Mt. Mazama's crater. It was quite unexpected and shockingly beautiful.

Crater Lake is one of the world's deepest freshwater lakes and is fed only by rain water. The depth and clarity of the waters produces an amazing cobalt-blue color not seen anywhere else. In the center of the lake lies Wizard Island, a remnant of its past eruption. The Rim Road encircles the entire crater and provides for breath-taking vistas. At an elevation of 8,000 ft we could see across the mountaintops to the horizon in any direction. We drove around the lake for a bit and then followed the road signs to the Mazama Park campground. It was 7 miles south of Rim Village, down the other side of the mountain.

At this campground, you don't select your site. They assign you one based on the size of your equipment and camping needs. We were not too happy with our small site - it was located next to the bathrooms which had a constant flow of people and even waiting lines to enter the showers. Thankfully, we had electric, and that night we ran the heater as it was now beginning to get cold. The campground was packed and surprisingly, there were a large number of young campers staying in tents. Judging by their accents, most were foreign visitors. I chuckled in the early morning as one of the young men left the freezing shower line to approach me and ask if I had any extra soap. It seems he was a "minimalist" and did not carry any. Trying to "minimalize" my responding laughter at the young man's request, I told him that the pumice ashes and sand he was standing on would probably work better and be more healthful for him. He gave me a sort of wry smile and wandered back to the shower line. Sometimes it's not easy being eco-friendly but I was proud of him. I jumped back into Bea and proceeded to have my hot coffee while pondering if we should also chuck our soap and other amenities and frolic in the outdoors. More power to the youngsters, but I don't think our old bones could handle it.

We took a beautiful hike through the old growth forests down into the nearby canyon. A small, gurgling stream meandered amongst the trees that were tucked in between the steep canyon walls and towering stone pinnacles - a result of the Crater's explosion many eons ago. We followed a thin trail that hung upon the edge of the mountainside as we traversed down the mountain between the huge trees until it reached a small green glade far below. We sat along the streamside in the cool shadows while listening to the birds and the merry murmurings of the flowing waters. It was exceptionally beautiful and probably one of our favorite hikes on the trip. After an early dinner of Steve's famous beef stew we relaxed in bed to read awhile, as it was now quite cold out and precluded any outdoor evening activities.

It was late September and I now had to start booking sites for next year's southwestern trip. There was no cell phone service in the Park and the next day we took an early morning drive 30 miles in either direction of the Park to find some. No success. This park is pretty far out in the boondocks. Returning somewhat disconsolately to the campground, I pondered visions of other campers grabbing up all the nice sights across the southwest as I lay stranded there on Mt. Mazama.

In the afternoon we chugged back up the mountain in 2nd gear until we reached the Rim Village and its scenic viewpoints. It seemed to me that Bea was doing an awful lot of "chugging" lately. My wife loves to collect rocks just like all the other crazy women in the world. Maybe it has something to do with their nesting instinct. I was hoping Jo might be different. Nope. Ever since leaving Nevada, the rock collection was growing and Bea was slowing. We probably had 500 pounds of rocks and boulders crammed under and in various cubby holes, cabinets, and odd spaces. Like a scene from "The Long, Long, Trailer", they clanked and clunked and rolled around our floor. We careened around hairpin turns, seemingly on two wheels, strained to scale the mountain peaks, and roared down to the bottom of the canyons as the weight of the small boulders shifted about. Some were stored underneath and behind Bea in the service and tool spaces. Bea groaned and strained like Sisyphus, only instead of pushing a great rock, she was dragging them along. I tried to address the situation, but backed off after a threat from my crazy copilot. Why couldn't she collect little, tiny gems or diamonds instead of 20 pound rocks? At least I would be amassing an investment instead of stones strewn about the yard that I constantly run over with the lawnmower. Why couldn't she just be happy with the piles of pine cones and driftwood? I secretly ditched a few as we rode along on our travels, but I was losing ground. It seems that my copilot suspected as much and just added to her collection. It was probably costing me a few miles per gallon at $4 a gallon and straining my already tired Bea, but the copilot would not or could not understand my perfectly logical observations. I am the one with, supposedly, no common sense – Ha! But, a happy wife means a happy life. In the end I demurred from further ranting and we rolled along with me chucking out the stones and her adding more. My only hope was that we could make it to the Mississippi River and thereafter just roll downhill all the way back to the east coast.

We roamed about the rim of the Lake for awhile, all the time scanning the waters below in search of the "Old Man of the Lake". According to information obtained at the Visitor's Center, it seems that back in 1896 an explorer discovered a large hemlock floating vertically in the Lake. It has been there ever since, calmly visiting various spots around the lake. The Park service tied it aground one time to study the lake and immediately the weather turned stormy and it began to snow – in August! Had they angered the Gods? After that incident, the Park released the prisoner and it has floated the lake unmolested for over 100 years. No one can figure out why it floats upright and how it propels itself about the lake. It makes for an interesting little side story about the lake, but we had no success in spotting him. We visited a few more vistas and then headed back to the campground. Somewhat disappointingly, we still had not seen much wildlife. On the way to Crater Lake we passed a small meadow with some female elk and stopped to take a few photos, but that was it.

On the way down we noticed the towering snow poles on the side of the road. In winter time, the Crater Lake area can get up to 40 ft. of snow. I was glad we were visiting in September. After Jo's wonderful chicken mushroom casserole, we spent a beautiful evening beneath a million stars visible from our mountainside perch. They twinkled like Christmas lights between the tall scraggly spruce tree limbs and it felt like we were in a giant planetarium. With a late chill in the air, we retired for the evening, burying beneath our warm blankets and enjoying peaceful dreams of craggy lofts and star-studded skies.

The next day we were on the move again heading for Silver Falls, Oregon. After a scenic drive through central Oregon we once again headed west and reached the campground late in the day. Jo made a big pot of chicken soup and we feasted on one of our back-home favorites. The campground was pretty nice and we were allowed to have campfires. We sat out beneath the stars and enjoyed the glowing flames and nighttime quiet. It was Monday so all the families with children and barking dogs had left.

In the morning we hopped on our bikes and headed to the falls. It was close enough so that we did not have to unhook and drive Bea over. The ride over was along a pretty trail wending its way through the spruce forest. We chained the bicycles at a small café along the trail and hiked down to the viewing area. The Falls were beautiful. They plunged 200 ft. into a dark green chasm and the sun was glinting off the spray, creating a beautiful rainbow. A trail, chiseled into the rock, went behind the falls, and offered a unique perspective of standing behind the falling waters and looking down into the large chasm. Huge Sitka spruce towered up and above the trails and enclosed the falls viewing area.

The hike back up was not so beautiful. I thought we were going to die as we climbed the steep trail, resting every once in a while to catch our breadths. I thought we were in shape from the hiking we had been doing, but obviously not enough. As we strained to climb up and up on our rickety joints, the pounding of our beating pulses synchronized to the tune of our wheezing lungs. Upon attaining the upper trail, we flopped into the cool bushes for a bit to recharge our weary limbs – somewhat embarrassed, but needing immediate rest. I thought I was going to die. We had seen only one of the nine waterfalls in the area, but the 8 mile hike to see the rest sounded quite arduous, so we skipped the rest and headed back to camp. After dinner we sat outside and Jo practiced on her guitar while I did a bit of reading. Just as it was getting dark we had a visitor. It seems that our bucolic campsite, with soft music floating in the air, had attracted one of the local fearless denizens of the forest – a skunk! He rustled about the edges of the campfire glow and then made a direct line to the picnic table where we sat. As you can imagine, even though he looked so cute and fluffy, we bolted into Bea and that was the end of our outdoor activities. We had finally seen some wildlife, but not exactly what we were hoping for. We retired to watch one of our favorite movies – "Chocolat". We left the striped intruder wandering outside, alone and friendless.

After checking that the coast was clear, we spent the next day hanging around the campsite. We took a few walks, caught up on Bea's maintenance, and spent most of the day nodding off in our recliners to the sound of the wind sighing through the giant spruce forest.

The next morning we were up and out early and headed for our next destination – Fort Stevens State Park. We enjoyed another delightful cruise along the Oregon coast and stopped at the creamery in Tillamook. The place was huge and packed with tourists. After perusing the hundreds of cheese and available dairy products, we wandered up to the counter to find some help in putting together a couple of gift packages for friends and family back home. Of course in this age of shit service, no help was forthcoming and we were informed that all gift packages had to be purchased online. Well, after insinuating where they could stick their hundreds of cheese varieties, we made our way back to Bea and continued on our trek. My belief in man was faltering, while my belief in nature was growing.

Fort Stevens State Park contains one of the largest campgrounds in the country and sits on a site commemorating a military installation that once guarded the mouth of the Columbia River in the far northwest corner of Oregon. We arrived in the late afternoon and after an early meal, sat outside for a bit and then hit the sack early. The next morning I was drinking my coffee out at the picnic table and heard another rustle in the brush – a big rustle. I nervously stared towards the source of the noise and in a few moments out popped a huge female elk. She wandered by, within a couple feet of the table and continued browsing on the brush alongside our site. It was quite an exhilarating moment. It was also a bit scary, but she kept to her nibbling and minded her own business, and by the end of the day we were quite comfortable with her presence in our site.

In the afternoon we bid leave of our new friend and took a 5 mile bike ride up to the old Fort. It was spread out atop a low hill overlooking the ocean. It is one of the few American places attacked by Germany during the war and was shelled by a German submarine. We toured the various gun emplacements and old fortifications and then sat for awhile eating a snack and watching the distant waves break on the shoreline. The bike ride itself was a beautiful ride through the forest and over small waterways. The trail was lined with wild blackberries and we eagerly feasted on them on our ride back to camp. Everywhere we had gone in Oregon had been loaded with wild blackberries and we hardly took advantage of the succulent treats. Most of the time we looked like little kids with purples stains on our hands and lips. We headed back to camp and saw a few more elk wandering the campground.

On the ride back, we passed quite a few electric bikes. We have been seeing a lot of electric bikes on our rides lately - only in America. I have a great idea – let's get some bikes for exercise and then buy electric ones so we don't have to peddle. I must be missing something....

We settled for some baked cod for dinner even though we had been hoping for a nice salmon dish. All the way up the coast I had been looking for a fish market to buy some nice fresh salmon. Disappointingly, we never did see any. It was the time of year for the salmon runs and I expected every corner we passed would be selling fresh salmon. Nope. We tried the supermarkets and all they had was farmed salmon – I couldn't believe it. We have a better selection of fresh seafood back home.

The next day we were planning on a visit to Ft. Clatsop which was nearby. We stopped in at the Visitor's Center the next day and learned some of the history of the Fort. Fort Clatsop was the winter encampment for Lewis and Clarks' Corps of Discovery in 1806. It is located at the mouth of the Columbia River and served as their final encampment before heading back east. It was named after the local Clatsop Indian Nation. The Corps spent the winter there, resting, gathering salt and hunting for wild game. They eventually abandoned the camp and headed back east, leaving the camp as a gift for the local Indians. The buildings rotted away over the years, but in 2006 state and federal officials reconstructed a replica near the original site. The Park itself had many trails branching out into the surrounding forest but the building was quite under-whelming. A small log building surrounded by log picket walls, it displayed various wooden furniture that would have been used by the original inhabitants. After our 10 minute tour we took a hike down to the river on one of the trails and feasted on some more blackberries while we rested under the shade of some trees. The whole Park only contained a few small displays and the gift shop was bigger than the Fort. We picked up a couple books and trinkets and headed back to the campground. On the way back, we stopped at a supermarket to pick up a few things.

What is with the bread out here? Ever since crossing the Mississippi it seems that the only bread that stores sell out here is made of sourdough. Maybe it's the new "thing", but I think it stinks. It is indeed sour and leaves a bitter taste in your mouth after eating it. Damn, if someone opened up a couple of decent bread stores up and down the west coast they would be millionaires. Where is the rye, pumpernickel, or Italian? Isn't this the age of diversity? I finally quit eating sandwiches on our journey because I couldn't take the sourdough anymore and it was starting to make me feel sick. What do they make their tomato sandwiches on? What do they use for French toast? What about a ham on rye? Sourdough and Kielbasa? I shuddered to think about it. I expected more from the greatest country on earth and pitied our western citizens.

The next morning, after saying good-bye to our huge, hairy visitors, we packed up and headed east to Ainsworth State Park, located within the Columbia River Gorge. It was a pleasant drive until we reached Portland and then we grimly made our way through the large city. One of the natural wonders that I vowed to visit on this trip was Multnomah Falls. I was stressed after reading about the skinny mountainous roads, the hordes of people and traffic jams, and the unavailable parking near the site, but was determined to see the Falls. Trying to forge those obstacles in a 24ft camper seemed impossible and I felt a bit flummoxed. Guess what? A wonderful surprise awaited us. As we were cruising down the highway, I saw a big sign – "Multnomah Falls Parking". My heart leapt. We pulled off and parked in a huge lot and proceeded through a tunnel beneath the road. There she was in all her glory. Spanning two tiers, the Falls plunge 620 feet through the basalt cliffs to a rocky pool below – twice as high as the Statue of Liberty. A beautiful stone bridge arches across the opposing rock cliffs for viewing. It was a breathtaking sight, even though we were surrounded by hordes of people. We stared up, at what looked like a liquid stream of silver plunging from the clouds above while sparkling veils of iridescent mists played about the cliffs. We took dozens of pictures and hiked the nearby trail up towards the top. We looked down upon the gushing waters as they plunged from the top of the cliff down towards the now little people clustered far below. It was an unbelievably beautiful sight rivaling the best on our journey so far. We headed back to Bea and I smiled, happy that we had gotten to see one of the vistas on my bucket list with little trouble and before we even got to our campsite.

The campground was pretty bad. The sites were very skinny, uneven and close, lying along a ridge above the highway and near a railroad track. All night we listened to car traffic and train horns blaring. It was very open and very noisy and pretty disappointing. I had read that this was one of the better campgrounds along the Columbia River Gorge. If so, I would hate to have seen the others. I guess they are somewhat limited in available space down in the narrow gorge.

The next day we took a ride up to the Vista House which provides for beautiful views of the Gorge. There are all kinds of advisories in the area that the trek along the scenic Columbia River Highway was not conducive for RV travel. It is an old, skinny road, built before the era of large campers and tractor trailers and the traffic can be overwhelming. I definitely wanted to see the views from above so I scouted out a shortcut up the mountain from the highway below. I found one and we proceeded - almost straight up to the mountain rim. It was so steep I thought Bea might start rolling backwards or blow a piston. I was scared to slow down, so pedal to the metal, we forged on. Eventually we reached the top and could see the Vista House down the road a bit. We fought our way into a parking spot and were rewarded with a bird's eye view of the Gorge, thousands of feet below as it makes its way 80 miles across the Columbia Plateau. A vast carpet of the mountains, the forest, and the Columbia River rolled out at our feet and the sun glinted off the wind surfer's sails in the Gorge below. We felt like we were soaring with the eagles. Vista House - an apt name for that building that provided for one of the most iconic vistas in our country. Since we were on top of the mountains, we now continued along the highway down to the campground. We stopped at a nearby Laundromat in town before heading home and finally got to wash a couple of weeks of dirty clothes. Back at camp, we heated up some fish sandwiches for dinner and spent the evening watching "Jeremiah Johnson".

In the morning we took a ride to the Bonneville dam. It was a bit scary at first as an armed guard approached us at the gate, clutching his M-16 rifle.

"Carrying any weapons"? He demanded.

I almost crapped my pants. They had us cold – two sixty-plus year old terrorists driving an RV which was filled with explosives, across the country from New Jersey. We got scared and Jo stammered out: "no sir, we were not carrying any weapons". Now my wife Jo is blessed with many fine attributes and abilities, but one thing she can't do is lie with a straight face. When she tries, she gets that look on her face that your pet gets after he has stolen the steak off the kitchen counter. The guard looked at her for maybe a second and then said he would have to look inside. We sat trembling as he opened the side door and took a peek inside. Would we be shot? Would we go to prison? Luckily, our well-hidden armaments were not discovered and we were given the ok to proceed. A trip to the federal penitentiary was not on our travel itinerary. The views of the dam were pretty but the best part was viewing the salmon in the underground fish ladder. Here they are counted, for tracking purposes, and you could watch them fighting their way through the powerful currents. It was very interesting. We took a ride up along the river and stopped for a quick lunch along its banks.

We left and headed up the road to the Cascade Locks Marine Park.

This is the home port of the sternwheeler "Columbia Gorge". The red, white, and blue vessel is a replica of the original paddle boats that once sailed our historic rivers and contained three decks as well as a small, full-service bar. We had been denied our chance at a sternwheeler cruise on the Mississippi, but wouldn't be denied again. We got our tickets and were soon "paddling" the Columbia River with 360 degree views of the Gorge. It was a beautiful, sunny day and we cruised beneath the historic Bridge of the Gods and watched the Native American fisherman netting salmon along the shores. As we travelled further into the Gorge, the boat was surrounded by dozens of the colorful kites used by the wind surfers and the shimmering white sails of the sailboats as they frolicked in the white crested swells. The hills were painted with a mauve colored brush as the sun was setting and we headed back to port. It was such a beautiful day, Jo even sprung for one of those kitschy photos to remember our visit by.

We headed back to camp, and still searching for a fish market, we finally found one. I picked up a beautiful filet of Chinook salmon and planned on having a feast in the near future. Whatever you do, don't waste money relying on your local restaurant hack to serve up your salmon. To prepare it, just give it a rinse, cover with a mixture of honey and mustard, add a bit of sea salt and some parsley flakes and sprinkle some breading and chopped nuts on top and bake for about 20 minutes. Serve it up with a baked potato and asparagus or spinach and a nice glass of wine and you will be a hero. The total cost of the meal was less than $20. Jo says it's the best meal she has ever eaten.

We got back to the campground late. Not having time to prepare my feast, we had a quick meal and watched a movie in the relative quiet of our moveable home. The next day we were pushing off to eastern Oregon and Baker City. Our visit to the Columbia River Gorge was fantastic and we could have easily spent a couple weeks there seeing all the sights and hiking the trails.

We took a somewhat round-about way to Baker City because we wanted to check out the Painted Hills of eastern Oregon. It was a long but scenic cruise through hills covered in sage and windswept grasses. There were very few trees. A few small towns were sprinkled, like an afterthought, along the way, as well as a few cows. It was a nice drive and soon we arrived at the Painted Hills. The road through the hills, which had been quite rugged, only allowed us to park at the overview near the edge of the park. Nothing really exciting here, but the colors were amazing. Red, purple, yellow and mauve striations ran horizontally across the sandy hills as if some crazed painter ran amok about the hillsides. It was beautiful and I was sorry we could not drive down into the Park for a longer, more expansive view. We hiked the area for a bit and then proceeded on to Baker City. We arrived at Unity Creek Campground late in the day after a nine hour trip.

Unity Creek was a beautiful campground with huge sites spread through a pine forest alongside a sizable lake. I love the forests out west. At home if you want to trek through the forests, you better be wearing leather chaps and ankle high boots. The neck high thorns will render your body like a filleted fish and your legs and ankles will be screaming after tripping over roots and the small limbs of the brushy understory. Slopping through the muddy cedar forests, you might find your self sinking in quicksand beneath the dark canopy.

Out here - gorgeous red-barked pines provided a backdrop for the tawny brown grasses glinting in the sun-filled meadows. You can walk through here barefoot. If I tried that at home I wouldn't have any feet left to walk on. I could easily follow the swooping flights of the hawks as they soared through the pines and over the glistening waters of the lake. It was a very secluded area and I had once again hoped to see some wildlife. Nope. I sat for hours in the early mornings quietly scanning the far side of the lake as the mists drifted across the waves and the sun rose into the sky. Nothing. I think I did see a small mouse scampering between the beautiful, blooming sage brush and lichen-covered rocks that covered the meadow, but that was it. Waves of yellow, brown and tan grasses danced to the morning light. If I was a great bull elk I would definitely move here, but none seemed to agree with me. I spent one morning chasing a large Pileated Woodpecker flitting from tree to tree, hoping to get a nice close-up photo. All we have at home are the little guys – the Red-headed and the Downy woodpeckers. We took a much-needed rest in the afternoon and as the sun began to set I practiced a little yoga beneath the swaying pines. My spirit soaked it all up and I felt content.

The next morning we took a ride to Baker City and visited the museum, which had been combined with the Oregon Trail Interpretive

Center. Though not being much of a museum man, I was greatly impressed.

We had originally intended to visit the Oregon Trail Interpretive Center. Through life-size dioramas, living history demonstrations and an amphitheater, the Center tells the story of the original settlers and pioneers that visited many years ago and settled in the area. The Center also offers up magnificent vistas of the Oregon Trail topography and wagon ruts along the interpretive trail system. Alas, our visit was not to be, as the center was closed.

Instead, we disappointingly made our way downtown to the local Baker Heritage Museum. We didn't expect to see much, but were pleasantly surprised. The 33,000 square foot site houses Baker City historical artifacts. Also, since the Interpretive Center was closed for renovations, some of their exhibits and artifacts were moved to the Museum. We spent a very interesting afternoon wandering the rooms of the exhibit. Various historic farm implements, medical equipment, printing press equipment, fire suppression equipment, mining gear and horse shoeing implements were on display. There were various rooms set up to display period pieces and gadgets including a dining room, kitchen, bedroom and living room. It also included a large vintage clothing display, stuffed animals, a huge gem and mineral section and a butterfly collection. As we wandered the lower floors we encountered vintage automobiles and an original covered wagon. I think the display was amazing. They had rooms set up as vintage retail stores including a pharmacy, gold assayer's office, dental office and a laundry. On display from the Interpretive Center are a recreated pioneer camp and Native American art and artifacts, including a teepee! I thought the whole place was exceedingly interesting and we spent the whole afternoon wandering the exhibits and chatting with the resident curators – 3 sweet little old ladies born and raised in the area. It was quite an enjoyable day.

We returned to camp where I finally cooked up our salmon and we enjoyed a superb repast out under the pines. I was going to start a campfire but it began to drizzle a little, so I packed the wood away and we retired to a quiet night of reading. We were soon lulled to sleep by the whispered pitter-patter of the raindrops on our roof.

Our visit to Oregon had ended. We had a fantastic time and were awed by the majestic scenery and friendly people. If I ever felt compelled to leave my native state of New Jersey, I would definitely consider moving here. A fantastically beautiful coastline, rushing rivers and soaring mountains, the high desert, waterfalls, wildlife and supposedly great fishing, all encompassed in this one area of the country. You could live a simple, beautiful life here and experience life the way it is supposed to be experienced. We would miss Oregon.

Oregon Coast

Crater Lake, Oregon

The Painted Hills, Oregon

Silver Falls, Oregon

Haceta Head Lighthouse, Oregon

CHAPTER 26

ROCKS AROUND THE CLOCK

The next morning we packed up and headed for our next destination – The City of Rocks National Reserve in southern Idaho. After a beautiful drive through the rolling, grassy brown hills we arrived at Castle Rock State Park, where we would be camped for a day. We had come in a big circle since leaving Nevada and once again we were parked on a sagebrush covered hill with sweeping vistas of the surrounding high desert. The sites were somewhat small, but the scent of juniper and sage once again reawakened our senses. A fantastic sunset erupted across the skies as we sat with our wine, watching the sun sink behind the Albion Mountains.

After a restful night, we awoke to partly cloudy skies and headed off to explore the Reserve. We stopped at the visitor's center to gather some information and then headed off into the tumbleweeds. An area favored by rock climbers, we passed amidst giant misshapen rocks larger than houses. Huge rock pinnacles, boulders and domes were strewn across the hills as if some ancient giant explosion had spewed forth the remnants of a nearby mountain. Some of the giant boulders contained signatures of the early settlers as they passed through the area. It was very picturesque. After several hours of climbing about the huge monoliths, we headed back to camp, exhausted by our outing. Following a peaceful evening, we hit the sack early knowing that the next day we would be on the move again – to Flaming Gorge National Recreation Area.

The 200,000 acre recreation area is located in the High Uinta Wilderness of northeastern Utah and stretches all the way into southern Wyoming. The namesake Reservoir stretches for 90 miles, cradled by steep red-walled canyons. We didn't have time to partake in any boating, fishing, or other aquatic activities, so we opted for the views. The remote area shuts down around the end of September and was very peaceful and quiet. I could not even reserve a campsite at this late date and I hesitatingly headed up the steep mountains toward Canyon Rim Campground wondering if we would find a site. Up until now most of the campgrounds we visited had been more or less packed with campers. Would this one be any different? No problem. Everything was deserted. The Visitor Center was closed. In the approaching darkness we searched for our site amongst the trees. It was a beautiful, spacious site in a small meadow sprinkled with pines. It was pretty cold, so we turned in early for the night and huddled under the blankets. There were no hook-ups and I didn't want to ruin the effect of this beautiful, woodsy site by running the generator. We were really out in "Gebip" and once again we drifted off to sleep with an evening lullaby provided by the local coyotes. Where is "Gebip"? It is so far out there that no one even knows it exists. That's where we were. It was beautiful, deserted, and totally "ours" to enjoy.

I jumped out of Bea in the crisp morning air and walked to the kiosk located at the entrance to the campground. A sign stated "Please place your campground fee in the accompanying envelopes". There were no envelopes. The Visitor Center was also closed. We hadn't seen a park ranger since yesterday afternoon, 50 miles south of our current position. I therefore affably accepted this small gift from God and headed back to Bea to tell Jo that we had finally beaten the system and saved $15 dollars to boot. We decided to take in the views from the canyon rim as the sun slowly warmed the meadow. We put on our hiking boots and headed to the rim. It was only 100 yards away! What a view! Crystalline blue waters, thousands of feet below, snaked between the steep canyon walls. The canyon sides plunged vertically in a riot of stones and trees. For a moment, my legs became wobbly as I stood at the cliff edge peering down from the dizzying heights. No ropes, no guardrails, we stood face to face with Nature in all her resplendent glory. Giant slabs of sandstone projected out above the abyss below. The winds swirled about, threatening to lift us like kites, to soar up above the great expanse. It was absolutely breathtaking – and only a few yards to the camper. It was totally quiet and all I could hear was the moan of the wind and a screech from a soaring hawk far down below in the canyon.

I hiked back around the meadow hoping to spy an early morning elk or big-horn sheep, but nothing was stirring. Up until now the wildlife extravaganza that I had hoped to see on our journey had not materialized. We spent the afternoon hiking back and forth to the canyon rim and relaxing at our campsite. All you could hear was the wind swirling the grasses and an occasional chirping bird. It was one of the quietest, most beautiful spots on our journey – and we got it for FREE! It might have been free but the ambiance was PRICELESS. Now I began to understand why some campers loved to boon-dock. It was something to consider for our future journeys.

A cold night and brilliant star-studded skies cloaked our peaceful slumbers that night.

We awoke to a frigid morning and ran the heater for a bit while we packed up Bea for our next jaunt. We were headed to Curt Gowdy State Park in eastern Wyoming.

Our stay at the Park was only a stopover for the night. It was a large Park, situated on the endless, rolling, sage-covered hills that we were now becoming used to. Parked on a prominent hill overlooking a small lake, we had a large, quiet site, festooned with small wildflowers and cacti, and shaded with one singular pine tree. We had a quick meal and I wandered down to the lake beneath the threatening, dark skies of an approaching storm. As the sun was setting, its rays reflected off of the dark black clouds in an extravaganza of yellows and reds that ended with an explosion of thunder as the storm passed over. A final salute as we headed east to South Dakota and the Badlands.

View from Castle Rock State Park Campground, Idaho

"Uncovered" Wagon at City of Rocks National Reserve, Idaho

Flaming Gorge Reservoir, Utah

CHAPTER 27

SOUTH DAKOTA
& THE BADLANDS

South Dakota is another state that, like Oregon, presents one with a myriad selection of places to go and visit. We had decided on visiting the Black Hills. On our long-ago trip out west, referenced in an earlier chapter, we had passed through this area but only stopped at Mt. Rushmore, before heading west to Devil's Tower. Since then I had read very positive commentary regarding the area and we wanted to see what we had missed the first time. We had booked a site at Stockade South campground in Custer State Park.

The ride from Curt Gowdy State Park was very picturesque and remote. Endless miles of rhythmic, rolling hills tinged with heather and the brown hues of autumn. Occasional herds of cows, scattered on the hills, were, for the most part, the only living things that we saw. My mind drifted off again, picturing the cowboys and settlers of years gone by. At one point we had to stop and wait while cowpokes drove a herd of cows down the road a bit. We were surrounded by a sea of bovines marching to the call of the cattlemen. Real, weathered men sat astride their steeds in their leather chaps, twirling their lariats and shouting commands as the dust billowed beneath the blazing sun. Out of nowhere, one particularly fetching young cowgirl trotted past my window and shot me a smile that almost melted the glass. As the silhouette of her form and the dark tresses flowing out from beneath her Stetson receded in my side view, I was almost tempted to jump out and "head for the hills". My mind began to wander again. I could see myself riding across the windswept plains with my gal: protecting her from the savage "injuns" and cattle rustlers, shooting rattlesnakes and sharing our grub and chatting around our lonely, glowing campfires. My reverie was once again broken by a sharp jab in the shoulder.

"Let's go. What are you waiting for?" inquired my copilot.

It seems the procession had passed and we were sitting in the middle of an empty road. I gave it the gas and on we rolled over the hills, my dreams fading in the windblown dust.

We arrived in the Black Hills as the sun was fading. Beautiful lakes lay scattered like jewels amidst the now forested, rocky hills. The campground itself was small and our nice quiet site backed up to a rock-strewn ridge that bisected the sites. A couple of pretty cabins rested up on the hill above us. We unpacked and enjoyed a peaceful night beneath the pines. I had planned a full itinerary for the next few days – taking a trip to the historic town of Lead, visiting Mt. Rushmore, the National Grasslands Visitor Center, and touring the Badlands with a quick trip to Wall Drug, that famous retail outlet of the Midwest. We also looked forward to cruising the Scenic Byway Loop which winds its way around the Hills, supposedly loaded with wildlife, and amidst which, we were now comfortably ensconced.

The next morning, after a late start, we headed off to the Badlands. It was quite a distance away from the campground, so we didn't arrive at our objective until early afternoon. Our first stop was going to be a visit to the National Grasslands Visitor Center, which was nearby, but it was closed. We proceeded on to the Badlands, which at first sight was a huge open plain populated by a few lone bison and hundreds of prairie dogs. We had never seen the furry little buggers before, so I jumped out of Bea and spent quite some time trying to chase them down and get a few good photos. As you approached the burrows, they would dive down inside, leaving you rushing to the next burrow to try and get a good shot, etc. etc. It was like playing "Whack-a-Mole" on the prairie. After a mostly fruitless pursuit, I gave up and headed back to Bea surrounded by chattering jeers and laughter – some from the prairie dogs and some from my fellow tourists.

On we proceeded, farther onto the plains. The Loop through the

Badlands extends for 30 miles and after a long drive through the native grasslands we approached the first of many colorful rock formations. Depending on the time of day you visit, the colorful striations offer up a palette of hues of white, grey, brown and pink. We curved and climbed our way between mounds, pinnacles, buttes and spires. It was other-worldly. We passed from one set of rock formations to the next on flat grasslands edged with eroded swells. There are 14 overlooks scattered about the Park and many trails to hike. It was very picturesque but also getting late in the afternoon, so we skipped any hikes.

We drove down the road and came to a private roadside attraction featuring an old settler's homestead built into the side of a hill. We stopped for a bit and it was an interesting stroll. The weathered old building contained old artifacts and implements of by-gone days. The inside walls of the shanty only rose about waist high. The rest of the wall was just dirt, carved from the hillside. A small bedroom was punched out of the back of the main room, deep into the hillside where there was no light. I could imagine sleeping in that totally black space at night, shivering in the cold and waiting for the bugs to crawl on my body. The sod roof draped over the rotted timbers. The occasional drip of water raised little dust puffs from the earthen floor. What those poor people must have endured in their struggles to settle the land.

I shivered and walked out into the bright light. We were once again in a little prairie dog town but since this one was privately owned, the cute, little buggers actually posed at their burrow entrances and allowed plenty of time for photos. They must have been on the payroll. We toured the old farm building and various implements and headed back to Bea. After a short ride, we popped out the other end of the Loop road and headed to Wall Drug.

Wall Drug is an internationally renowned cowboy-themed retail mall situated off highway 90, east of the Black Hills. It was in "the middle of nowhere" and purchased by Ted Hustead in 1931, who hoped to establish a successful business in the small town. Things were not going so great until his wife came up with the idea of offering free ice water to the thirsty tourists passing by. Things soon began to boom and through additional creative marketing the original business has now grown into a huge mall featuring retail stores, galleries, a restaurant and an amusement park. Were we impressed? Not so much. One of my favorite authors, Bill Bryson, has stated "it is an awful place, one of the world's worst tourist traps". I agreed. It was a monument to retail vulgarity and in-your-face crass commercialism. Of course he also finished the quote by saying "but I loved it and won't have a word said against it". I therefore will hold off any further criticism in honor of Mr. Bryson, but suffice it to say that we didn't drive three quarters of the way around the country to see some kitschy stores. In one of the stores, the cashier literally tried to rip us off for $20, but my sharp-eyed co-pilot caught the error on the sales receipt and we were eventually reimbursed after a long argument. On we sailed across the ocean desert, out from beneath the giant dinosaur sculpture, and towards our encampment. We needed a breath of fresh air.

The sun was starting to set when we arrived back at the Park, but I cajoled my wife into taking a quick ride around the Wildlife Loop "before dinner" to see some "wildlife". Well, as usual on this trip, it was not to be. We saw nothing. Bea putted up and down the hills as we searched. I sat atop the grassy knolls scanning the hills with my binoculars. We still saw nothing. We sat and waited and searched until the sun went down. Realizing we were once again defeated in the quest for wildlife, we jumped into Bea and headed home in the dark, rushing to get out of the hills and back to dinner. I took a wrong turn somewhere and we proceeded up some skinny, little, curved strip of tar with hair pin turns and huge hills rising into the dark mountains. After squeaking beneath a low bridge, we came to a warning sign advising RV's to turn back. Cursing and swearing, I managed to turn Bea around in the dark and headed back from where we had come, suppressing my pangs of hunger, fearful of never finding our way back, and even more fearful of getting a slap on the head from my co-pilot who was now fidgeting, mumbling and showing signs of severe distress from lack of food. Eventually, about 3 hours after we started the 18 mile loop we stumbled on to the back entrance to our campground and thankfully retreated to our site. It was now 8:30 at night and by mutual agreement, too late to eat anything much. It had been a long day. We were exhausted and grabbed a quick bite to eat before falling into bed. Our gastric clocks were once again askew.

We drove into Custer City the next morning. It was actually a very nice town, not crowded with hordes of people, and had some nice small shops. We picked up a few things, grabbed an ice cream cone and walked the few city blocks. I paused in front of the local barbershop for a moment, but continued on, fearful that some young novice might be trying to master his skills on some unsuspecting tourist.

I told Jo I didn't want to ruin my "Clampett" image. My hair was now down to my shoulders as I had not gotten a haircut for 2 months. The clothing supply was running low because we had not seen a Laundromat recently and I strolled around in sweatpants, an old shirt and hiking boots. I had originally brought 3 pairs of shoes on my trip. Two of them literally fell apart during the first couple weeks and all I was left with were hiking boots and flip-flops, the latter being more comfortable but not suited to the 40 degree temperatures we were now experiencing. My glasses rested askew upon my nose as I had stepped on them a few weeks prior and the stubble on my face looked like an ad for a barbed-wire company. I thought that by looking like bums and crazy people, it would keep us from getting robbed or harassed by the local street vendors or wild mountaineers. Bea also played the part. She was by now covered in grime and you could not see into her dust laden windows. A missing hubcap, the dent in the back from me hitting a rock somewhere in our travels, and the little branches hanging off of the water spouts completed the "hillbilly" look. Of course my co-pilot still insisted on looking prim and proper and tried to distance herself from me on our occasional public outings. She didn't quite "get" my line of reasoning, and only responded with a long sigh and that far-off look in her eyes that seemed to suggest she could have done better in the husband selection department.

We headed back towards camp once again planning to tackle the Wildlife Loop, but this time in the daylight. We slowly cruised about the Loop, scanning the hills for wildlife. This time was a success. Far off in the distance I spotted a big brown thing. I presumed it was a Bison, but being so far away I could hardly tell. An hour later we came upon another and this one was only a few hundred feet away. His thick dark matted hair let off puffs of dust as he trudged through the shimmering grasses beneath the blazing sun. He was a big boy and I restrained from getting too close, fearful of getting crushed by a charging onslaught. I took quite a few photos, scared that he might be the only bison we saw. It was indeed worth the effort as we in fact saw no more on our journey.

But we did see some more animals. Rounding a bend later in the day, we came upon a cute quartet of donkeys wandering the roadside. They quickly charged towards us expecting some handouts, but alas we had none to offer. After braying their dismay, off they wandered into the nearby brush, nibbling the leaves as they went. I didn't know if I could consider the donkeys as "wild animals", but since recent pickings were slim, I jumped out and shot a few photos. Off we ventured into the hills again. This time we were slowly cruising along a large grassy meadow and spotted some movement further up the road. A family of antelope now graced us with their presence. I pulled along the roadside and got a few great photos. The sun was now sinking in the distance and I managed to capture a few last images of the antlered male silhouetted by the setting sun, his family trotting along behind him atop the glistening ridge. It would be a very nice remembrance of our visit.

We headed back to camp as the sunlight waned. We passed through a couple more prairie dog towns in the gathering darkness but did not stop. Like riotous punks in a small town, they whistled and jeered at us as we passed, knowing we could not get any photos in the encroaching darkness. We soon arrived at camp, had a hot meal of Chicken Paprikash and settled in for the evening with a movie. A beautiful day, but it was about to come to an abrupt end.

I awoke in the middle of the night to visit the "loo" and then pressed the flush pedal. Nothing happened. What the hell? I went to the sink – couple of gurgles and nothing. It dawned on me at 3:00 in the morning that we had no water. Something must be up with the pump as I couldn't hear it working. I grumpily gathered some jugs and headed down the road to the water spigot. I was freezing to death, having only grabbed a light shirt and slippers. Of course I forgot the flashlight and in the pitch blackness managed to douse myself with gallons of water before filling the jugs. Fearing attack from a mountain lion or a bear, I hurried back to Bea and climbed under the warm covers. The next morning I awoke, grimly preparing for the task at hand, while I used bottled water to make the coffee. The water still would not come on and the pump was not running. My highly mechanical mind swept into action – I checked the switch, the breaker, and looked for any loose wires on the pump.

Everything seemed fine and I was stumped.

Today was to be our last day at Custer State Park. I had planned a drive up to visit the historic town of Lead and had hoped to possibly make it to Mt. Rushmore by the end the day. Obviously my plans were now all down the drain as I surfed the internet looking for a mobile RV mechanic. I found four. The first 3 calls resulted in messages to the effect that they had ended the season and retired down south for the winter. Oh God. The last call was a success. The individual was packing to go down south but was here for 2 more days. I pleaded my case and he agreed to come out to the site.

An hour later he showed up. After checking things out, he discovered that the converter was not working and the batteries were dead. After a few more checks it was determined that we needed a new converter. Scouting around the area he managed to find one that fit and left to procure it. I was left with instructions to clean up the battery posts and connections which were looking a bit corroded. The converter must have quit the previous day. All night long the batteries were running down and now they were basically drained. After a while he returned, the converter was replaced and all was well with the world. Of course I almost choked to death on the $700 bill. I don't mind paying $100/hr for technical wizardry, but $100/hr for travel? It took a total of about 1/2 hr to replace the part. The rest was travel time. He only accepted cash. After some wrangling I convinced him to take a $200 check and $500 in cash and off he went. After putting a big hole in my cash stash, I convinced myself that shit happens, it was still a beautiful day and life goes on. My travel plans for the day had been thwarted, but we could still hang out and relax.

"Wait Mr. Glass half-empty, that's not how it is supposed to work". Well, you're quite right Mr. Observant Reader, and, as usual, my philosophy on life proved true once again. After a couple of hours the water stopped flowing. I checked the batteries again, but this time they were fully charged. I decided it must be a pump problem. Staring somewhat incoherently at this new technological marvel hanging beneath the bedroom, I peered intently at it with my flashlight. The wires were attached and nothing seemed to be leaking. It looked ok to me but the usual purring sound was not heard. After a bit of swearing and a couple raps with a rubber mallet which usually works at home, discussions were had with the co-pilot and the decision was made to call back my high-priced friend. The next morning we were supposed to leave and we didn't want to risk having to cross half the country without a water supply. As the sun was setting, he pulled into our site again. Now working by flashlight, it was determined the pump had died and we would need a new pump. Once again he called around and left to retrieve us a new water pump. In the meantime we gulped down a quick dinner and waited for him to return. Upon returning, he changed out the old water pump and proceeded to exclaim - "I've never seen anything like this before. The housing has completely separated and water was leaking out. The pump probably burnt out".

After another $300, off he went into the dark night. This time with a check, as my cash situation was now getting a bit precarious. Of course the delightful idea popped into my head that maybe I had been scammed. I never could really see what he was doing, crowded into the small storage spaces and working in the dark. Maybe it was just a hard-to-believe coincidence. Being a mechanical idiot, I couldn't tell. All I know is that at the end of the day, I was out $1,000 and he was on his way south with half of his vacation paid for, compliments of my naivety. At least everything was now working. I put the supposed "broken" parts, which I had requested to keep, into the storage bay, vowing to have them checked out by my reliable mechanic back home. We plopped into bed, dirty, cold, and broke - so ended our visit to the Black Hills and Custer State Park. There were many interesting and beautiful sites to visit and we had a grand time. We didn't quite accomplish the planned itinerary, but suffice it to say we enjoyed our time there immensely. That was it for most of the grand sites on our journey, and early the next morning we headed east, towards home.

Our first stop was at Northpoint Campground. The campground is located in the southeastern area of South Dakota, along the banks of the Missouri River. After driving about 200 miles through the rolling plains, we drove another 200 miles through the cornfields of the Midwest. Once more we were out in the middle of nowhere. Finally, after bumping down a rutted 10 mile dirt road we entered the campground. It was very large, almost deserted and right on the water. I backed into where we could hear the mnemonic lapping of the waves on the shore and we set up camp for the evening. I could see the campfires of our only neighbors, glimmering far away, at the other end of the campground. It was totally dark and quiet and I was starting to feel a bit unsettled.

Coming into the campground we had passed a large trailer park tucked up into the neighboring woods. Why would anyone live out here? The nearest place of employment or grocery store was at least 30 miles away. Judging by the condition of some of the trailers, I would guess that most of its inhabitants were unemployed. Had we stumbled on some secret sect living out in the middle of nowhere? What did they subsist on? Maybe it was the flesh of unsuspecting travelers? Maybe they pillaged and burned their victim's campers and then feasted on their bodies in all-night orgy of grotesquely evil horror (with a side of corn). The night was cold and black and totally silent, except for the lapping of the waves. My mind was running rampant again and an eerie tingling sensation crept up my body. I vowed to protect my love, and my belongings, and perched myself outside of Bea with a large butcher knife in my hand. At one point I thought I heard muffled voices down along the river bank. I flitted about the shadowed trees, ears straining for any perceptible sound. Thankfully no one approached to ask questions or to chit-chat or I would have hacked them into little pieces. I was stressing and tense. Of course no one can stay in a state like that for long, so after a few hours I retired to the camper, exhausted and bleary-eyed, ceding our lives to our good Lord above. Jo just shook her head in dismay, vowing to get me some psychiatric help when we got home.

I awoke the next morning to a beautiful sunrise glowing on the hills across the river. Fog was creeping across the waters and a couple of large "vee's" of geese were honking and passing overhead. I took a few photos while noticing a few small fishing boats gliding through the mists on the water. Maybe they were responsible for the voices I thought I heard the prior night. I put on the coffee and started packing up Bea. I also noticed a young couple walking hand-in-hand atop the hill, near the boat landing. Maybe we weren't parked in some satanic hell-hole back in the cornfields of South Dakota. I awakened Jo and described my horrific concerns of the previous night. She chuckled and stated something to the effect that if I was approached in the dark of the night, I probably would either have had a heart attack or plunged screaming into the endless surrounding fields, leaving her defenseless. I didn't quite understand her somewhat snide minimalization of my heroic efforts, but concluded that she was just an unknowing, innocent rube. She didn't quite understand the perils of everyday life, but thankfully God had placed me at her side to protect and take care of her. She's a lucky girl.

Hoping to see some of the kitsch of Americana, we had decided to take a drive for the day to Mitchell to see the Corn Palace. Now, in case you haven't heard of this place, the Corn Palace is a large arena-type structure decorated with murals and art work consisting of corn and various grains. The designs are changed every year and are supposedly, quite beautiful. The Arena hosts various festivals and activities showcasing South Dakota heritage. After a long drive we arrived at our destination. It was indeed beautiful and we wandered around taking a few photos. Then we went to the front door to check out the inside of the building. It was national Indian day or something and the arena was closed. Once again, are you kidding me? They close one day a year to honor the local Indian tribes and that is the day we had picked to visit. My timing on this trip had been a little off. After wandering about, somewhat morosely, we headed off in Bea to find somewhere interesting to stop on our way back to camp. We decided on the nearby Lakota Indian Museum.

Guess what? Their museum was open. They must have actually wanted to share a part of their heritage with their visitors on National Indian Day. The grounds outside were decorated with a large teepee, medicine wheel and water fountain. The exhibits were beautiful and housed many historic artifacts and artwork. Original beadwork, carvings, and dress were displayed along with gems, paintings, tapestries and bowls. Dioramas depicting Indian culture were also stationed about the museum. We wandered about until I eventually made the mistake of asking one of the curators about the history of the Akta Lakota. In response I was rewarded with a one hour dissertation describing the various sub-tribes of the Lakota, their history and culture.

The Lakota were a sub-culture of the Sioux tribes. They mostly inhabited the Great Plains after being pushed south and west, a result of skirmishes with the northern native tribes. Some of the more well-known

Lakota were "Crazy Horse", "Black Elk", "Red Cloud" and "Sitting Bull". In the early 1800's the tribe was estimated to consist of approximately 8,000 natives and their culture depended mostly on the buffalo. They eventually settled in the Black Hills area after battling the local tribes. They considered the area sacred and were not very friendly when encountering settlers crossing their land. They were constantly having small skirmishes with the U.S. government until a treaty was signed granting them sovereignty over their lands in exchange for allowing for safe passage through the Hills for the settlers "as long as the river flows and the eagle flies". Well, we know how treaties worked out and after the gold rush of 1872 settlers and miners once again started settling in the area. Of course this really pissed off Sitting Bull and Crazy Horse and skirmishes once again broke out between the Indians and the settlers. The government then ordered the Indians onto reservations. The Indians resisted and eventually 10,000 settled into an area known as the "Greasy Grass". Of course they probably called it that because you can imagine thousands of families camped in a small area with no indoor plumbing. Reinforcing the "Peter Principle" theory, Lieutenant Colonel George Custer, a graduate of West Point who was promoted to the level of not knowing what the hell he was doing, decided to attack the Indians and forcibly remove them with a force of 200 men. Well, following the principle of "200 men can't defeat 10,000 men in a battle" theory, Custer and his battalion were wiped out. The U.S. Government would not give up and eventually defeated the Lakota and confined them to reservations after the battle at Standing Rock and the Wounded Knee Massacre put an end to the fighting. It was a very interesting, if somewhat sorrowful story. By now, after walking all day around Mitchell and the museum, my legs were aching and we edged our way toward the exit, despite the curator's best efforts to keep us enthralled. I picked up a book and Jo picked up a few remembrances and off we went, back to camp. After a quiet dinner, I once again hopped outside and patrolled our dark, eerie campsite. I eventually retired to a fitful sleep, dreaming of Indian raids, scalping and war parties.

Pronghorn Antelope, Custer State Park, South Dakota

Settler's Cabin, Badlands National Park, South Dakota

Badlands National Park, South Dakota

Custer State Park, South Dakota

CHAPTER 28

HOMEWARD BOUND

The next morning, off we roared, headed to Prairie Flower Campground in Iowa. All day long we passed through endless cornfields as far as the eye could see with huge combines and tractors making their long sweeps through the brown stalks. Dust was billowing and blowing across the highway and the wind shrieked. I was getting scared that the wind might even overturn us as we cruised upon the endless ribbon of tar. I fought the wind all day, and as we finally approached the campground, my arms and my back ached terribly. Our beautiful, lakefront site was in the open but we gladly soaked up any of the warming sunlight. The day had been quite chilly. This place was packed as opposed to the previous night's lonely remoteness. An endless parade of retirees strolled past our site, creeping out like zombies from their Class A's as the light waned. I feared that our peaceful sojourn was coming to an end.

I was right. After a peaceful night I was awakened by a huge crash and screeching as the local trash truck emptied the contents of the container near our site. As I sat sipping my coffee, hordes of mowers descended from the hilltop and roared about our Bea – shattering any of our hopes for peace and quiet and a sign for us to get going.

We drove off from the offending noise, seeking peace at our next site in Illinois.

Moraine View Campground was quite pretty. After another 300 miles of cornfields, we were finally approaching some forests and were rewarded with the colors of an approaching autumn. Brilliant white birches flashed amidst the pines and the maples were sprinkled with bright yellow and orange foliage. Like usual, I had picked the best site in the campground and basked in the glowing compliments proffered up by my co-pilot. Snuggled up under the colorful canopy, our site lay along the waters edge and no other campers were near us. I wandered about gathering up some firewood from the nearby fallen trees and longingly watched the bass boats ply the calm waters of the shimmering green lake. Once I again I cursed my stupidity for not bringing along my kayak.

The next morning I tried a few half-hearted casts from the bank, but to no result. I did scare up a brown weasel and he scared the shit out of me as he raced passed and vanished into the dark shadows of the woods. That was my exciting moment for the day and the rest of my time was spent relaxing and reading at the site. It was a sunny, but chilly day and the encroaching cold spell impelled us to think about heading home fast. That night the temperature fell to 32 degrees and we were flirting with frozen water tanks and possible disaster.

The next day, bright and early, we headed off to Deer Creek Campground in Ohio. We drove all day through eastern Iowa, across Illinois and into western Ohio. The drive consisted of mostly more fields and scattered woods. Arriving late in the day to our lakeside campsite, I shimmied our way between the neighboring campers and into our tight spot. The campground was jammed and the "lake" was a tiny little pond with a small dock, upon which, the little kids from the campground sat and fished for bluegills. It looked like a Norman Rockwell painting and for a moment brought back distant memories. It was now cold and we spent the evening watching a movie before turning in for the night. The following day we were headed to our last stop before home – Cowan's Gap State Park in western Pennsylvania.

Home. Like the pull from an outgoing tide on the shore, the desire to get home was getting stronger and stronger. I missed fishing in the small lakes with my kayak, hiking through the Pine Barrens, and, though I hate to admit it, the friendly faces of my family and the neighbors. At home, there would be no more worrying about breaking down on the road, getting assaulted or running out of cash.

Those were my thoughts as we sped over the mountains of eastern Ohio and western Pennsylvania. One minor incident marred the whole day. After driving for 7 hours, we pulled in tired and weary from our travels, for some gas. I ran in to buy some cigarettes and the middle aged women asked me for an I.D. Even though I do sport a somewhat youthful look and physique, unless the woman was blind I find it hard to believe that she thought I might be under 18 years of age. Well, after our long arduous trek and hours behind the wheel, before I could stop myself I exploded with: ARE YOU SOME KIND OF FUCKING IDIOT?" She stared at me in stupefied wonder and then retorted "NO SIR, I AM NOT A FUCKING IDIOT". I Stalked out of the building, steam coming off my head, as I once again cursed the stupidity of government. It was not her fault, she was only following instructions. I felt sorry and shameful and driving to the campground I prayed that the Lord would forgive my stupid outburst.

After driving up and down the steep hills for about 10 miles, we arrived at the campground. It was very nice, sprawling across the face of the mountain, with large, wooded sites. By now the leaves were in full, blazing color and shimmering red and orange leaves drifted down upon us as we set up camp. After a quick dinner of home-made stew, we sat out at the campfire amidst the encroaching darkness. We soon heard the laughter and screams of approaching groups of children as their flashlight beams lit the surrounding trees. Being somewhat off of a time schedule, we had forgotten it was Halloween. We were immediately in a panic as we had no treats to offer. I suggested we fill their bags with some of the hundreds of stones we were carrying. That didn't go over too well with the co-pilot. I then considered donating quarters to the little beggars, but we did not have the 100's required and pennies seemed a tad cheap. Up until now we had made it mostly intact and I feared hordes of children in the black of night ravaging our poor Bea, after they realized it was us who threw the pennies in their sacks. We were embarrassed since we had nothing to offer and we surreptitiously slid behind Bea as the children passed by. We felt terrible and hid in shame. After awhile, the throngs petered out and silence reigned again. We edged back to the fire and enjoyed our last night camping, listening to the hiss and crackle of the logs.

The next morning, bright and early, we headed for home. We rolled up and down the hills, Bea no longer "chugging" but bounding towards home and the distant Jersey Shore.

We crossed the Delaware Memorial Bridge and entered the flat lands and small farming communities of Southern New Jersey. The trees were exploding in color as if to salute our return. An autumnal fireworks display. We had made it home.

EPILOGUE

On our journeys, we had watched the sun slowly sink into the Pacific from our perch on the craggy hills of Haceta Head Lighthouse and had watched its glorious rise along the thunderous coast of Maine. We had hiked and biked and climbed and were renewed and our steps a bit lighter. The memories will be forever etched into our minds and our spirits were now reinvigorated from the overwhelming beauty of this great land. In our long trek, we had crossed rivers and deserts, climbed steep mountains and plunged into deep canyons. We had experienced rain, thunderstorms, hail, cold and blistering heat. As we struggled up the steps dragging our belongings behind us we couldn't help grinning at each other. We made it!

That night as I sank into the welcoming cushions of my couch, I was reading a book and sipping on a hot cup of tea. It was the one I had purchased on our travels detailing the hardships and adversity that the early settlers endured on their trek along the Oregon Trail. It struck a chord in my heart. A restless spirit cannot be stilled until it finds what it is seeking, or it will die.

Jo and I had struggled to overcome our own adversity. We had managed to heal our bodies and our minds, but something was missing. Our spirits also would not be stilled.

We sought a sense of solace and decided we would travel the country in hopes of finding it.

Did we find the solace that we were seeking? Yes we did:

Beneath the great canopies of the giant Redwoods

On the quiet, sage-covered hills of the High Desert.

In the wild-flowered meadows of the Rockies.

On the windswept coast of Maine

But solace is not only to be found in the magnificent National Parks. You can also feel it in the wind that caresses the boughs of the pines, you can see it in the twinkling of the stars and you can hear it in the chuckling waters of a mountain stream. It is all around us. It is found in the rhythms of nature. We must all find a connection to that rhythm if we hope to do more than just survive in this life.

Could we have embraced these rhythms at home? Possibly, but the myriad distractions of everyday life make it almost impossible. Sometimes you cannot gain fulfillment only by looking within or about you. You must seek it out and grab it. After 10's of thousands of miles, we had found it and we were finally at peace and our spirits were stilled. The feeling of calm and solace that we were able to experience might only last for a moment in our lives, but it felt good.

Upon our return, I felt as one with the birds that greeted me every morning and the trees that shaded my yard. We had managed to tap into that constant flow that emanates from the natural order of life and it cleansed our spirits like a giant breath of fresh air. For a short period of time we were able to throw off the shackles that bind us to the modern world. No longer surrounded by the stifling, depressing pallor of everyday life in the modern world and the bullshit and banality that we are normally faced with, we had experienced true peace and joy and wonder.

Now we are like addicts. We will continue to seek a greater and greater high and we will not be denied by the pressing weight of societal norms. The peace and serenity invigorated our spirits and once again made life worth living. We were enjoying life and that's what it's all about.

So yes, our journeys will continue. As I sit here writing this, I can already feel the strong, salty breezes from atop the Acadian highlands and can smell the flowered fragrances of the Cascadian meadows. More adventures are being planned:

American Southwest – currently in the planning stage, we will be visiting Oklahoma, Utah, Arizona, New Mexico, and Texas.

Northwest Passage – following our American Southwest trip, we will be training our sights on the northwestern parts of the country including but not limited to Wyoming, Idaho, Montana, Washington State, Vancouver Island, and North Dakota with planned stops in Yellowstone, the Olympic Rainforest, the Cascades, Glacier National Park and Theodore Roosevelt National Park.

Also in the preliminary planning stages are journeys to Nova Scotia and New Brunswick and a final trip down to the Deep South to explore

Georgia, Florida and Louisiana.

Life is too short. We still have a lot of places to visit. Let's have some fun together. We welcome you to join us on our future journeys and I hope you enjoyed my book. Stay tuned for part 2 and our continuing search for solace.

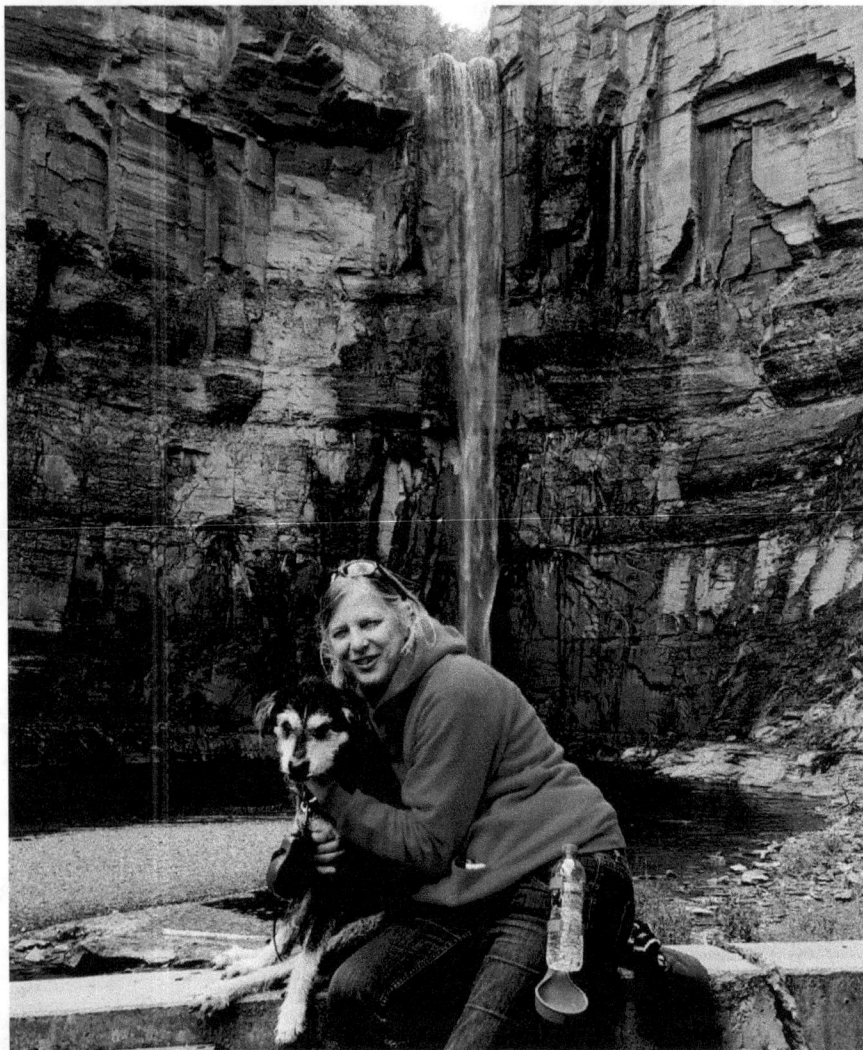

"My Girls"

APPENDIX A - TRIPS REVIEWED

Approximate total cost $15,000
(gas, campsite fees and entrance fees)

Approximate number of miles travelled 22,346

Approximate number of nights camped 160

States camped in:

California	Massachusetts	Pennsylvania
Colorado	Michigan	South Carolina
Delaware	Minnesota	South Dakota
Georgia	Missouri	Utah
Idaho	Nebraska	Vermont
Illinois	New Jersey	Virginia
Indiana	New York	Wisconsin
Iowa	North Carolina	Wyoming
Maine	Ohio	
Maryland	Oregon	

National Parks & Recreation areas visited:

Acadia National Park	Cherokee National Forest
Badlands National Park	Ashley National Forest
Crater Lake National Park	Fremont-Winema National Forest
Great Basin National Park	Tahoe National Forest
Great Smoky Mountains National Park	Mark Twain National Forest
Redwood National Park	Siuslaw National Forest
Rocky Mountain National Park	Green Mountain National Forest
Yosemite National Park	Sawtooth National Forest
Black Hills National Forest	Medicine Bow National Forest
Flaming Gorge National Rec. Area	Whitman National Forest
Oregon Dunes National Recreation Area	City of Rocks National Reserve
Columbia River Gorge Nat. Scenic Area	Mark Twain Caves Nat. Monument
Hiawatha National Forest	Sleeping Bear Dunes Nat. Lakeshore
Humboldt-Toiyabe Nat. Forest	Scott's Bluff National Monument

*Favorite Campgrounds:

> Jedidiah Smith Redwoods State Park in California
> Sleeping Bear Dunes National Lakeshore in Michigan
> Hamilton Branch State Park in Georgia
> Canyon Rim Campground at Flaming Gorge National Recreation Area in Utah
> Northhampton Beach Campground in the N.Y. Adirondacks
> Unity Creek Campground near Baker City, Oregon

* The goal in our travels was to find beauty, peace and serenity. Our favorite campgrounds provided for that. If your idea of the perfect campground is water and electric utilities, restaurants, a pool, a Laundromat, a golf cart and other amenities, our selections would probably not be for you.

APPENDIX B - FAVORITE RECIPE'S

I have noted a few of my favorite recipes in the following pages. As previously discussed, we cook most of our meals in the oven of our RV. We're not that couple that cooks out over the fire every day in their cast iron stoves and barbeques. That's okay for steaks, burgers and hotdogs, but not our favorite meals. That might be something that I will work on in the future, but as of now we stick to our home recipes and utilize our RV equipment – it's rain-free, easier, expedient and I don't have to worry about some bear running off with my piece of salmon. Campfire cooking might work in your local KOA, but when we're out in the woods, I don't want the aroma of our dinners wafting through the forest for all the local wild animals to hone in on. Unless otherwise noted, most of the following recipes are for 2 servings. Some of our favorite meals include:

Potato Pancakes

Ingredients:

4 or 5 medium potatoes
1 egg
1/4 to 1/3 of a cup of flour
Dash of salt and pepper

Grate potatoes very fine, add egg, flour, and salt and pepper and mix in bowl. Cover large cast-iron skillet with oil and heat to very hot. Dollop in mix and flip when brown. When finished, soak on paper towels for a minute. Some people like to add diced onions into the mix. Various toppings include sugar, applesauce, catsup or you can experiment with your own toppings. I prefer applesauce.

Crepes

Ingredients:

1 cup of milk
1/2 teaspoon of salt
3 eggs
2 tablespoons of melted butter
1 cup of flour

Beat eggs until foamy with milk and salt added. Add flour and mix. Cover and let sit for 1/2 of an hour. On a buttered cast-iron skillet, pour in the mixture and turn the pan until you cover the entire pan with a very thin coating. Flip when browned. Remove the crepe and ladle a thin portion of your favorite jam or jelly on the crepe and roll it up. Our favorites include blueberry, grape or strawberry jam. If you want to get fancy, you can sprinkle with powdered sugar.

Chicken Mushroom Casserole

Ingredients:

2 bone-in chicken breasts
1/4 cup of flour
Paprika, onion salt and garlic powder
Butter
One small onion
Two or three potatoes
Broccoli and/or cauliflower
Couple of carrots
1/2 can of mushroom soup
1/2 can of water

Pour the flour onto a sheet of wax paper. Add the paprika, onion salt and garlic powder to the flour. Caramelize the onions in a pan until they turn yellow. Wash the chicken breasts and remove any fat. Cover the breasts with the flour and then brown both sides in a buttered cast-iron frying pan. When browned, place into a sprayed baking dish along with the vegetables and pour the combined mushroom soup and water over the dish. Add salt and pepper to taste. Cover the dish with aluminum foil and bake @375 for approximately 50 minutes.

"Steve & Jo's Excellent Sausage Sandwich"

Ingredients:

Two long rolls
2 small potatoes
1/2 of an onion
Green pepper
Sweet Italian Sausage

Cut the onion and green pepper into long slices of approx. two to three inches. Fry the peppers and the onions in an oiled pan and add the sausage and brown. Halve and slice the potatoes approx. a quarter of an inch thick. After the sausage is browned, cover with water in the pan, add the sliced potatoes and cook for approximately 45 minutes at a high simmer with a lid on the pan. The Sweet Italian sausage is a variation. To make it even quicker and simpler, use hot dogs, in which case you would only simmer for about 20 minutes. A great simple meal.

Beef Stew

Ingredients:

Package of beef round cubes for stew
2 bouillon cubes
1/2 small onion
3 potatoes and 3 carrots
Sage
Dried mushrooms (I use my own Bolete's that I pick, but can be purchased in store)
Parsley flakes

Put a little oil in a large pan. Cut the onion into large slabs and then slice into approximately one inch pieces and caramelize the onions in the pan. Add the bouillon and beef chunks cut to the desired size and brown. Add some salt and pepper to taste. Coat the meat with a good sprinkle of sage and throw in a handful of dried mushrooms. After browning, fill the pan with water. Heat to a simmer and cook for approximately 2 hours (Keep checking and adding water as it will slowly boil out). After two hours, add the vegetables, cut to the desired size and sprinkle with garlic powder and parsley flakes. Simmer for another 1/2 hour. You can add a little corn starch or flour to thicken up the sauce but I like it the way it comes out. In addition I usually remove some of the cooked, browned beef cubes and juices before adding the vegetables and freeze them for a quick pepper steak meal in the future. For that, just heat up the beef in a small pot, add some dried ginger, soy sauce and pepper and onion slices and pour over rice.

Baked Honey-Mustard Salmon

Ingredients:

One pound of wild salmon
1/8 cup of melted butter
1 1/2 tablespoons of mustard
1 tablespoon of honey
1/4 cup of dried bread crumbs
1/8 cup of chopped nuts
Parsley flakes

In a bowl, stir together the melted butter, honey and mustard. In another bowl, mix the bread crumbs and nuts. After rinsing off the fish, season with some sea salt and pepper. Brush the salmon pieces with the honey-mustard and butter mixture, and then coat with the bread crumbs and chopped nuts. Add a couple squirts of lemon, some parsley flakes and bake in a heated oven @ 350 for approximately 30 minutes or until easily flaked. Add sides of baked potato or wild rice and a heap of coleslaw and you will be in heaven! To keep the honey from sticking to your measuring spoon, first coat it with a little vegetable oil.

Stuffed Flounder Filet Roll-ups

Ingredients:

2 medium or 4 small-sized flounder filets
3/4 cups of steamed spinach leaves
1/8 teaspoon of garlic powder
1/4 cup of mayonnaise
1/4 cup of mustard
Bread crumbs
Carrot
4 ounces of lump crab meat
Lemon

First rinse the filets and check for and remove any bones. Place the spinach, carrot shavings and crab on the flounder filets. Sprinkle with garlic powder, then roll up the filets and hold together with a toothpick. Cover the filets with a mixture of the mayonnaise and mustard. Top with some bread crumbs and a squirt of lemon. Bake in a buttered baking dish @ 350 for 25 to 30 minutes. When finished, place on a bed of wild rice. If trying to save money – just leave out the crab. The result still tastes pretty good.

Jersey Shore Crab Cakes

Ingredients:

8 ounces of lump crab meat
1/2 cup of diced onions
1/4 cup of diced red peppers
1 egg
2 tablespoons of mayonnaise
1/2 teaspoon of dried mustard
1/2 cup of crushed, salted Ritz or Townhouse crackers
1/8 teaspoon of cayenne pepper
1/2 teaspoon garlic powder

Sea salt, pepper and Old Bay seasoning to taste
1/2 cup of breadcrumbs

Mix together the crab meat, onions, red pepper, egg, mayonnaise, dried mustard, crushed crackers, cayenne pepper, garlic powder, salt, pepper, and old bay and form into 1/2 inch thick patties. Place on baking sheet and coat lightly with bread crumbs. Place in refrigerator for an hour or so. Heat some oil and butter in a frying pan and cook patties until browned on both sides, approximately 5 to 6 minutes a side. When finished, drain on paper towels. Served with home-made French fries and coleslaw or salad and you are a hero!

P.S. – If you really want to be frugal (not cheap!), just replace the crab meat with a 1/2 pound of diced cod filet and leave out the cayenne pepper. I personally think it tastes just as good and you can have 2 great meals for about $10.

Shrimp and Penne Pasta Salad

Ingredients:

1 cup of penne pasta
1 lb. of shrimp
2 strips of bacon
Salad ingredients

First, cook up 1 cup of the penne pasta, and fry up the bacon strips. While they are cooking, mix yourself up 2 servings of a simple salad. I usually use red lettuce, tomato chunks, cucumber chunks, a couple of red onion slices and a little arugula and spinach. Drain and rinse the pasta and mix in with the salad, then sprinkle with crumbled bacon bits. When finished, fry up the shrimp in a little butter, oil, and garlic. While cooking, add a little sea salt and Old Bay seasoning to taste, then sprinkle with a little dried Tarragon. Add to the salad (I like the shrimp to be a little warm on the salad, if you want it cold, cook it up ahead of time). When all mixed together, add some coarse ground pepper.

For the salad dressing, take a 1/3 cup of olive oil and add 2 teaspoons of minced garlic and 2 teaspoons of parsley flakes. Add a couple squirts of lemon juice to taste. This is a great summer meal.

Steve's World-famous Pizza

Crust Ingredients:

1 packet of Rapid Rise Yeast
1 cup of very warm water
1 tsp. of salt
1 tsp. of sugar
1 dollop of olive oil
3 cups of flour

Dissolve the yeast in the water in a large metal bowl. Add the salt, sugar, and olive oil and stir until well combined. Add the flour, a cup at a time until well incorporated. Knead the dough for a few minutes. If sticky, add a bit more flour. When done kneading, place the bowl on a small warming pad and cover it with a dishtowel. Let it rise for an hour or two. When finished rising, it should be 2 or 3 times the original size. This makes 1 large pizza and 1 small pizza. We usually freeze the small pizza and eat it on the road.

Sauce Ingredients:

1 small can of tomato paste (6 ounce)
1 tsp. of Italian seasoning
1/4 teaspoon of pepper
1/8 teaspoon of garlic powder
Dash of olive oil
1 teaspoon of salt

Mix the above ingredients in a small bowl. Fill the empty tomato paste can 3/4 of the way with water and add to mix. Place bowl in refrigerator until the dough is risen and ready to go.

Roll out the pizza dough on a floured pizza mat in 2/3 and 1/3 portions. Place on Pam sprayed pizza pans (1 large, 1 small). Cover with tomato sauce. If you are adding vegetable toppings, add now, before adding the cheese (this will keep the vegetables from burning). Jo usually adds sliced mushrooms and/or spinach on her half. Cover both pizzas with pizza cheese (approx. 16 ounces). For myself, I then add pepperoni and/or sausage. Sprinkle with olive oil and oregano. Place in the oven @415 for around 15 minutes. This is a great meal with plenty of leftovers for snacks. Just reheat frozen slices in toaster oven (or microwave if you have to – but then it tastes like crap) whenever you want a nice hot snack. We always bring our toaster oven on camping trips.

Chicken Parmigiana

Ingredients:

2 small boneless chicken breasts
1/4 cup of flour
1/4cup of bread crumbs
1 scrambled egg
1/2 package of mozzarella cheese (8 oz.)
Tomato sauce*
Linguine
Parsley flakes

Place flour, egg and bread crumbs in separate bowls. Rinse chicken and remove all fat. Notice I said "small breasts" as some of them now-a-days look more like turkey breasts and neither Jo nor I can eat a whole one. If they are real big, just cut one in half. Season the chicken with salt and pepper to taste. Dip the breasts in the flour, the egg, and the bread crumbs in that order. Place on buttered pan and brown both sides. Then place the chicken breasts in a sprayed baking dish and coat with tomato sauce. Cover with foil and bake for approximately 20 minutes @350. After 20 minutes, take out of the oven and cover the breasts generously with cheese. Sprinkle with parsley flakes. Place back in the oven, cover with foil and bake for another 10 minutes. In the mean time, cook up a batch of linguine. When it's done, make sure to drain and rinse it off with hot water and add a little butter to it to get rid of that starchy taste – unless you like that starchy taste, in that case have at it. The chicken breasts, linguine, and maybe some garlic bread will make you the king of the kitchen!

* I can't divulge my tomato sauce recipe until my death or maybe never. Even my Italian friends can't beat it. So you will just have to buy some or use your own. Maybe, if you buy all 3 of my planned books, I will hide the recipe somewhere inside the books. It will be worth the cost.

Well, that's it for the recipes for now. In my future books I will be adding some of Jo's baking and soup recipes, my special, quick, artisan bread recipe and, if I threaten Jo's life, maybe she will divulge her special Chicken Paprikash recipe so that I can sell a few more books. She has always told me to give her some on her death bed as it would probably resurrect her. It's better than anything the doctors can come up with.

Well, I hope I got them all right. Forgive me if I screwed up, I am a CPA, not a chef. Eat at your own risk. I make no guarantees with my cooking, but I will tell you that Jo and I would probably rather have any of the listed meals for about $5 - $10 per serving than go out to a restaurant for a $100 plus meal. Cooking is fun, you control the freshness, taste and the portions and it's healthier. If you eat at home you will probably also lose a few pounds seeing the size of some of the portions they serve in restaurants. Instead of going out to eat a few times a week, put that money aside - it would probably make your RV payments and you could join us on the road! Stick with me and you'll be traveling for free! Bon Appétit!

www.ingramcontent.com/pod-product-compliance
Lightning Source LLC
Chambersburg PA
CBHW062205270326
41930CB00009B/1654